Reading the Cozy Mystery

ALSO BY PHYLLIS M. BETZ
AND FROM McFARLAND

---

*Katherine V. Forrest:
A Critical Appreciation* (2017)

*The Lesbian Fantastic:
A Critical Study of Science Fiction, Fantasy,
Paranormal and Gothic Writings* (2011)

*Lesbian Romance Novels:
A History and Critical Analysis* (2009)

*Lesbian Detective Fiction:
Woman as Author, Subject and Reader* (2006)

Reading the Cozy Mystery

Critical Essays on an Underappreciated Subgenre

Edited by PHYLLIS M. BETZ

McFarland & Company, Inc., Publishers
Jefferson, North Carolina

ISBN (print) 978-1-4766-7727-9
ISBN (ebook) 978-1-4766-4169-0

LIBRARY OF CONGRESS AND BRITISH LIBRARY
CATALOGUING DATA ARE AVAILABLE

Library of Congress Control Number 2021003060

© 2021 Phyllis M. Betz. All rights reserved

*No part of this book may be reproduced or transmitted in any form
or by any means, electronic or mechanical, including photocopying
or recording, or by any information storage and retrieval system,
without permission in writing from the publisher.*

Front cover image © 2020 Stock-Asso/Shutterstock

Printed in the United States of America

*McFarland & Company, Inc., Publishers
Box 611, Jefferson, North Carolina 28640
www.mcfarlandpub.com*

For Diane Giovinetti, a wonderful friend.
Rest in Peace

Acknowledgments

Any project is built on of the support of many others; this is especially true with an anthology.

I must first thank Dr. Pamela Barnett, Dean of Arts and Sciences, at La Salle University for granting me a sabbatical for the Fall semester of 2019. This allowed me the time to give my full attention to the work of reading, editing, and writing that eventually became the current collection.

I must thank all of the contributors who provided the scholarly work that forms the core of this study, the first to examine the cozy mystery from a critical lens.

As always, I owe thanks to the people of McFarland who answer my questions, no matter how trivial, and provide the assistance that has helped me clarify and articulate my own critical interests.

It goes without saying that Joan's love and support for me and this project, as well as her patience, must be acknowledged.

I also want to acknowledge the women and men who work in La Salle's Food Service—Debbie Jennings, Kiko Jennings, Glen Jones, Joanne Kitchen, Wanda Mayhugh, Bryant Simpson, Lois Hunt, Vanessa Speight and all those whose names I don't know. During my time at La Salle they have kept me grounded, been my cheering squad, and added a little lagniappe every now and then when I order lunch.

Table of Contents

Acknowledgments   vi

Introduction: A Cat. A Craft. A Cookie. A Cozy.
    Phyllis M. Betz   1

Contemporary Cozy Mysteries, Agatha Christie and
the 1990s: Six Steps Toward a Definition
    Marty S. Knepper   17

The Cozy from the Margins: The Archetypes of Home and
Heroism from Inside and Outside the Modern Cozy
    Susan Rowland   49

Counterpointing the Cozy: Louise Penny's Three Pines
    Paula T. Connolly   65

Is the Cozy a Tailor-Made Style for Historical
Crime Set in the 1920s and 1930s?
    Jennifer S. Palmer   79

Displaced Controversies: The Paradoxes of the Cozy Setting
    Phyllis M. Betz   94

This Cozy England: England and Englishness
in Cozy Mystery Series
    Susan K. Martin *and* Kylie Mirmohamadi   113

Extending Cozy Boundaries
    Kathryn Heltne Swanson   130

The Body in the Library: The Library in the Cozy Mystery
    Mary P. Freier   144

Aurora Teagarden, the Cozy and the Southern Gothic
    Jessica Gildersleeve   156

Clara and Solange: Two Very Modern Detectives in a Very Cozy World
    Jon Wilkins   169

A Likeable Man: Columbo as Cozy Detective
    Stephen Cloutier   188

The Best of Both Worlds: Being Cozy and Hard-Boiled in Rex Stout's *Nero Wolfe*
    Sally Beresford-Sheridan   204

About the Contributors   225
Index   227

Introduction
A Cat. A Craft. A Cookie. A Cozy
Phyllis M. Betz

The debates surrounding the value of popular culture and the texts that culture produces seem to be cyclical; each new popular form of expression reignites concerns about the cheapening of aesthetic values. From the romance to the western, from the detective story to the graphic novel, popular fiction has had to defend its writers and readers from negative comments. Interestingly, in spite of the tendency to dismiss such work as hardly worth noticing, such fiction has also been labeled as dangerous and debilitating: "If literature is to be judged by a plebiscite, and if the plebs recognize its power, it will certainly by degrees cease to support reputations which give it no pleasure and which it cannot comprehend. The revolution against taste, once begun, will land us in irreparable chaos" (Strinati, qtd. Leavis, 20). From the end of the nineteenth century to the present, cultural critics like Matthew Arnold, F.R. and Q.D. Leavis, and others have held that these works cheapen the artistic production of culturally acknowledged masters. They either throw a mind-numbing pall over readers due to the lack of innovation and complexity or they exert a subversive influence, especially on young readers, with idealized portraits that feed unrealistic expectations of life. Contemptuous or dismissive attitudes about this literature, especially popular romance, continue to be found in the pages of academic criticism as well as in popular magazines. Even today, academics who study popular fiction are often asked when they will turn their attention to serious (and more legitimate) work. While some popular genres, particularly the detective and romance novel, have begun to receive academic and mainstream approval, other types of popular fiction continue to be treated as uninvited guests at the wedding. The current subject of this debate over the value of a popular literature is the cozy mystery.

Despite being much maligned and frequently parodied, however, the cozy mystery has become one of the most popular forms of the detective story. A clear illustration of the form's appeal and dominance can be found in my local Barnes & Noble; cozies have been separated from the other detective stories and placed in their own section of the mystery titles, filling an entire shelving unit on the floor. Another sign of the growing impact of the cozy mystery can be seen in how these stories have become staples of television: for example, they dominate the schedule of the Hallmark Murder & Movies cable station lineup. In fact, many of the movies are based on well-known cozy series, such as Joanne Fluke's Hannah Swensen series and Charlaine Harris' Aurora Teagarden mysteries. The popularity of these novels is also reflected in the number of publishers, both mainstream and specialized, producing such work, as well as the establishment of Malice Domestic, a national organization that brings writers, readers, and critics of the traditional and cozy mysteries together at an annual conference. Even though the cozy mystery has gained a wide audience, the works themselves receive very little critical attention. Somewhat like the romance novel, cozies are frequently regarded as little more than light entertainment, a beach read to be quickly read and as quickly forgotten. They are viewed as being nothing more than formula fiction with the same few ingredients thrown into a well-worn plot. The cozy tends to be seen as repetitive, redundant, and to have relatively limited merit as a novel. Such a description, though, begs the question: if the cozy is only seen as little more than a frothy entertainment, what accounts for its strong appeal for the reader? If the narratives offer little in the way of innovations in plot or character, what do the stories provide that maintain reader interest? The essays in this anthology intend to correct this dismissal of the cozy by offering a range of critical analyses showing that, like other popular genres, these mysteries respond to the interests of their readers by commenting on contemporary social and cultural issues with an unexpected depth and complexity.

My purpose in this introduction is to situate the authors' essays against a set of theoretical concepts that will, I hope, establish a base on which the cozy can be reexamined. The authors in the anthology have not been required to engage specifically with my own position; their essays will approach the examinations from a range of critical viewpoints. This variety of ideas about and interactions with cozy mysteries offered here will provide an introductory exploration of the writers and narratives typical of the cozy that will counteract the tendency to overlook these texts. In an important way, this anthology aims to reframe the discussions of these texts by looking at the various components of the genre and the ways authors use and adapt them to create novels that provide both the familiarity all genre writing depends on as well as the reinterpretations that keep the genre fresh.

The starting point for this reevaluation confronts the stereotype of the readers of any genre text as mindless consumers of their preferred fiction. Because popular fiction relies on the same tired conventions, the idea goes, readers become inured to clichéd plots heavy on coincidence and flat and unbelievable characters. The steady diet of these books dulls the readers' ability to appreciate finely crafted literature and portrays them as mindless consumers who purchase the next book with little discernment.[1] A number of contemporary scholars of popular literature have debunked this notion of readers as passively engaging with their books: Peter Swirski asserts that "[r]eading popular fictions is not a mindless and submissive process. On the contrary, it requires the constant exercise of one's interpretative powers" (70). Reading is primarily an individual experience with the readers selecting books they feel connect to their own interests or desires. But as Scott McCracken posits in his essay "Reading Time: Popular Fiction and the Everyday," reading is also a complex of the individual's interaction with the physical as well as the temporal and spatial contexts tied to the act of taking up a text, in whatever form, and engaging with it outside the reader's private reading experience. The connecting of the place and time of the reader's engagements with a book are particularly important when the reader selects a work of popular fiction:

> The seriousness of popular fiction lies in the everyday dissatisfactions of our lives, not just in what we are denied, but our inability to know what we want. Its pleasures (the gift of popular fiction) lie not in giving us what we want, but in providing a space, a time, a condition within the everyday in which we can consider what we might want, even if we then decide that what occurs is, after all, a disappointment.... Popular fiction offers a structure through which such large and abstract events and ideas can be perceived and understood within the context of the ordinary events of everyday life [118].

Reading popular texts creates a space for readers to articulate desires, try out behaviors, and take on various roles that allow for the temporary reimagining of their lives. McCracken has described this relationship in his earlier study, *Pulp: Reading Popular Fiction*, as a triad of world, text, and reader that "has the capacity to provide us with a workable, if temporary, sense of self" (2). Such views as Swirki's and McCracken's should put to rest the conception of readers of popular literature as passive consumers.

Any attempt to quantify the reasons why people choose a particular novel, therefore, must be recognized as a complicated task. In her well-known study of popular fiction, *Reading the Romance: Women, Patriarchy, and Popular Literature*, Janice Radway's examination of the reading habits and preferences of the Smithton women reveals the complex relationships between the women's interests in a book, how they interpreted the working out of the story and development of characters, and the satisfaction they felt at the novel's conclusion. The women in Radway's study were active participants in deciding which romances they read and discriminating about the effectiveness of an author's ability to meet their expectations. Cozy readers, like every other consumer of popular fiction, reflect the make-up of society; they look for books that may address issues related to their personal experience, a favorite place, or a hobby that adds to the value of the text. It is probably no accident that many cozies, especially those where main characters quilt, bake, or run a bed and breakfast, include recipes mentioned in the narrative or knitting or quilting patterns as a bonus. Perhaps one of the most compelling attractions of the cozy for its readers stems from the prominent position of a female protagonist who faces the same challenges of balancing work, home, and relationships, which should not be surprising given that the majority of mystery readers are women.

Swirski also notes these reading choices are based on "the constant exercise of one's interpretive powers" (70). The ability to consider how a text works and evaluate whether a book matches one's requirements to be successful is not restricted to some professional group of "official" readers who are said to function as a society's arbiters of taste. According to Dominic Strinati, early critics of popular culture and production saw the efforts to grant equal cultural status and value to popular art as "a danger because [they] can undermine the distinctions, established between elite and popular culture. [They] can co-opt, while at the same time debasing and trivializing, what high culture has to offer" (Strinati 15). Such attitudes have relaxed since the early years of the twentieth century, but there is still a tendency for some to sneer at the woman on the bus reading a romance novel, especially if it's a Harlequin. A number of reasons have been offered as the source for this elitist view of popular fiction and its readers, ranging from a lack of intellectual capability or curiosity in readers, an inability to appreciate the aesthetic qualities of a "real" literary work, and the poor creative talent of its author. This particular criticism reflects a certain troubling strain among academic and some cultural critics; the underlying assumption asserts that only some are capable of the exacting aesthetic judgment that separates a sophisticated reader from everyone else. Popular fiction's audience has been accused of lacking the ability to discern the excellent work from the ordinary one. Radway's study of the Smithton readers, however, shows that they would challenge a novel that failed to meet their criteria for being a good one; they were just as ready to drop a text as enjoy it.

The same disdain is directed not only toward the cozy mystery reader but the writer as well. Genre fiction's reliance on the use of established conventions has caused its writers to be labeled as craftsmen rather than artists; series authors, especially, have even been accused of phoning it in, maneuvering a set of stereotyped characters around a predictable narrative that offers little innovation in how the story develops. As long as the writer includes the expected components of the particular genre, she has done all that is needed to produce the text.[2] A frequent claim made by its critics is that anyone could write a genre novel, as long as the text contains a sufficient number of the appropriate conventions. Implied in such a characterization is an assumption that such books don't have to be good; once the author checks the necessary genre boxes, the texts will find their readers. Such audiences, after all, aren't interested in the quality of the work, merely the fact that it meets readers' expectations. In a May 9, 2019, blog post Sherry Harris, the author of the Sarah Winston Garage Sale mysteries, addresses these frequent negative comments:

> So to all of you who mock the cozy mystery genre, I invite you to write one, find an agent to represent you, get it published by a major publisher, get nominated for a major award, earn out your royalties, get positive reviews, get your contract renewed multiple times, have your editor ask you to write a second series, and hit a bestseller list. Maybe then you'll understand that *all* writing is hard and give cozy writers a little respect [emphasis in text].

Interestingly, Harris highlights the hard work that follows the writing of the novel and points out the rewards that come with maintaining the artistry that keeps both publisher and readers looking forward to the next work. But, without the actual text "that fit[s] the parameters of the cozy genre" and also includes portraits of "emotional depth with complex male and female characters who are trying to live their lives when a murder interrupts it," none of the succeeding stages of the process can be realized (Harris, May 9, 2019). Her comment underscores the often overlooked reality of the importance for the writer to produce work that keeps readers' interest; if a writer cannot, they will look for the writer who can.

The link between readers, and how they choose their texts, and writers, and their ability to create satisfying work, centers on the role the conventions of a genre play in developing and maintaining that connection. The key issue in examining the way genre writers rely on the particular conventional components of their chosen literature is tied to the complicated meaning of the term and its use. Outside the context of literary analysis, the term tends to have a somewhat negative connotation: conventional attitudes are the sign of an old-fashioned way of thinking; conventions reflect the trite, the hackneyed, or the overused aspects of any art form. Yet, Shakespeare's *Hamlet*, considered one of the world's greatest literary works, relies heavily on the conventions of the revenge tragedy popular during the late Renaissance; in fact, much scholarly work has been written tracing the influence of them in the play. One can select any number of classic texts and discern the same outlines of conventional plots, characters, and settings. The importance of literary convention to one's understanding of how a text works technically as well as aesthetically remains the foundation of my own, and others', introductory literature courses. A writer's use of conventional techniques slides from being a necessary aspect in the development of the work to the subjective response that depending on them becomes a sign of creative laziness.

In addition to the double-edged notion of conventions is the way many critics and commentators react to the word formula. Unlike the term convention, which has an understandable and accepted context due to its use in literary criticism, formula suggests a rigid set of steps that must be followed exactly. A well-known example of this notion of formula appears in the set of rules Harlequin has required its authors to follow. Interestingly, at one time these rules allowed for little deviation from the template; however, due to changing reader preferences, Harlequin has expanded its catalog to include narratives that would once be considered inappropriate for the brand. Like any text relying on conventional forms, formula fiction tends to be regarded as the worst kind of popular fiction, the romance novels that can be bought five for a dollar at second-hand stores.[3] Many writers of popular fiction, particularly romance writers, bristle when accused of writing to a formula. Throughout the Jayne Ann Krentz edited anthology *Dangerous Men and Adventurous Women*, the contributors, all well-known romance writers, react strongly to the accusation that they are at the mercy of a formula.[4] To a woman, these authors stress the importance of the romance formula to the expectations and enjoyment of readers. As Sherry Harris affirmed above, the cozy writer also understands the importance of the formula to creating her novels, but she, like every other writer, is not a slave to them.

George Dove, one of the earliest critics of the detective story, begins his examination of the role and use of convention in the detective novel in his extensive study *The Reader and the Detective Story* by noting that "[t]he writer writes (and a reader reads) with an understanding of what is acceptable within the limits of the literary form, of what inventions and experiments are permissible, and what traditions must be observed" (2). Dove's statement indicates that between reader and writer exists a compact that guarantees both parties will bring the necessary attributes for the creation and enjoyment of the novel. When readers pick up the detective novel, they already come prepared, based on their previous reading of the genre, with an understanding of what techniques the writer has at her or his disposal in order to create a narrative that will entice them. During the time spent with the text, an exchange between what is written and what is read is undertaken; this engagement will both encourage readers to become involved in the pursuit of the solution while at the same time challenging them with permissible alterations in the formulation of the investigation, for example, the use of red herrings:

> A genre can be defined simply as a group or class of works that meet a given set of expectations. A different kind of definition starts from the assumption that the generic horizon is not exclusively in text or reader but in the interchange between the two, whereby the reader responds to the signals of the text on the basis of expectations inherited from an earlier reading experience [Dove 71].

Doves' analysis is based on the ides of reception theory developed by Hans-Georg Gademar, Wolfgang Iser, and Robert Jauss. In the first two chapters of *The Reader and the Detective Story*, he examines and discusses a complex set of ideas regarding the ways in which the reader's understandings and expectations of the text are addressed in the text by the writer. An important component of this theoretical framework is Gademar's idea of "transformed play" (14). A basic feature of this play is the importance of knowing and understanding the rules by which the game is played. For Dove, the rules of the game are found in conventions of the detective genre. Dove distinguishes these conventions as "constitutive, ... which define the genre and are essential to it; ... regulative, which characterize a genre but are not essential to it; and third—by far the largest in detective fiction—the recurrent stereotypes" (75-76). The first set of conventions concern the explicit aspects of the detective story that can only be found in this particular narrative; Dove uses the fact that unless the story has a detective it cannot be a detective novel; regulative conventions are those that describe the detective story, especially the sequence of the plot's movement, the conscious reference to other detective narratives, and its handling of time—the tension between the present of the investigation and the past of the crime. Dove uses the example that while murders dominate detective stories, they are not absolutely necessary for the investigation that propels the story, but once the plot has been started it follows a standard pattern. Finally, the recurrent stereotypes are those devices—character, locations, methods—that are most recognizable, such as the hard-drinking private eye or the rundown police station (76-82). These features also most often become the target of negative criticism as they are the dominant aspects of the text recognized by readers.

The major difficulty with how people respond to the use of conventions in genre literature rests, I believe, on the conception that a convention remains static; once articulated and used by an author, the device is fixed and cannot be altered in any way. If this were true, then there might be some justification in seeing popular literature as merely recycling the same tropes over and over. However, such a view is undercut by the constant reevaluation and reinvention of conventional forms that any genre text may participate in. George Dove explains that the "bounds of a genre *naturally* offer a challenge, to which creative authors respond by probing those limits and seeking points of breakthrough. What takes place then is a continual founding and altering of horizons. If the reading public accepts these alterations, the rules of the game will be revised and new horizons of expectations established" (96, emphasis added). Dove's use of the word naturally opens, for me, the obvious point that the techniques available to a writer for constructing a text are paradoxically fixed and fluid. A genre is recognized due its utilization of standard tactics and formulations, but those same standards must continually be reevaluated since popular literature is the most responsive to social and cultural shifts in belief and behavior. Philip Fisher's essential, for me, articulation of the idea that popular literature has the important function for its readers of making the revolutionary familiar offers another support for seeing the relationships between popular fiction and its readers as an evolving practice: "The popular forms colonize entirely new terrains They enter what are only temporarily exotic configurations of experience as a necessary practice for a transformation of moral life that is approaching" (20). Whether it is Warhol making viewers re-see the ubiquitous soup can as art or the lesbian romance showing the beauty of two women in love, popular art, because it contextualizes radical possibilities within a well-known frame of reference, provides a space for the awkward or strange to become ordinary. This process, of course, is not straightforward or without reaction: when Muller, Paretsky, and Grafton reframed the portrait of the hard-boiled detective as a woman, many critics castigated the authors and the novels as a dangerous and damaging trend. Today, detective fiction reader will see the shelves of any bookstore well-stocked not only with these authors, but many others who have taken this new model and made it their own.

Perhaps the main critique of the cozy centers on the notion that these texts are too tied to their use of convention. However, if one accepts Dove's analysis of the role and use of conventions within the detective story, then such a criticism must be seen as skewed toward the negative. Applying Dove's three categories of convention to the cozy shows how these novels are actually successfully participating in the genre's push and pull between convention, "tradition, structure, those things that change very little if they change at all," and invention, "the variations, the innovations that give each story its special character" (Dove 75). Many critics tend to forget that the cozy is, in fact, a detective story, and thus it must adhere to the same constitutive conventions as any other detective narrative; any deviation in them means the text is not a detective story. Dove lists four: "the protagonist is a detective, detection is the main plot, the mystery is an inordinately difficult one, and it is always solved" (76). Whatever cozy title one selects, it adheres to these criteria. Notice that the detective is not identified as a professional by Dove; the cozy protagonist is typically a member of her community living an uneventful life who, often reluctantly, only becomes the detective in order to solve the murder that has intruded into her well-run routines. Since most cozies have their main character accidentally caught up in the death that instigates the narrative, she must pursue the investigation in order to identify the perpetrator to clear her or a close friend or family member's name. Many cozies, unlike more traditional texts, do not present the search for the solution in a straightforward trajectory; the pursuit of a solution is frequently side-tracked by new information or suspects; motives shift as the protagonist evaluates her progress; often a sub-plot intersects the main storyline that interrupts the detective's efforts. Finally, the protagonist, usually with help from friends and official investigators, discovers who the murderer is and the reason for the death. Not coincidentally, the woman at the center of the cozy narrative also brings a happy resolution to events in her personal life, such as finding a career, establishing herself in the community, and the beginning—or possibility—of a romantic relationship.

Like every detective story, the cozy builds its narrative along standard regulative patterns. The cozy usually opens by introducing the protagonist dealing with her daily routine; her life may be running smoothly until the unexpected death disrupts her routine. A variation is meeting the protagonist at a point of transition where she is trying to regain a sense of stability. She becomes involved in the crime generally by accident or because she is peripherally connected to other characters. Once the main emphasis of the plot is laid out, the protagonist finds herself becoming more enmeshed in the circumstance involved in the death and must use her skills to resolve the crime. As the narrative develops the protagonist's particular skills will give her a way to intrude into the official investigation (caterers, for example), use her training to provide insight into the crime (as an herbalist who knows poisons), or give her access to places or people the police may not (knowing the wife of a commander on a military base). Her behavior tends to disrupt the standard investigative procedures of the police, but these differences in approach are reconciled with the apprehension of the killer. These variations in the novel's basic structure provide the necessary reconfigurations that keep the genre fresh. Not surprisingly, many of the women at the center of these novels are aware they are participating in a mystery; of course, they are at the center of the actual investigation either as suspect, witness, or participant in the investigation. References to other detective writers and novels frequently appear, too; protagonists who own a bookstore (usually one specializing in mysteries) have a wide knowledge of the genre. Other protagonists are readers of mystery novels and will occasionally compare their situation to their favorite author or fictional detective. The last regulative convention found in the cozy is the juxtaposition of the past, when the crime was committed, and the present. Here cozies adhere to the standard dual representation of time as all other detective stories, although the length of time between these events is often short.

The incorporation of stereotypes, as in other popular genres, remains the source of some of the more intense criticism of the cozy. The characters who populate the novels seem to be the target of the most disdain; they are said to be two-dimensional, showing little depth in personality or perception. The issue here, as with the word *convention* itself, hinges on the context in which a stereotype is understood. For example, used as a technical description of standardized character types—the hard-drinking police officer or the serial killer—stereotypes through constant repetitive use become a form a short-hand during the construction of the text since they bring a set of recognized behaviors the author will use to serve the needs of the novel. Each popular genre relies on these consistent characters or situations that serve a range of narrative functions particular to its own requirements, and one specific type can have several iterations related to its appearance in a novel. The problem with the response to stereotypic characters arises when they are taken out of the confines of the technical sphere and instead become an indication of laziness or lack of talent on the part of the writer. The stereotype is a walking cliché offering little reason for the reader to feel connected to the character's experience or feelings. The same negative response applies to the structuring of the plot and thematic implications incorporated into the narrative. Many popular texts are criticized for lacking any ingenuity in the construction of the story; the revelation of the criminal, it is claimed, is clear from the first pages. The protagonist's movement through the plot will include being misidentified as the murderer, being abducted by the villain, or leading the police in the wrong direction. Dove argues, though, that these standardized plot points are necessary components of the frame: "One of the most informative principles of the conventionality of the detection formula is that the conventions themselves have structure, and that they are absorbed into the structure of the genre as a whole" (82).

An additional problem is noticeable with stereotypic characters, particularly the negative cultural meanings that have been attached to them. Characters' race, gender, sexuality, and class become immediate targets of critical challenge due to the long history of how these parts of a character's make-up have been represented. The many vile portraits of such characters must be acknowledged; they have too frequently been used to denigrate the particular group being portrayed. Popular fiction is just as guilty of relying on such representations. Yet, often popular fiction paves the way for re-imagining them and provides a more positive role of the character in the text. My earlier work has examined the way lesbian popular fiction has operated within and without not only literary standards, but cultural perceptions. Lesbian writers through their utilization of the necessary genre conventions of the mystery, the romance, and fantasy/science fiction have begun the process of familiarization by taking the negative stereotypes of lesbians and repositioning them in familiar narrative frameworks. When the butch lesbian, for example, becomes the hard-boiled detective, her masculine traits enable her to deal with the investigation in the way readers have come to expect. As long as she solves the crime and metes out justice, her sexuality fades into the background. This is the one area that seems to have been left underdeveloped in the cozy, but perhaps because of the specifically configured settings typical of the genre, the cozy appears to remove the complications that could result from including characters with the most discernable signifiers of otherness—race and sexuality. However, other stereotypes do appear, such as the nosy neighbor, the eccentric older relative, the rebellious teenager. What the exclusion of race, sexual identity, or economic differences means in the cozy, for me, becomes an important issue to consider. Yet, these same omissions of diversity can be seen in other mysteries besides cozies; many of the Golden Age novels also lacked such diverse characters. Some differences may be coded, I think sexuality is a major one, so there is room for ambiguity in a reader's awareness, giving the reader the option of how to integrate that knowledge into the response to the character.

Scott McCracken offers a succinct evaluation of the relationships developed between readers and their particular choices of genre texts. McCracken has often described this relationship as a negotiation of desire, expectations, and satisfaction, and readers look for books that provide them not only entertainment but a way to evaluate their sense of themselves as individuals and as part of the wider world. Popular fiction can often provide guideposts of what to do or not to do: "The text, the popular narrative itself, is produced in the world and becomes a part of the world.... The reader is also a product of the world, but at the same time, she or he is an agent in that world, changing it through her or his actions.... Popular fiction can supply us with the narratives we need to resituate our*selves* in relation to the world" (*Pulp: Reading Popular Fiction* 16–17, emphasis in text). The conventions used by the writers to organize the experiences of their characters are the mechanisms through which this connection begins and is continually remade as readers find, through them, the reassurance that the world is familiar and knowable. Cozy mysteries have attained their popularity, I believe, because they replicate this relationship; by using the well-known conventions of the detective novel, the cozy reader is welcomed and encouraged to stop by the café and have a cookie, pop into the local bookstore to pet the owner's cat, and support the protagonist's search for the killer who has disrupted the daily routine of the community.

This anthology begins with essays that engage with the question of what, exactly, is a cozy mystery? As do many genre texts, the cozy mystery slips between genre categories: is it a romance that revolves around a mystery; is it a mystery the involves two characters becoming romantically involved; does it include aspects of the supernatural? One issue often raised when discussing the cozy centers on when did this form of detective narrative appear. Marty S. Knepper's essay, "Contemporary Cozy Mysteries, Agatha Christie and the 1990s: Six Steps Toward a Definition," addresses a mainstay of commentary on the cozy, that Agatha Christie was one of the earliest writers, indeed creator, of the cozy. Knepper counters this view by carefully developing a definition of the cozy through a thorough analysis of criticism on the detective novel, the available commentary of the cozy, and a statistical survey of 56 contemporary cozy novels. She then compares the novel *Three Blind Mice* by Christie that, on the surface, would seem to adhere to this definition, with Amanda Flower's *Assaulted Caramel*; however, Knepper's discussion counters the prevailing view of Christie as a writer of cozy mysteries.

Susan Rowland's essay, "The Cozy from the Margins: The Archetypes of Home and Heroism from Inside and Outside the Modern Cozy," addresses one of the main critiques of the cozy, that it underplays the role of violence and complex social and political issues in its narrative. Rowland places the cozy novel against other female authored mysteries that represent distinctly different detective genres to illustrate the ways in which the cozy, working against its expectations, engages with topics not usually seen within its pages—spousal abuse and domestic and racial violence. To combat the potential of such actions to create fissures in the narrative, Rowland sees major characters as incorporating qualities of the Jungian archetypal figures of four Greek goddesses. (Rowland's study, *The Sleuth and the Goddess*, provides a more detailed discussion of these figures and their influence in shaping the personalities and behaviors of the cozy's main characters.) Hestia, the goddess of hearth and home, dominates the cozy narrative, thus allowing the resolution of the novel to restore the balance threatened by the intrusion of physical and emotional violence.

In "Counterpointing the Cozy: Louise Penny's Three Pines," Paula T. Connolly problematizes the standard definition of the cozy by examining how Penny's Three Pine series both engages with while at the same time interrogating some of the cozy's main conventional requirements. Connolly examines how Penny's series seems to rely, on the surface, on some of the standard tropes associated with the cozy mystery; however, her analysis shows how the novels question the validity of these conventions as typical expectations of setting, characters, and other cozy requirements are challenged by the darker impulses described in the narratives. Beneath the seemingly benign surface Three Pines presents at first sight reside deep-seated resentments and questionable pasts that undercut this serenity.

The next essays tackle the way the setting of the cozy mystery influences how it shapes the development of the narrative, determines the behaviors and relationships of characters, and constructs the social contexts that underpin how the inhabitants conceive of themselves and their world. The dimensions of the cozy setting can encompass a whole community as well as more limited spaces. An important point raised in these essays is the insistence that a cozy novel's setting is neither limited to the small town nor set in the present day. Jennifer S. Palmer's essay asks the question "Is the Cozy a Tailor-Made Style for Historical Crime Set in the 1920s and 1930s?" To answer her question Palmer first establishes the historical and critical frameworks: briefly describing the key events of the time period and a summary of the cozy conventions. Palmer takes care to point out that the novels she is examining are contemporary ones that use these years as their setting, not works produced during those years. Palmer then discusses the work of four authors who write historical mysteries by examining how each writer incorporates standard cozy techniques in their texts to support her assertion that the cozy is a suitable form for historical crime stories.

My own essay, "Displaced Controversies: The Paradoxes of the Cozy Setting," addresses the lack of racial, ethnic, and class representation in the cozy mystery. Since the majority of cozy novels are set in small towns or restricted environments, their populations tend to be homogeneous. When characters of a different race or class do appear in these books, their appearance paradoxically emphasizes their absence. This situation creates a tension between the somewhat hermetically sealed environment of the cozy and the economic and racial reality of such places, which forces the reader to question the reasons for such omissions.

An idealized English village, like Agatha Christie's St. Mary Mead, has been accepted as the model for any cozy situated in a small town. Susan K. Martin and Kylie Mirmohamadi's essay, "This Cozy England: England and Englishness in Cozy Mystery Series," challenges the accuracy of this position. The authors compare an American series set in an English country house that has been literally brought to America piece by piece, with the Agatha Raisin series set in the Cotswolds region of England. Martin and Mirmohamadi show how the American version of England embodies a narrow and fantastic portrait of what England and Englishness are, invoking an old-fashioned idea of proper English manners and behaviors. In contrast, the authors illustrate how the Agatha Raisin books not only rely on the cozy conventions of setting but at the same time challenge them to reflect the changing social and cultural experience of England.

The setting of the cozy mystery is not limited to the small town; many cozies take place in other locations that embody most of the expectations connected to their inhabitants and their various relationships. Kathryn Heltne Swanson's essays shows how the dimensions of the cozy setting can be expanded beyond the typical small town. In her essay "Extending Cozy Boundaries," Swanson examines how the environments of the university and the hospital utilizes the conventions of the cozy with a particular emphasis on the role of the protagonist who is a member of the community. This character, typically but not always female, brings an expertise which allows for the resolution of the crime. Likewise, Mary P. Freier focuses on the specific setting of the library as the scene in which the crime and investigation occur in "The Body in the Library: The Library in the Cozy Mystery." Freier begins by pointing out Agatha Christie's use of the library in her mystery novel *The Body in the Library*; however, the library in the cozy is a public place, which serves the entire community, rather than a private one. Just as the dead body threatens the peace of the community, the library itself is often faced with threats of closure or reduction of services that would have a negative impact on the people who use it. Solving the crime, usually by the librarian who feels a strong sense of responsibility for the library's survival, restores both the sense of order to the community and the assurance of the library's survival.

The final set of essays in this collection center around the character who becomes the investigator of the crime. Typically, this character is an amateur, most often a woman who becomes entwined in the crime by accident. She either owns her own business or has close ties to the town which gives her access to the scene of the crime and the ability to solicit information from those involved in the crime. Her interference in the investigation puts her at odds with the police, but she is likely to become romantically involved with the detective as the case develops. Rather surprisingly, two of the essays presented here suggest that the cozy detective need not be a woman and need not be an amateur.

Jessica Gildersleeve's essay, "*Aurora Teagarden*, the Cozy and the Southern Gothic," suggests that the standard portrait of the accidental detective is problematized in Charlaine Harris' series. Aurora Teagarden is unlike other such figures: she is a librarian with well-developed research and investigative abilities, and she has an ongoing interest in crime as a founding member of the "Real Murders Club." Just as Teagarden counters the prevailing portrait of the cozy heroine, the novels themselves undercut the typical narrative emphasis on a clear resolution to the crime that restores the community's sense of equanimity. Gildersleeve's discussion shows how the Teagarden novels, by engaging with the idea of the Southern Gothic, reveal a darker side to the conventional notion of the cozy.

Not all cozy detectives are amateurs and not all professional detectives are male. Jon Wilkins' essay, "Clara and Solange: Two Very Modern Detectives in a Very Cozy World," discusses two early twentieth century professional female investigators, who, Wilkins claims, present characteristics of the cozy even though the genre had not yet been defined. Lady Clara, Baroness of Linz, is the proprietor of an investigative agency in London; Solange Fontaine in a professional detective whose investigations are set in France and England. Like many cozy characters, Clara and Solange work within closely defined environments, suited to their social status. Violence, when it appears in their stories, is brief and most often take place off-stage. Solange and Clara use their talents to resolve their cases successfully, thus bringing about the expected cozy ending. Both women seem ill-suited for detective work: their physical beauty is what most other characters notice and respond to and is often used by them to advance the progress of an investigation. Of course, their appearance masks the keen intellect and observational powers they bring to their cases

Stephen Cloutier contends that the cozy detective can just as easily be an official member of a police department in his essay "A Likeable Man: Columbo as Cozy Detective." Cloutier's contention, at first, seems to be unworkable; Columbo's status as a detective in the Los Angeles Police Department would disqualify him. Cloutier discusses how the character's background—he represents the everyday, working class individual who is often invisible in society—and his methods of investigation—rejecting the hard-boiled stance more typical of the police—suit him for placement in the cozy category. Columbo's association with the cozy is enhanced due to the successful resolutions to his investigations which bring unscrupulous criminals, who rely on their wealth and social status to protect them, to justice, thus restoring order and decency to the community.

Nero Wolfe is another fictional detective not typically associated with the cozy mystery. Sally Beresford-Sheridan's "The Best of Both Worlds: Being Cozy and Hard-Boiled in Rex Stout's *Nero Wolfe*" presents an examination of both Wolfe and his assistant, Archie Godwin, that supports her reading of them as balancing both detective genres. Even though the setting of the novels is New York City, Wolfe's self-imposed limitations on his movements works to establish a cozy-like setting for his investigation. Wolfe stays inside his brownstone, using his intellectual powers to reach a solution, while Archie does the legwork associated with the active hard-boiled detective; Wolfe is a connoisseur of food, wine, and orchids, while Archie chases suspects, engages in violence, and becomes involved with women. Most notably, Beresford-Sheridan points to the importance of the relationship that develops between Wolfe and Archie over the series as the rationale for seeing them as suitable cozy characters.

As the authors of these essays show, the cozy, like any other genre text, offers readers more than passive, momentary entertainment. Looked at closely these works, through the involvement of the characters in pursuit of their investigations, provide insights into and comments on the world in which their audience resides. The cozy is more than just a simple book for whiling away an afternoon; as Scott McCracken notes in the conclusion to his study *Pulp*, "Popular fiction feeds the desire for something beyond the limitations of our lives, for something new. At its most successful it is able to seep into the cracks of contradictions of social reality and demonstrate the possibility of a better world" (187).

Notes

1. For a concise overview of the major theories of popular culture see Dominic Strinati, *An Introduction to Theories of Popular Culture*, 2nd edition (New York: Routledge, 2004). Chapters One and Two, particularly, lay out the key areas of conflict regarding the production and consumption of works of popular art.

2. I use the feminine pronoun deliberately as the majority of cozy mystery writers are women.

3. Just as criticism of popular fiction and the detective story use the terms convention and formula interchangeably, I will refer to these literary practices throughout the introduction with both.

4. In her contribution to the anthology Krantz confronts one of the most frequently criticized parts of the romance—the alpha male: "Why [do] we dig in our heels and resist the effort to turn our hard-edged, dangerous heroes into sensitive, right-thinking modern males? ...We [do] it because, in the romance genre, the alpha male is the one that works best in the fantasy" ("Trying to Tame the Romance: Critics and Correctness," 108).

Works Cited

Dove, George. *The Reader and the Detective Story*. Bowling Green State University Popular Press, 1997.
Fisher, Philip. *Hard Facts: Setting and Form in the American Novel*. Oxford University Press, 1987.
Harris Sherry. "Can We Just Stop?" *wickedauthors.com*. May 9, 2019. Web. 11 July 2019.
Krentz, Jayne Ann, "Trying to Tame the Romance: Critics and Correctness." In *Dangerous Men and Adventurous Women*, ed. Jayne Ann Krentz. University of Pennsylvania Press, 1992.
McCracken, Scott. *Pulp: Reading Popular Fiction*. Manchester University Press, 1998.
_____. "Reading time: popular fiction and the everyday." In *The Cambridge Companion to Popular Fiction*, eds. David Glover and Scott McCracken. Cambridge University Press, 2012.
Strinati, Dominic. *An Introduction to Theories of Popular Culture*, 2nd edition. Routlegde, 2004.
Swirski, Peter. *From Lowbrow to Nobrow*. Montreal: McGill-Queen's University Press, 2005.

Contemporary Cozy Mysteries, Agatha Christie and the 1990s

Six Steps Toward a Definition

Marty S. Knepper

ALEX TREBEK: "She's a fan of a type of mystery I haven't heard of—the cozy mystery. What is it?"
CONTESTANT: "It's like an Agatha Christie, without a lot of blood and guts."
—*Jeopardy*, 22 November 2018

Introduction and Definition 1: The Problematic Soundbite Definition

In 1986, Sara Paretsky and others founded Sisters in Crime, an "advocacy organization ... established to promote and connect women writers, editors, reviewers, publishers, booksellers, librarians, and readers in the crime and mystery field" (Kinsman 21). In 1989 Malice Domestic was founded to celebrate at their annual conferences "the traditional mystery, books best typified by the works of Agatha Christie" and containing "no explicit sex, or excessive gore, or violence" (*Malice Domestic*, "About" page). In a 1992 *New York Times* article, Jean McMillan describes these two organizations' "sense of militancy" on behalf of "the traditional mystery" and their "demand [that it receive] respect and attention" (qtd. in Stasio 2), which paved the way for the emergence of a new type of female-oriented mystery, the cozy, a contemporary spin on classical detective fiction. Since the early 1990s, the cozy has developed into a best-selling genre in the United States, squeezing out psychological thrillers, police procedurals, P.I. novels, and other whodunits on the limited, competitive shelf space of Barnes & Noble stores.

Obviously, the brief definition of the contemporary cozy offered by the

Jeopardy contestant echoes Malice Domestic's definition of the traditional mystery: the cozy is an Agatha Christie–style traditional mystery characterized by a lack of violence and sex (**Soundbite Definition 1**). This common cozy definition misleads more than it elucidates. While "no violence, no sex" characterizes both Christie's mysteries and contemporary cozies, these traits reveal little about either form. The genre term *cozy* originated in the 1980s and 1990s to describe both the contemporary cozy and post–World War I Christie-style whodunits, which share few traits.[1] The genre term *traditional mystery*, introduced about the same time as *cozy*, usually refers to Christie-style whodunit puzzles, though cozy influencer Carolyn G. Hart describes the traditional mystery as a morality tale, using Christie as a source for this definition (129–30). Besides problems with cozy-connected terminology, evoking Christie to explain the cozy creates more definitional confusion, especially for post-1980s scholars who resist the notion that Christie's mysteries are simple, unvarying in their formula, and culturally insignificant. If frequent allusions to Christie by those attempting to define the cozy perplex many, using Christie as a lens through which to view the cozy can also clarify the situation of women writers of popular fiction and highlight unique qualities of the cozy, which from here on will refer to the contemporary cozy mystery, not its ancestors.

To reach a more comprehensive definition of the cozy in this essay, we will move through four more definitions beyond the soundbite definition. First, we will identify the marketing definition of *cozy* and then test its accuracy against my survey of 56 popular cozy novels, in the process discovering key traits marketers do not emphasize. From there, we can shape a formulaic definition of the cozy as popular literature. Disentangling the historical confusion over the term *cozy* and then contrasting Agatha Christie's *Three Blind Mice* and Amanda Flower's *Assaulted Caramel* will lead to a literary definition asserting that the cozy is more about character and community than identifying a murderer among suspects. Finally, we will develop a cultural definition that claims that the cozy, written and read mainly by women,[2] directly repudiates trauma-inducing trends in the United States[3] since the early 1990s by providing fantasy narratives with alternative values needed to create a safer, more humane democracy. This step-by-step process will lead to a final composite definition of the contemporary cozy mystery.

Marketing Definition 2

Covers market books. Even if Barnes and Noble didn't put cozies in a clearly labeled section within the general category "Mysteries," the distinctive covers alert browsers that they are in cozy country and reveal other traits of the cozy beyond "no violence, no sex." The front and back covers of Amanda Flower's[4] *Assaulted Caramel*, published in 2017 by Kensington, a major cozy publisher, typify cozy packaging. The front cover has a punning title, a series description ("An Amish Candy Shop Mystery"), bright pastel colors (caramel gold, bright yellow, and aqua), and a picture of an old-fashioned store full of candies and cakes, handmade quilts, Amish hats, a friendly cat, a horse and buggy glimpsed outside the large window, and signs advertising "Buggy Rides" and country newspapers. The back cover introduces amateur sleuth Bailey King, who has left her job as "assistant chocolatier at world-famous JP Chocolates" in NYC to help her Amish grandparents who run a sweet shop in Harvest, Ohio. The blurb is full of candy language: "[s]ometimes you need a sweet tooth to take a bite out of crime," "a yummy deputy with chocolate-brown eyes," "living the sweet life," and "a cunning killer tries to fudge the truth." Below the blurb we see the announcement, "Recipe included!"[5]

Such playfully domestic, nostalgic cover art and text lead browsers to embrace, or dismiss, the cozy mystery genre with its apparent light humor, non-violent murder mystery, and ordinary female hero open to adventure and romance while dedicated to operating a "traditionally feminine" small business in a small town or neighborhood where people enjoy foods, pets, crafts, family, friends, and community events. A blending of these cover traits with other traits from representative online and print sources[6] yields **Marketing Definition 2**, which highlights these features of the cozy:

- A bright, likeable, independent, nearly always female amateur sleuth with a strong support group of eccentric family and friends and a fun, "feminine" business (such as floral arranging or staging homes for real estate agents) or hobby (such as knitting or baking);
- A non-gory, often offstage crime, nearly always murder, that the intuitive sleuth solves mainly by talking with community members and often relying on helpers;
- An ordinary person turned murderer for personal motives (e.g., greed, jealousy, revenge, covering up a secret) and a victim whose death pulls the sleuth into the investigation;
- A small town setting or a neighborhood or small business in a city or suburb—where people know each other and the number of suspects is limited;
- A fast-paced plot with dialogue and humor but no graphic violence, explicit sex, or profanity;
- A mystery, with clues and red herrings, that readers can try to solve along with the sleuth;

- An intriguing setting such as a New England coastal village or a former plantation in Mississippi;
- Punning titles such as *Moss Hysteria, Yews with Caution*, and *A Rose from the Dead*[7];
- Frequent inclusion of pets, recipes, and holiday celebrations in the narrative;
- A romance element;
- A focus on relationships among ordinary people; and
- The sleuth and various other characters developing throughout a series.[8]

Why do cozies appeal to readers, mostly women? In an online article, Amanda Flower says, "In a cozy, there is a happily ever after and justice is served. That does not always happen in the real world. A cozy is a brief escape from the troubles of the real world and I, for one, plan to take that escape over and over again" ("What Exactly is a Cozy Mystery?" 2). Flower's ability in *Assaulted Caramel* to deliver to readers a comforting narrative that transplants Bailey King from the stresses of Manhattan to rural Ohio may explain the success of her 22 cozy novels in 7 series published between 2010 and 2019 ("Amanda Flower—Book Series in Order" 1). Yet Flower's acknowledgment that the real world is troubled and Bailey's deep dissatisfactions with work and romance in Manhattan suggest that cozy mysteries may tap into readers' frustrations with the world as it is and may be more complex and less comforting than they seem, despite the alluring promise of their covers.

Background: Agatha Christie as Writer and Cozy Writers

As indicated earlier, the cozy is strongly associated with Christie. A review of popular views of Christie and her work can illuminate our study of the cozy. For decades, readers have described consuming Christies as comforting and an escape from the dark, complex, stressful real world. Written between two brutal world wars, the so-called Golden Age Mystery portrays a threatened Edenic world, a concept W.H. Auden promotes in his influential 1948 essay "The Guilty Vicarage." Murder must take place in what appears "to be an innocent society in a state of grace.... [T]he more Eden-like it is, the greater the contradiction of murder" (403–04). The detective's role is "to restore the state of grace" (406). But Christie's novels, published between 1920 and 1976, are not so morally simple or predictable; neither are her characters and settings innocent. Miss Marple constantly reminds her nephew

Raymond West that "[t]here is a great deal of wickedness in village life" ("The Bloodstained Pavement" 57). The end of a Christie mystery reveals not just the murderer(s) but also the secrets and crimes of other characters. The end of *There Is a Tide* (1948) reveals not only poisoning but also perjury, embezzlement, gambling, drug-taking, violence, blackmailing, living a false identity to inherit an estate, spiritualism, suborning perjury, a possible faked death, eavesdropping, and hiding crimes. Christie's novels create the illusion of coziness because the dark side generally reveals itself on the last few pages. This erroneous idea that Christie's fictional worlds are innocent should provoke skepticism about the coziness of the cozy.

Cozy readers and writers have elevated Agatha Christie to queen of the cozy, the epitome of popular success, but popularity doesn't equal critical respect. A Dame of the British Empire (Sanders and Lovallo xx), Christie was also dubbed "Mystery Writer of the Century and the Poirot books Mystery Series of the Century" by Bouchercon in 2000 (Curran 7–8). Christie's "seventy-eight crime novels, approximately 150 short stories, six 'straight' novels, four nonfiction books, and 19 plays" are nearly all still in print, outselling even Shakespeare, and have been translated into 104 languages (Gill x). At her death in 1976, Christie reigned as "best-selling novelist in history" (Bernthal 1). Julius Green calls Christie the "most successful female playwright of all time," noting that her 1952 play *The Mousetrap* "holds the record for the world's longest-running theatrical production" (1). In 2016, Mark Aldridge notes that "there is no sign of her appeal diminishing, with new attempts to bring her stories to a general audience continuing to appear," mainly on screen (1).

Cozies, collectively, are also a publishing phenomenon. Although the exact sales figures for cozies cannot be established, the larger category of mystery/detective fiction in 2017 sold approximately 12.1 million copies, ranking below suspense/thrillers and romances and above fantasy and science fiction (Amy Watson 1). Websites such as *cozy-mystery.com*, *kensingtonbooks.com*, and *mysterytribune.com* list hundreds of cozy writers and series, as do listings on Kindle and Nook. Libraries stock plenty of cozies. They are obviously very popular in the U.S. Yet cozy writers find themselves in a similar situation to Christie at the time of her death: popular but not taken seriously.

Few writers have received as much critical neglect and abuse as Christie did in her lifetime. Tillie Olsen in *Silences* and Joanna Russ in *How to Suppress Women's Writing* catalog the ways women writers, popular writers, and in particular popular women writers have been silenced, erased, or dismissed as sub-literary. Despite or perhaps because of her sales, Agatha Christie's reputation during her lifetime suffered at the hands of journalists, scholars, and even mystery historians who frequently criticized her characterization, style, and literary worth.[9] Christie contributed to the demeaning of her work by describing herself as a literary "sausage machine" (qtd. in Gill 133) and stating that "I regard my work as of no importance—I've simply been out to entertain" (qtd. in Sanders and Lovallo vii). Yet, starting in the 1980s and 1990s, once scholars such as Earl F. Bargainnier and Allison Light began approaching Christie with the critical rigor they would use with a canonical writer, they discovered her artistry in manipulating the detective story formula, modernist sensibilities, and shrewd commentary on how England changed in terms of gender, race, class, and "Englishness" between and after the world wars.[10]

Writing in 2015 about Christie and her Detection Club colleagues, Martin Edwards states that "[t]heir novels are often sneered at as 'cosy'" (8). Sherry Harris laments online that the contemporary cozy genre has similarly received scorn from both mainstream writers and other crime fiction writers (1–4). In her writing guide, Nancy J. Cohen warns aspiring cozy writers that "you may experience a lack of respect for your talent and hard work" (81). Until now, no book-length academic study of the cozy has been published.[11] Like Christie, cozy writers who describe their books as "fun" and "escapist" and readers who imply that cozies follow a predictable formula, like sausage production, may boost sales but discourage scholarly treatment of cozies as a significant form of popular literature with something valuable to say about contemporary society and the lives of ordinary people, especially women. But where to begin? First, we need to situate the cozy as popular literature and identify useful scholarly concepts and approaches for studying popular literature. Then we can turn to the cozy texts themselves.

Background: Popular Literature Concepts and Methods

Distinguished scholars have articulated principles and methods that have shaped popular literature study and can guide us in considering the cozy as a popular fictional formula. Jack Nachbar and Kevin Lause observe that "the greater the popularity of the cultural element" ["object, person, or event"], ... "the more reflective of the zeitgeist this element is likely to be" (5). In the U.S., for example, blockbuster superhero movies reflect deeply held American ideas about masculinity, violence, and distrust of government.[12] The popularity of the cozy is, therefore, a sign of its cultural importance.

Gary Hoppenstand observes that popular fiction serves as "the union between commercial success and storytelling," "two things that Americans seem to love the most" (1). He notes further that "'[e]scapism' is a term that perhaps best expresses how popular fiction functions as entertainment" (2).

He cites as an example the 1974 popular all-star movie version of Agatha Christie's *Murder on the Orient Express* that allows viewers to "temporarily escape the day-to-day routine of their lives by climbing on board" the luxurious "Istanbul-Calais coach" and ride into an imaginary world of "exotic suspense." When a murder takes place, viewers can "match wits with the great detective's [Poirot's] 'little grey cells'" (2). While popular fiction's escapism and mass appeal "usually disturb ... literary critics" (2–3), it has "many of the same qualities that we often praise in 'respectable' literature: effective use of language, interesting settings, distinctive characterizations, and sophisticated plotting" (2). It also "affects, as well as reflects, society" (5). Cozies tell good stories, both reflecting and affecting our society and era.

John Cawelti defines popular culture formulas: they use both "novelty and familiarity" to allow us to enter the "controlled landscape of the imagination" in which "tensions, ambiguities, and frustrations of ordinary experience are painted over by magic pigments of adventure, romance, and mystery. The world for a time takes on the shape of our heart's desire" (1). Formula study provides a tool for studying the psyche of a particular culture and time in history. Cawelti warns that formula definitions should be based on "the widest possible range of literature and other media" (33) and must take into account the "literary whole" (34). By this he means looking at how characters, settings, themes, plot, and symbols work together to "successfully articulate a pattern of fantasy that is at least acceptable to if not preferred by the cultural groups who enjoy them" (34). What, then, is the appealing formula of the cozy?

To look at the cozy as a "literary whole" (as opposed to selected traits) and base the formulaic definition of the cozy on a wide sample, I conducted a trait-based survey of 56 cozy novels,[13] starting with a list of 50 recommended cozy writers I found in May 2018 on *cozy-mysteries.com*. I added 6 more cozies to the study based on recommendations by members of my Booked on Crime group and other cozy-reading friends.[14] The results confirm that the marketing definition traits are accurate but do not include several very significant, overlooked cozy features that provide the bread crumbs leading us to a definition of the cozy as a significant popular literature fantasy formula.

Survey of 56 Cozy Novels Leading to Popular Literature Definition 3

Description of Novels in the Survey

- The 56 books are each by different authors.
- In some cases, the book is the first in a series, but often not.

- 96 percent of the authors use female or androgynous names; I found a few men hiding behind pseudonyms.
- 4 percent of the books appeared in the late 1980s, 13 percent in the 1990s, 27 percent in the 2000s, and 57 percent in the 2010s.
- 73 percent were set in the U.S.; 23 percent in England, Ireland, Scotland, or Wales; 4 percent in Canada and Africa.
- 16 percent of the books have paranormal elements (talking animals, vampires, witches, ghosts).
- 14 percent of the books have historical settings. (All but one of the historical books were set in England.)
- 14 percent of the books identified LGBTQ characters; 13 percent non-white characters; most were middle class.

Comments: (a) Further study might focus on how series develop characters and plotlines. (b) The number of cozies has risen each decade, or the recommended list included more recent books. (c) Paranormals fit the cozy pattern better than historicals, 86 percent of the latter fitting the classical whodunit pattern rather than the cozy pattern. (d) Further cozy study might focus on gender, race/ethnicity, and class.

Support for the Traits in Marketing Definition 2

A bright, likeable, independent, nearly always female amateur sleuth with a strong support group of eccentric family and friends and a fun, "feminine" business or hobby.
- 95 percent of the sleuths are amateurs. (1 sleuth is a constable; 2 run or are partners in a P.I. agency.)
- 98 percent of the sleuths are female. (1 is a gay male vampire.)
- 91 percent of the sleuths appear to be in their 20s, 30s, or 40s, none as old as Miss Marple.
- 86 percent of the books include family members of the sleuth.
- 96 percent of the sleuth's jobs/hobbies can be considered "fun" and 75 percent "stereotypically female."

A non-gory, often offstage crime, nearly always murder, that the intuitive sleuth solves mainly by talking with community members and often relying on helpers.
- In 96 percent of the books, the crime is murder, always non-gory and often off-stage.
- Crimes are solved mainly by conversation and observation, with help from cops and friends.

An ordinary person turned murderer for personal motives and a victim whose death pulls the sleuth into the investigation.

- 89 percent of the murderers are ordinary persons who kill for personal motives. (Two books have mentally ill murderers, 1 assumed murder is an accident, 1 murder is an international revenge situation, and 2 books have no murders.)
- In 98 percent of the books, sleuths (including 1 cop and 1 P.I.) are pulled into the investigation by deaths connected with the sleuth or her family, friends, or community.

A small town setting or a neighborhood or small business in a city or suburb—where people know each other and the number of suspects is limited.
- 63 percent of the books are set in rural areas/small towns; 38 percent in urban areas, including suburbs.
- The suspects are nearly always within a closed circle of the sleuth's or victim's acquaintances.

A fast-paced plot with dialogue and humor but no graphic violence, explicit sex, or profanity.
- None of the cozies rehash the crime, possible methods, and suspects at length; conversations with suspects nearly always integrate with the sleuth's daily life activities.
- Emphasis is on action and dialogue. Dialogue is often humorous, never laden with profanity.
- Sex scenes rarely appear in cozies, and, if they are alluded to, there are no details, and the couple is nearly always married, engaged, or in a long-term relationship.

A mystery, with clues and red herrings, that readers can try to solve along with the sleuth.
- 100 percent of the books have a mystery with clues and red herrings.

An intriguing setting.[15]
- 75 percent of the books have intriguing settings.

Punning titles.
- 30 percent of the books contain titles with puns.

Frequent inclusion of pets, recipes, and holiday celebrations in the narrative.
- 54 percent of the books have pets or animals; 23 percent include recipes; holiday celebrations are common.

A romance element.
- 73 percent of the books contain romance between the sleuth and one or more other characters; 16 percent of the sleuths are married; 5 percent are not married; 5 percent are not in a position to marry (e.g., nun, child).

A focus on relationships among ordinary people.

- Except for the occasional witch, vampire, or talking cat, cozies focus on conversations and connections among regular people, with their own histories, flaws, aspirations, and temperaments.

The sleuth and various other character often develop throughout a series.
- 100 percent of the books are part of a series.

Comments: (a) A few judgments involved subjectivity: fun jobs/hobbies and intriguing setting, for example. (b) After completing my survey, I concluded that 11 books in the sample are not cozies: 9 are more like classical detective stories, 1 a police procedural, and 1 a spy/adventure thriller. If these books are eliminated from the sample, the percentages skew even higher in support of these cozy traits. (c) This survey strongly supports the traits in Marketing Definition 2, … but it does not tell the whole story.

Other Significant, Seldom Mentioned Cozy Traits

The following traits were not mentioned or emphasized in sources that contributed to Marketing Definition 2 of the cozy mystery, surprising omissions because they are obvious in the cozy texts.

Romance

- With 89 percent of the sleuths married or in one or more romantic relationships, romance is a *major* element in cozies.[16] Even when a married woman is a sleuth, other men admire or tempt her.
- Only 52 percent of the novels focus significantly if not exclusively on the mystery. The other 48 percent give more space to work, family, community, and especially romance.
- In 84 percent of the books, the sleuth has a close relationship with a police officer, lawyer, or P.I. Often this official is the sleuth's husband, boyfriend, ex, friend, lover, admirer, or connected to a close friend or relative. While these concerned official investigators sometimes discourage the sleuths from crime investigation, they usually provide help and protection when needed.
- While some sleuths are described as beautiful, most are ordinary women who could stand to lose ten (or more) pounds,[17] wear ordinary clothes, have character flaws, and value their independence. Yet men love and respect them as they are.[18]

Dark Elements

- 54 percent of the plots involve sexual abuse/coercion of women, men, girls, or boys (for example, rape, assault, domestic violence, homophobia, forced marriage, witch torture, predatory vampirism, or family/spousal pressures leading to anorexia, alcoholism, or drugs). These dark elements usually occurred in the past, but they influence the present. Sometimes, not always, the dark elements motivate murder. As in Christie's novels, cozy readers generally feel comfortable until the end of novels when the sleuths may be threatened and dark elements reveal themselves.

Face-to-Face Communication

- 89 percent of the books have little technology in them beyond occasional cell phone calls or website mentions. This would be expected in the 14 percent of the novels set in earlier historical periods. But books set after 1990 almost exclusively present face-to-face communications. When computer research is needed, professional investigators generally do the research, not the amateurs.

Rejection of Corporate/Urban Life

- 0 percent of the sleuths work for corporations or within a bureaucracy, 13 percent work as part of a tiny business or non-profit operation (literary agency, book shop, convent, the White House kitchen, library, rural middle school, domestic service); 87 percent are small businesses owners, nearly all entrepreneurial, female-oriented ventures they have established or inherited.
- 63 percent of the books are set in small town/rural areas; only 38 percent are set in cities or suburbs.
- In the 35 rural/small town books, 49 percent of the sleuths decided to relocate from an urban area, leaving a high-pressure corporate job such as law, finance, media, or prestige food service to settle in a hometown or place where relatives live. Since not all the books were first in a series, a larger percentage of sleuths may have left cities for a less stressful life.[19]

Based on these mostly unacknowledged but significant aspects, another definition of the cozy emerges (**Popular Literature Fantasy Definition 3**): While cozy mysteries reveal dark deeds in the past and characters are troubled by crime in the present, they provide an appealing fantasy world in which lovers, families, friends, and community members interact in healthy and supportive ways; women are respected and nurtured; technology has not destroyed intimacy and empathy; and economically viable small businesses in small towns or neighborhoods offer goods and services that make people happy.

In the last section of this essay, we will explore how the U.S. cultural trends since the 1990s can explain the development and popularity of this particular fictional fantasy formula with women. Before we can do that, however, we must resolve confusions about the term *cozy*, which has also, since the rise of the contemporary cozy, been used to describe classical detective stories of the past, like those of Christie. Only by distinguishing the classical detective story formula from the cozy formula can we see clearly the unique elements of the cozy within its contemporary cultural context.

Problems with the Use of the Term Cozy in the 1990s and Since

Popular literary genres evolve and provoke reactions throughout time and across national boundaries. In the late 19th and early 20th centuries, in the Sherlock Holmes stories, for example, terror and suspense often mixed with reasoning. In the post–World War I Golden Age, mystery readers craved whodunit or howdunit puzzles that later transformed in the direction of the comedy of manners. In reaction, the American *Black Mask* school created tough, violent male PIs who tried to create some measure of justice in a deeply corrupt, materialistic world. These hard-boiled detectives softened or became even more violent over time and even became women. From the 1960s through the 1980s, the more non-violent detective story resurged as what might be called the "puzzle plus mystery": the "plus" including, for example, religion (Harry Kemelman), diverse cultures (Tony Hillerman), occupations (Simon Brett, Amanda Cross), and history (Ellis Peters).[20] In the 1990s, the cozy emerged as another kind of "puzzle plus mystery,"[21] a distinctive subgenre of what came to be called the traditional mystery.[22]

In 1998, Carolyn G. Hart defined the traditional mystery as embracing the earlier mysteries of Christie, her peers, and her successors. The traditional mystery, she claims, is no more about murder than the hard-boiled mystery, which she categorizes as a crime novel. Defined in contrast to the hard-boiled tradition that portrays a knightly hero and his code, the traditional mystery, Hart argues, which "Agatha Christie once compared ... to the medieval morality play," shows what happens "to lives dominated by ... the deadly sins." Today's traditional mystery is a morality story "in a more sophisticated guise.... [It] reveals the intimate, destructive, frightening secrets hidden beneath what so often seems to be a placid surface." It focuses less on ripped-from-the-headlines brutality and more on righting wrongs at work and at home (129–31). The term *traditional mystery* has caught on among Malice Domestic attendees and surfaced in more recent published sources. I will use this term from here on. Although Hart's definition of the traditional mystery provides a useful umbrella category, it does not clear up definitional confusion about the cozy as a subgenre or indicate how it is unlike earlier traditional mystery formulas.

An essay on the cozy written by Susan Oleksiw and published in *The Oxford Companion to Crime and Mystery Writing* (1999) exemplifies confusion over the *cozy* definition. Attempting to cover nearly 80 years of what she calls cozy writing from E.C. Bentley (1913) through Barbara Neely (1992) in a very limited space and writing before the contemporary cozy had become recognized as a new subgenre, Oleksiw did the best she could, but her definitional essay thoroughly mixed together older detective story traits ("intricate" plots, "literary allusions," "idiosyncratic sleuths," country house settings, references to servants) with traits in books by writers now identified as early contemporary cozy writers such as Carolyn Hart and Lillian Jackson Braun (intriguing settings such as a Cape Cod tavern, "a light tone," humor, and explorations of "questions of community") (97–98). Oleksiw's broad use of the term *cozy* to cover a wide spectrum of crime writing is still very common but problematic because it does not specify what makes the contemporary cozy unlike what has come before.

Probably using the *Oxford English Dictionary* as her source, Oleksiw claims that the first use of the word *cozy* as a genre descriptor appeared in a review by Maurice Richardson in the [London] *Observer* on May 25, 1958, but the citation is to *cozy* as a descriptive adjective, not a genre category: "a cozy little murder mystery" (Oleksiw 97; 1958 Richardson 16).[23] Fairly certain that *cozy* was not used as a genre term until the 1990s, I surveyed 55 detective fiction histories and anthology introductions on my bookshelves, published between the 1920s to the 2010s.[24] I found that the most common terms used for traditional mysteries were the adjectives *detective, mystery, classic,* or *Golden Age* followed by the nouns *story, fiction,* or *novel.* Some other terms were *whodunit, murder mystery, formal detective story, puzzle story,* and *tale of ratiocination.*[25] Other than the 1958 reference noted above, I found no references to cozies in these sources before 1971, when Colin Watson remarked that the term had been applied to the Mayhem Parva writers "in no pejorative sense" (171), and 1972, when Julian Symons spoke of "[c]ozy detective stories and bloody thrillers" (6). In these cases, *cozy* again seems to be a descriptive adjective, not a genre label. I found two mentions of the cozy in the 1980s and five in the 1990s that clearly reference Christie-era detective stories[26] and only three extremely brief sources, from 1998 to 2006, that used *cozy* to refer to the contemporary cozy. In *Deadly Women* (1998), Ellen Nehr's tiny essay mentions aspects of the contemporary cozy: novices who become sleuths for personal reasons, interesting occupations and settings, and believable plots (127–28). A 2004 mystery reference guide cites a single link to cozies by Susan Wittig Albert, Cleo Coyle, and other cozy writers (Bleiler 54). In *The Longman Anthology of Detective Fiction* (2005), Deane Mansfield-Kelley and Lois A. Marchino present an introduction to the culinary mysteries of Diane Mott Davidson that really describes cozy series: a protagonist interested in food and eating, appealing titles, recipes, a recurring cast of characters, "fast-paced and intricate" plots, and a sleuth "good at thinking about people and situations" but not a "tough cookie" (185–86). By 2006, Chris Roerden assumes readers know *cozy* means contemporary cozy (11).

This research shows that (a) the genre term *cozy* was not used when Christie and her peers were writing; (b) it began to be used retroactively in the 1980s and early 1990s to describe Christie-era mysteries, and (c) only in the late 1990s was the term used in print to describe the growing subgenre of contemporary cozies, the same time that the term *traditional mystery* emerged in print sources.[27]

The source of confusion over the term *cozy* now identified, we can examine the difference between Christie era detective fiction, illustrated by her novella *Three Blind Mice (3BM)*, and the contemporary cozy, represented by Amanda Flower's *Assaulted Caramel* (AC), both popular texts. *3BM* was originally a short radio play written for Queen Mary, which Christie later adapted into a novella with the same title (1948) and then into the 1952 record-setting stage play, *The Mousetrap* (Green 303–04). Flower's books were nominated for four and won two Agatha Awards and have appeared on the *USA Today* bestseller list ("Amanda Flower," "Agatha Awards").

Distinguishing Classic Detective Fiction from the Contemporary Cozy: Literary Definition 4

To highlight what makes Christie's mysteries distinct from the cozies, I chose two mysteries more alike than different. Cozy lists often include Miss Marple and Hercule Poirot novels, but these two sleuths are old, frequently outsiders, and focused on justice, very little on their own personal lives. Christie's young adventurer novels such as *The Secret Adversary* and *The Man in the Brown Suit*[28] at first seem closer to the cozies in spirit, with their younger female protagonists and the romance element, but these women are desperate to escape small villages for metropolitan areas and the world outside England, and the plots involve adventure more than detection. Christie's *Three Blind Mice* and Amanda Flower's *Assaulted Caramel*, however, share many common elements beyond skillful writing.

Both texts have as central figures a young couple just getting to know each other, with the young woman as the central character. Both young women are inventing new lives for themselves as entrepreneurs. Married for only a year after a two-week courtship and now living in rural England post–World War II, Molly and Giles Davis in *3BM* have transformed a Victorian house Molly inherited from an aunt into a guest house. In *AC*, Bailey King flees a high pressure, high profile chocolatier job and a bad boyfriend in Manhattan to help her dying Amish grandfather and his aging wife run their sweet shop in Harvest, Ohio, where she immediately meets her eventual love interest, Deputy Sheriff Aiden Brody. Bailey loved spending childhood summers in Harvest, and Aiden found a loving temporary home at the sweet shop when he was a child, fleeing with his mother from an abusive, drunken father/husband. Both mysteries have rural settings with an old-fashioned flavor. The guest house in *3BM* is full of Victorian ambiance, comforting to survivors of a traumatic war. Bailey's grandparents and their Amish friends drive buggies, do not use telephones except for work, and live a 19th-century lifestyle in a 21st-century world. Both couples confront a murder in their own domestic space. A disagreeable lady guest is murdered at Molly and Giles's guest house while a snowstorm rages outside; an underhanded developer who wants to turn Harvest into a commercial Amishland is killed in the sweet shop kitchen. Both stories weave in the theme of abused children and have memorably eccentric characters such as the flamboyant Mr. Paravicini in *3BM* and Aiden's mother, Juliet, in *AC*, with her polka dot clothes and polka dot pig. Both narratives present social history of different places and times. Most astonishingly, both have exactly the same surprise ending. Because these texts have so much in common while representing their own eras, the differences between the two mystery formulas appear in sharper focus. The context of each story (post–World War II vs. 2017) and what drives each story (situation vs. character and community) define the difference between the traditional mysteries of Christie and contemporary cozies.

Situation drives *Three Blind Mice*. Midway through the first half, the two proprietors of Monkswell Manor, four guests, and police sergeant Trotter are snowbound in a house with no working telephone. Having arrived on skis, Trotter tells them that a Mrs. Lyon murdered two days ago in London was actually Maureen Gregg, recently released from prison, sentenced for abuse and neglect of three evacuee children in her care during World War II, one of whom died. The suspected killer is the dead boy's grown up, mentally unstable brother, who left a notebook near the crime scene indicating Monkswell Manor as his next stop. He may already be there, one of them. When Mrs. Boyle, a thoroughly unpleasant, bossy lady in charge of placing children in temporary homes during the war, is found dead, the gravity of the situation increases, especially for Molly, the only woman still alive in the house. As in Christie's *And Then There Were None*, all are trapped, and one of them is a murderer.

Besides the snowstorm and the threat of murder becoming a reality, what creates tension for the mice trapped in this Victorian cage is suggested early in the narrative when Molly describes the husband she married after only two weeks as a stranger. On page 5, Molly repeats the words "strange" or "stranger" three times before the shadow passing her window reveals itself as Giles. On the same page, Molly realizes she doesn't know herself either: three times she repeats the phrase "playing a part" or "playing a role" to describe herself. Everyone trapped in Monkswell Manor is a stranger, has secrets, plays a role, and behaves queerly: any one of them could be the murderer.[29] Once Mrs. Boyle is killed, it gradually emerges that several other characters, besides her, know about or have ties to the notorious wartime child abuse case, paralleling the situation of the characters snowbound in a train in Christie's *Murder on the Orient Express*, all of whom connect to the Daisy Armstrong kidnapping.

While developing the characters and their interrelationships (for example, Molly's growing bond with the "queer" Christopher Wren and Giles' jealousy of him), Christie weaves together clues and red herrings on every page, making the narrative a kaleidoscope that changes the reader's perceptions of guilt and innocence with each new development. The shadow of World War II contributes to the tension because so many people were damaged, displaced, or morally compromised by the war and now engage in illegal black-market activities. A final reenactment of the crime leads to the surprise exposure of the murderer's and others' secrets and later, according to J.C. Bernthal, to an implied reconciliation and conventional gender realignment among Molly, Giles, and Christopher (109).

Christie and the classic detective story emphasize the situation of a murder set in a closed society with interestingly developed, secretive characters existing mainly to make a baffling mystery. The cozy, in contrast, focuses much less on the whodunit tension and more on the character and journey of the female protagonist—less a sleuth and more a professional, friend, relative, romantic partner, and community member. Solving a mystery in a cozy showcases the protagonist's intelligence, people skills, independence, courage, and determination to protect those she loves.

Assaulted Caramel begins with Bailey King's friend Cass's shouted words, "I still can't believe you left!" transmitted through Bailey's cell phone (1). Cass panics because the board of prestigious Manhattan JP Chocolates is about to name Bailey head chocolatier. Cass doesn't know that Bailey is also leaving her secret rich and famous boyfriend, TV celebrity Eric Sharp, a self-absorbed, unfaithful, image-obsessed jerk with poor cell phone etiquette. While Bailey at first sees her departure from NYC as temporary, by novel's end, she has given up her 100-hour-a-week job and glamorous Sunday junkets with Eric. What has changed her? Partly it is spending time with loving, principled people in Harvest—her grandparents, Jebidiah and Clara King; Deputy Brody and his mother; humorously fish-out-of-water Cass with her purple bangs and trendy fashions who gamely plunges into the Harvest lifestyle to help Bailey; young Emily Esh, whose hushed up teen pregnancy and mistreatment by her Amish siblings has not made her bitter; and a group of church ladies who assist Bailey with an overnight catering job. Aiden Brody, the ultimate good son and potential good boyfriend, opens Bailey's eyes to Eric's flaws, especially when Aiden comforts her during dying Jeb's last moments. The murder investigation shows Bailey how obsessive greed and status-seeking poison human relationships. Finally, Cass's honest anger shows Bailey she has not been a good friend by keeping secrets about Eric and her father's Amish heritage. At novel's end when faithful Jeb has died, the mystery is solved, and Bailey has recommended Cass as JP's new head chocolatier, Bailey says to Clara: "My time here forced me to take a hard look at my life, and I didn't like what I saw. I need a fresh start, and the best way to get that fresh start is to be as far away from New York as possible. I can't think of a place any farther away than Harvest, Ohio" (327).

In Amish country, Bailey has seen a morality play enacted, as Carolyn Hart puts it, and her role has been Everywoman. She rejects the materialistic values of her Manhattan life for the more humane values embodied by her grandparents and their rural community. While too independent a modern woman to accept the patriarchal strictures and old-fashioned lifestyle of the Amish religion, she rediscovers what she knew as a child, that Harvest, while not perfect, nourishes her soul as Manhattan never could.

This character-based storyline and contemporary setting drive *Assaulted Caramel*. The investigation Bailey takes on to clear her name and the reputation of her grandparents propels her into the community to meet both Amish and English. A few people become suspects because of their connection to the victim or their questionable ethics, but not everyone is a threatening stranger or role-player as in *Three Blind Mice*. Many are obviously ordinary, struggling, sometimes eccentric and humorous, sometimes annoying human beings simply living their lives. While blackmail and coercion of Amish business owners cause stress in Harvest, people go about their business during the murder investigation, not terrorized like blind mice fearing a carving knife. I appreciated the clever patterning of clues, red herrings, and surprise ending in Flower's book, but much of the narrative raises non-whodunit issues with wit and style. I suspect readers who have, like me, gobbled up other novels in the Amish Sweet Shop Series care less about the intellectual puzzles and more about the emotional lives of Bailey and Aiden, Clara, Cass, Emily, ornery Jethro the pig, and their community.

Assaulted Caramel also illustrates the important and consistent but not always acknowledged elements of the contemporary cozy noted earlier: romance (Bailey and Aiden, Juliet and Pastor Brook, Clara and Jeb), dark elements (child abuse and domestic violence, forced marriage, blackmail), face-to-face communication (Eric's abuse of Bailey via her cell phone vs. Bailey's conversations with the Amish who do not use telephones except for business), and rejection of urban/corporate life (Bailey's choice of Harvest over Manhattan).

The contrast between two remarkably similar mysteries, one classical detective fiction by Agatha Christie and the other a representative cozy by Amanda Flower, leads us to **Literary Definition 4:** Unlike the situation-driven classic detective story in which characters and other literary elements, however artistically handled, primarily exist to serve the whodunit plot, cozies are character-driven. Within a small community of ordinary people with ordinary human virtues and vices, the amateur sleuth protagonist learns about herself in relation to others as she solves the crime that threatens her world. Human (and sometimes animal) relationships are the compelling interest in the cozy.

Conclusion: Why are Contemporary Women Drawn to the Cozy Formula? (Definition 5)

What factors propelled the rise of the female-oriented contemporary cozy formula in the 1990s? To put it in John Cawelti's terms, how does the cozy formula embody "the shape of our heart's desire"? (1). In marketing terms, what do today's women want that the cozy delivers?

Early cozy writers like Hart and Davidson and their readers saw the second wave of feminism transform into a feminist backlash in the 1970s and 1980s.[30] Cozy writers of Flower's generation grew up in the 1990s, a virulently misogynist era when "girl power" meant buying makeup, not making political change, computers and media transformed our lives, and unregulated capitalism dominated American life. These 1990s trends persist, creating problems for women, families, and communities and suggesting why cozies are so popular: women want "older" values, not our current mainstream values.

Is the cozy's appeal, then, primarily nostalgic? Personal and cultural nostalgia increases in stressful times, as reflected at 1990s Iowa film sites where tourists flocked to relive nostalgic film fantasies inspired by *Field of Dreams* and *The Bridges of Madison County*.[31] The opening chapter of *Assaulted Caramel* is full of longing for the past. After the anxiety-inducing cell phone exchange with Cass and discovering that bad boyfriend Eric has not texted her, stressed Bailey drives into Harvest, which she loved as a child and now views with nostalgia: the apple trees, "an Amish woman pushing a double stroller" with two giggling children, gas-powered lamps, store fronts advertising homemade and locally grown products, and a town square where community events are held (2–6).

But it is not enough to say that nostalgia is an explanation for the cozy's popularity. For one thing, Chapter 1 of *Assaulted Caramel* quickly yanks Bailey out of her reverie. The greedy developer threatens her grandfather to sell the family business so he can transform the town into a fake, profitable Amish theme park for tourists; the stress of this confrontation causes Jeb to collapse. This tiny scene suggests the immense, often traumatic cultural changes of the 1990s, which have increased exponentially since. They have made us all, especially women, desperate to escape to a world with values unlike those that dominate our lives—specifically, misogyny, sexual abuse, and the media's objectifying women to sell products; the technology explosion that has led to stress, depression, and a loss of intimacy and empathy; and the dramatic transformation of U.S. economics, politics, popular culture, and workplaces, prioritizing corporate profits over quality of life and social stability. Returning to Harvest, no Eden, Bailey, and readers, can escape the intensity of modern life. New forms of popular fiction emerge during times of cultural stress. As the whodunit emerged after World War I, the 1990s led to the birth of the cozy.

Several recent books illuminate these dramatic cultural changes since the early 1990s that have made women's lives stressful. In *90s Bitch: Media, Culture, and the Failed Promise of Gender Equality* (2018), journalist Allison Yarrow presents convincing evidence showing that in the 1990s, as women gained power, the pejorative *bitch*, either directly stated or conveyed through images or demeaning labels, "undercut [women's] achievements and stop[ped] their progress" as well as punishing women who spoke truth to power (viii). Examples are the harsh media treatment of Hillary Clinton, Janet Reno, Madeleine Albright, Marcia Clark, Anita Hill, and Monica Lewinsky (Chaps. 3 and 6, 89–95). Yarrow also demonstrates that the 1990s was "the decade that destroyed women and poisoned girlhood" (xvi) through creating anxiety about appearance to sell products, leading to an epidemic of eating disorders and consumer spending, and glamorizing passive sexualized females as objects of male desire, normalizing crimes against women (Chaps 1, 2, 10). In *That's What She Said: What Men Need to Know (And Women Need to Tell Them) About Working Together* (2018), Joanne Lipman claims that she does not shame men (x) and is optimistic about promising workplace experiments (240–41); nevertheless, throughout the book she paints a dismal picture of women in the business world who, though having risen to higher positions, constantly experience unthinking as well as overt discrimination beyond hiring, promotion, and compensation. They encounter, for example, double standards in speech situations (Chap. 1), lack of respect (Chap. 5), masculine office culture (chap. 4), and high costs for appearance maintenance (2–4).

Psychologist Sherry Turkle's book *Reclaiming Conversation: The Power of Talk in a Digital Age* (2015) is based on extensive interviews and studies about living with technology and its effects on solitude, self-reflection, family, friendship, romance, education, work, and the public sphere. While Turkle works with and respects technology leaders at M.I.T., her book recounts harrowing anecdotes and statistics demonstrating that by letting technology control every aspect of our lives, we are losing intimacy and empathy with others (103–207), conversation and reflection skills (18–56, 79–99), courtesy (345–46), and a knowledge of ourselves shaped by reflection rather than electronic feedback (345–62). She concludes, "This is our nick of time and our line to toe: to acknowledge the unintended consequences of technologies to which we are vulnerable, to respect the resilience that has always been ours. We have time to make the corrections. And to remember who we are—creatures of history, of deep psychology, of complex relationships. Of conversations artless, risky, and face-to face" (362).

The dominant paradigm of the U.S. after the Great Depression was that of the Keynesian "regulated economy" with government at its center (Naomi Klein 25). Taking 1970s inflation as evidence that that this paradigm was no longer valid, economic thinkers such as Friedrich Hayek and Milton Friedman, Nobelists in 1974 and 1976 respectively, supplied market-biased answers in the 1980s that, according to Ryan Poll, led the "economic elite" to make "neoliberalism the official regime of global capitalism" (456). Neoliberal ideas about unshackling markets and privatizing government responsibilities have been significant forces in global and U.S. culture and politics for more than 40 years, ripening during the Reagan-Thatcher era and growing ever since. Poll defines the complex, contested term *neoliberalism*[32] as "a political and economic commitment to an unfettered free market that opposes all forms of collectivism (such as unions) and all forms of centralized state planning (such as regulations)" (447). Neoliberalism is characterized by Stegar and Roy as "an ideology, a mode of governance, and a policy package" that promotes "deregulation (of the economy), liberalization (of trade and industry), and privatization of government state-owned enterprises" (11, 14). In *The Shock Doctrine* (2007), Naomi Klein emphasizes privatization of civic functions such as education, homeland security, and warfare as conducted now by private contractors

(3–25). Although a decade of neoliberalism brought about the economic boom of the 1990s and, as Klein acknowledges, a market economy need not be brutal and totally unregulated (25), she documents that unchecked corporatism has led to undemocratic exploitation of disasters (such as 9–11, Hurricane Katrina, the Middle East wars, and political instability in Latin America) to convince traumatized people to accept extreme neoliberal initiatives (3–17). While creating wealth, rewarding entrepreneurship, and making our lives easier in many ways (e.g., cheap flights[33] and express shipping), capitalist initiatives, Klein shows, have too often led to long-term disasters of another type such as worldwide extremes of wealth and poverty, corporate takeover of media and political processes, "skeletal social spending," "exploding debt," perpetuation of profitable war, environmental crises (18–25), and the 2008 global financial crisis. Robert McChesney sums up the effects of unregulated markets under neoliberalism: "Instead of citizens, it produces consumers. Instead of communities, it produces shopping malls [now online shopping sites]. The net result is an atomized society of disengaged individuals who feel demoralized and socially powerless" (11).

How has this dramatic economic paradigm shift affected the cozy mystery? It explains why nearly all the cozy sleuths are small-scale entrepreneurs. Neoliberalism promotes the idea each of us is a marketable product and sells entrepreneurial dreams that promise financial success, what Poll calls "a damaging, dangerous fantasy" (460). No wonder cozy readers like books about hard-working, talented cozy sleuths following their passions to establish successful tea, candy, book, or knitting shops.

Directly countering the values of some corporations, however, cozies espouse values such as caring for others, community, ethics, justice, conservation of the past, and environmental sustainability. Cozies can be read as a female critique of corporatism. No cozy heroine in the surveyed books works in a bureaucracy or corporation. Bailey King and many cozy sleuths have deliberately fled successful urban careers because they can no longer live a profit-driven life. What was the point of working at JP Chocolates, Bailey reflects, "[m]aking chocolate creations that most people could never afford" (104) and trying to satisfy "Upper Eastside supermoms planning their daughters' million-dollar birthday blowouts" (88)? While heroines range from poor to rich with most in the middle, all are committed to success, but what they value most is not wealth but family, community alliances, intimacy, communication, safety, and the welfare of the humans, animals, and environment that surround them. They value quality, handmade products that give pleasure and comfort. They detect crimes without pay for the sake of justice and to protect the innocent. They do favors for neighbors because that is the humane way to live.

While cozies reflect the neoliberal spirit of their times in the emphasis on entrepreneurship, they embody values that run counter to the dominant paradigm of the last forty years by providing a model of involved citizenship, not disengagement and demoralization. While not as overtly feminist as Sara Paretsky's V.I. Warshawski, who regularly takes on corporate institutions such as insurance companies and homeland security, cozy sleuths, in a less overtly feminist way, often expose individual capitalists, whose greedy schemes threaten communities, and promote the "female" value of caring.[34]

Cozy readers of the millennial generation have grown up feeling the effects of misogyny, technology, and corporatism. At the 2019 Popular Culture Association conference, two young feminists presented moving papers, suggesting how these disturbing changes have impacted their generation of women. Tessa Davis presented a gender analysis of Tinder, noting men often use the dating site for sex, while women more often crave meaningful relationships. She confessed her own three-year addiction to Tinder, despite disastrous experiences which led her to doubt herself, even while knowing the superficiality, lies, and sexual predation that characterize online match services. Ali Place grew up with girl power: the idea girls can become anything, maybe even the first female president. The 2016 election defeat of Hillary Clinton catalyzed her into action, having come to realize for some time that girl power and its "grown up version, empowerment" is a way to sell products, "not the same thing as power." She conducted interviews of other millennial women and discovered that gender inequality was a personal issue for them and many identified as feminists. They said the 1990s "girl power" narrative was not only false but "detrimental to their views on gender and society," leading them to "feel helpless and unsure," view reality as disappointing, lose faith in state and federal government and large corporations, and focus locally. She sees as a solution an online revival of 1960s-style feminist consciousness raising groups because conversation can convert shared personal stories into self-confidence and political action. These women aspire to lifelong careers in higher education, which has felt the pervasive effects of corporatism in the form of emphasis on outcomes, the growth of part-time workers, and careerist curricula.

If these women's lived experiences represent their generation of cozy writers and readers,[35] it makes sense that they would delight in (**Cultural Definition 5**) a fantasy formula that, contrary to current realities of women's lives in the U.S., shows respectful men loving women as they really are; women, families, and communities in intimate, empathetic, and face-to-face relationships; independent women fighting for justice and safety for victims of violence and mistreatment; women making a good living in a small community or neighborhood in a larger city, doing what they love; and a world not poisoned by corporate-controlled politics, media, and technology. The fictional fantasy of the contemporary cozy highlights what life should be like for women—and everyone—in our democracy.

The five definitions presented so far in this essay form a multi-faceted picture of the contemporary cozy mystery, a picture that draws from secondary and primary sources, popular culture formula analysis, a comparison with traditional mysteries like Christie's, and disturbing historical and cultural trends in the 1990s. While contemporary cozies share traits with older and more recent traditional mysteries, they provide a new and different fantasy formula that provides a current generation of readers with their "heart's desire" (Cawelti 1). As Amanda Flower puts it, cozies, like all popular fiction, give readers "an escape from the troubles of the real world" ("What Exactly is a Cozy Mystery?" 2).

Epilogue: Composite Definition 6 of the Contemporary Cozy Mystery

A descendent of the classic detective fiction of Agatha Christie and her Golden Age peers, the fast-paced, dialogue-driven, often humorous, female-oriented contemporary cozy mystery subgenre of the traditional mystery emerged in the early 1990s with its unique formula. Unlike mysteries in which all literary elements are subordinated to intellectual crime detection, cozy mysteries emphasize in their series the life journey of a (usually) working-woman amateur sleuth within the context of her colorful small town or urban/suburban neighborhood as she interacts with friends, acquaintances, family, and police to solve a personally motivated murder that affects her community. Personal relationships, including romance, are equally or more important than detection of crime. While cozies often allude to past dark deeds (including sexual abuse) that impact the present, the books do not show explicit violence and sex. Murderers and other characters are seldom evil but humans with moral flaws who succumb to emotion or temptation. Just as Christie-era mysteries provided an appealing fantasy after the traumas and rapid change after World War I, cozies provide a fantasy that repudiates U.S. values and social changes that have emerged since the early 1990s: mass-mediated normalizing of misogyny and sexism, loss of empathy and intimacy due to 24/7 technology obsession, and capitalist economic policies and priorities which have poisoned human life, personal relationships, family stability, and communities. Cozies show an alternative set of values. Working women sleuths reject corporations and bureaucracy for entrepreneurial small businesses or tiny operations that allow them to earn a stable living doing what they love, often traditional feminine pursuits dealing with food, books, and handicrafts. They enjoy life in a smaller community or urban neighborhood among friends, family, and pets, where people know and help each other and communicate face-to-face. The sleuths generally have supportive love relationships with partners (often official investigators) who respect them as they are, independent, flawed women determined to protect their communities. The world of the cozy is not perfect, but it provides an escape from factors making contemporary life increasingly stressful and dehumanizing.

Notes

1. Prior to the 1980s, *cozy* was used as a descriptive adjective, not as a genre descriptor.
2. Peg Johnson of the Sioux City Public Library confirms that mainly women check out cozies.
3. I limit discussion to the U.S. since my survey includes only books available in the United States. A study of the global reach of cozies would enhance our knowledge of this genre.
4. Amanda Flower also writes under the pseudonym Isabella Alan.
5. Cozy mysteries generally avoid the cutesy language that marketers put on their covers.
6. Besides the marketing on cozy covers, the marketing definition is based on these print and online sources: "Cozy Mystery" (*Wikipedia*), Flower, Houghton, Klems, Ius, Oleskiw ("Cozy Mystery"), Rosett, Rogers, Stasio, Teel, and "What Makes a Cozy Just That?"
7. All three titles are cozies by Kate Collins.
8. Flower's acknowledgments (containing a thank you to "my Heavenly Father") and the Amish setting of *Assaulted Caramel* may suggest that all cozies contain heavy emphasis on religion and personal spirituality. Although a sub-genre of Christian cozies exists and churches and ministers may pop up as part of a cozy's community, mainstream cozy marketers don't stress religion as a major trait.
9. In her 1990 Christie biography, Gillian Gill remarks that if she had "relied on Christie's critics rather than immerse myself in the writer's own work, I should probably have done no more than skim one or two of her novels..." (ix). Prior to the 1990s, many Christie critics (e.g., Barnard, Panek, Symons, Wilson) praise her plotting but insult her characterization and style and refuse to grant her work literary significance (Knepper 43, 51). Allison Light remarks in *Forever England* (1991) that "[c]ritics of all political hues" tend "to pass Christie by" (64).
10. In the 1990s and since, besides Gill and Light, these critics and others have rehabilitated Christie's literary reputation: Mark Aldridge, J. C. Bernthal, Julius Green, Sophie Hannah, Allison Light, Merja Makinen, Gill Plain, Susan Rowland, and Melissa Schaub.
11. A 2007 Paul Tomlinson how-to book for aspiring traditional mystery and cozy writers includes mystery history and criticism, but less than 20 pages on the cozy.
12. See Robert Jewett and John Shelton Lawrence's *The Myth of the American Superhero*.
13. I chose to focus on novels in my survey and not include short stories or TV cozies. Nancy Cohen mentions TV cozy series such as *Murder She Wrote* and Hallmark's *Mystery Woman* in *Writing the Cozy Mystery* (4). The novels I used in my survey are listed separately in the works cited.
14. Linda Healy, Helen Lewis, Deanna Mumgaard, Cathy McKnight, Pat Simmons, Mike Nichols.
15. "Intriguing" implies a distinct, memorable setting, not necessarily a charming one.
16. Tomlinson argues that romance novels and romantic comedy helped shape the cozy sleuth (98–99).
17. The amount of comfort food consumed by cozy sleuths may be one of its fantasy appeals.

18. "I like you very much ... just as you are," Mark Darcy tells Bridget in *Bridget Jones's Diary*, the film of the famous chick lit book. Chick lit arose simultaneously with the cozy. A comparison of the two genres would illuminate two complementary directions that 1990s cultural factors drove women's popular literature. *Chick Lit: The New Woman's Fiction* analyzes this genre.

19. These significant cozy elements—romance, abuse, lack of technology, and rejection of urban/corporate life—marketers may not choose to highlight when hyping the cozies in order to distinguish cozies from romances, hide the prevalence of abuse and other dark elements, and appeal to younger readers.

20. Charles Brownson labels what I call the1960 to 1990 "puzzle plus mysteries" the "neoclassical revival" in Chap. 6 of *The Figure of the Detective*.

21. The "plus" the cozy adds is romance, work, community culture, and/or geographical setting.

22. The term *traditional mystery* is problematic since pioneering works in the hard-boiled, police procedural, thriller, and spy subgenres could also be called "traditional mysteries."

23. Adam Fullerton found an even earlier use of the descriptive adjective *cosy* by Maurice Richardson in a brief review titled "Crime Ration" in the Sunday [London] *Observer* on 8 Mar. 1953: "cosy, consequential murder mystery with snug old-fashioned flavour...."

24. The authors or titles of sources I surveyed to find when the genre label *cozy* began to be used include the following, in chronological order: (1920s) *14 Great Detective Stories*, *The Omnibus of Crime*; (1930s) Thompson; (1940s) Haycraft, *101 Years' Entertainment*, Rodel, *The Art of the Mystery Story*; (1950s) *A Treasury of Great Mysteries*, Murch; (1970s) *The Mystery Writer's Art*, Barzun and Taylor, *Murder Most Foul*, Watson, Routley, Symons, *Detective Fiction: Crime and Compromise*, *Crime on Her Mind*, *A Mystery Reader*, *Dimensions of Detective Fiction*, *Encyclopedia of Mystery and Detection*, Ousby—*Bloodhounds of Heaven*, Haining, *Murder Ink*, *The Great Detectives*, *Bedside, Bathtub, and Armchair Companion*, *Murderess Ink*, *Women's Wiles*; (1980s) *Detective Fiction: A Collection of Critical Essays*, Knight, Craig and Cadogan, *The Poetics of Murder*, *Roots of Detection*, *Great Detectives*, *Colloquium on Crime*, Pronzini and Muller, *The Black Lizard Anthology of Crime Fiction*, Panek, *Masterpieces of Mystery and Suspense*, Binyon, Keating, *A Reader's Guide to the Classic British Mystery*, Schwartz; (1990s) *Women of Mystery*, *Murder Is Academic*, *The New Mystery*, DeAndrea, Kathleen G. Klein—*Great Women Mystery Writers*, Munt, Ousby—*Guilty Parties*, *Deadly Women*, Hoppenstand, Oleksiw—"Cozy Mystery"; (2000s) Scaggs, Bleiler, Mansfield-Kelley and Marchino; (2010s) Edwards.

25. Some other terms for the classic detective story used in the above listed sources include *howdunit, whydunit, house party story, domestic detective story, fictive mayhem, Mayhem-Parva school, comedy of manners, country house mystery, domestic malice,* and *village mysteries*.

26. Earl F. Bargainnier (7), Dorothy Salisbury Davis (66), Kathleen G. Klein (4), William DeAndrea (64), Ian Ousby—*Guilty Parties* (160), Neil McCaw (41), and Teri White (127).

27. In 2017, Paul Tomlinson confidently uses *traditional murder mystery* to refer to Agatha Christie-style whodunits and *modern cozy mysteries* to describe a distinct subgenre of the traditional mystery (7).

28. Other Christie young adventurer books include (American title first): *The Secret of Chimneys* (1925), *The Seven Dials Mystery* (1929), *Partners in Crime* (1929), *The Boomerang Clue/Why Didn't They Ask Evans?* (1934), *They Came to Baghdad* (1951), and *So Many Steps to Death/Destination Unknown* (1954).

29. In "Agatha Christie: Modern and Modernist," Nicholas Birns and Margaret Boe Birns argue that "pretense, disguise, play-acting, and outward show" are "essential to the [classic] mystery genre and given a special intensity in Christie's work...." (122).

30. See Susan Faludi's *Backlash* (1991) for a discussion of 1980s anti-feminism.

31. See Knepper and Lawrence (1–40). While 1990s rural nostalgia tanked in the new millennium, cozies have increased in popularity since the 1990s, suggesting that their appeal transcends nostalgia.

32. Daniel Rodgers and Dag Einar Thorsen write about problems with the term *neoliberalism*, which has worn different guises in different times and places and been defined mostly

by fierce defenders or supporters. *Neoliberalism* is neither new nor liberal in the more recent popular use of the term *liberal*.

33. Poll discusses the airplane industry, showing that deregulation, lowering prices, and keeping corporate profits high have led to decreases in safety, worker training, and worker salaries, according to the real Captain Sully, whose memoir Clint Eastwood transformed into the neoliberal heroic film *Sully*.

34. Whether the cozy is feminist and what definition of feminism it might fit are debatable issues beyond this paper's scope. Catherine Rottenberg's *The Rise of Neoliberal Feminism* (2018) might provide a starting place, with her skeptical view of recent media feminism that aligns with neoliberalism.

35. Another definition of the cozy, beyond the scope of this essay, might focus on cozy readers' experiences. Janice Radway's *Reading the Romance* provides a model for studying reader interactions with popular fiction and shows that stereotypical assumptions about why readers like a popular genre don't necessarily prove accurate when in-depth interviews with readers are conducted.

Contemporary Cozy Mysteries in Survey

Adams, Ellery. *Murder in the Locked Library*. New York: Kensington, 2018. Print.
Albert, Susan Wittig. *The Tale of Hilltop Farm*. New York: Berkley, 2004. Print.
Alexander, Ellie. *Caught Bread Handed*. New York: St. Martin's, 2016. Print.
Arlington, Lucy. *Played by the Book*. New York: Berkley, 2015. Print.
Atherton, Nancy. *Aunt Dimity: Detective*. New York: Viking, 2001. Print.
Bartlett, Lorraine. *A Crafty Killing*. New York: Berkley, 2011. Print.
Blackwell, Juliet. *Tarnished and Torn*. New York: Obsidian, 2013. Print.
Bowen, Rhys. *Royal Blood*. New York: Berkley, 2010. Print.
Bradley, Alan. *The Sweetness at the Bottom of the Pie*. London: Orion, 2009. Print.
Brightwell, Emily. *Mrs. Jeffries Plays the Cook*. New York: Berkley, 1995. Print.
Brown, Rita Mae. *Pawing Through the Past*. New York: Bantam, 2000. Print.
Cahoon, Lynn. *Killer Green Tomatoes*. New York: Lyrical Underground/Kensington, 2018. Print.
Carlisle, Kate. *Once Upon a Spine*. New York: Berkley, 2017. Print.
Cates, Bailey. *Spells and Scones*. New York: Berkley, 2016. Print.
Cavender, Chris. *A Slice of Murder*. New York: Kensington, 2009. Print.
Chesney, Marion. *Hasty Death*. New York: Minotaur, 2004. Print.
Childs, Laura. *Scones and Bones*. New York: Berkley, 2011. Print.
Collins, Kate. *Moss Hysteria*. New York: Berkley, 2016. Print.
Connolly, Sheila. *Many a Twist*. New York: Crooked Lane, 2018. Print.
Coyle, Cleo. *Holiday Grind*. New York: Berkley, 2009. Print.
Daheim, Mary. *Silver Scream*. New York: Morrow, 2002. Print.
Daley, Kathi. *Turkeys, Tuxes, and Tabbies*. Lake Tahoe, CA: Kathi Daley Books, 2014. Print.
Davidson, Diane Mott. *Catering to Nobody*. New York: Minotaur, 1990. Print.
Davis, Krista. *Diva Steals a Chocolate Kiss*. New York: Berkley, 2015. Print.
Delany, Vicki. *Among the Departed*. Scottsdale, AZ: Poisoned Pen Press, 2011. Print.
DiSilverio, Laura. *The Readaholics and the Poirot Puzzle*. New York: Berkley, 2015. Print.
Duncan, Elizabeth J. *Murder on the Hour*. New York: Minotaur, 2016. Print.
Dunn, Carola. *Anthem for Doomed Youth*. New York: Minotaur, 2011. Print.
Flower, Amanda. *Assaulted Caramel*. New York: Kensington, 2017. Print.
Fluke, Joanne. *Devil's Food Cake Murder*. New York: Kensington, 2011. Print.
Frazer, Margaret. *The Apostate's Tale*. New York: Berkley, 2008. Print.
Goldenbaum, Sally. *Death by Cashmere*. New York: NAL, 2008. Print.
Haines, Carolyn. *Them Bones*. New York: Bantam, 1999. Print.
Harris, Charlaine. *Shakespeare's Christmas*. New York: Minotaur, 1998. Print.
Hart, Carolyn G. *The Christie Caper*. New York: Bantam, 1991. Print.

Hart, Ellen. *Hallowed Murder*. Seattle: Seal Press, 1989. Print.
Hess, Joan. *Pride v. Prejudice*. New York: Minotaur, 2015. Print.
Hyzy, Julie. *Foreign Eclairs*. New York: Berkley, 2016. Print.
James, Dean. *Baked to Death*. New York: Kensington, 2005. Print.
Kelly, Sofie. *Paws and Effect*. New York: Berkley, 2016. Print.
MacLeod, Charlotte. *The Balloon Man*. New York: Mysterious Press, 1998. Print.
Martin, Nancy. *Cross Your Heart and Hope to Die*. New York: NAL, 2005. Print.
Maxwell, Edith. *A Tine to Live, A Tine to Die*. New York: Kensington, 2013. Print.
McKinlay, Jenn. *Copy Cap Murder*. New York: Berkley, 2016. Print.
Meier, Leslie. *Bake Sale Murder*. New York: Kensington, 2006. Print.
Page, Katherine Hall. *The Body in the Boudoir*. New York: Morrow, 2012. Print.
Perona, Elizabeth. *Murder on the Bucket List*. Woodbury, MN: Midnight Ink, 2015. Print.
Peters, Elizabeth. *Naked Once More*. New York: Warner, 1989. Print.
Ross, Barbara. *Fogged Inn*. New York: Kensington, 2016. Print.
Sefton, Maggie. *A Killer Stitch*. New York: Berkley, 2007. Print.
Shelton, Paige. *Of Books and Bagpipes*. New York: Minotaur, 2017. Print.
Smith, Alexander McCall. *The No. 1 Ladies Detective Agency*. Johannesburg: David Philip, 1998. Print.
Smith, Karen Rose. *Silence of the Lamps*. New York: Kensington, 2016. Print.
Swanson, Denise. *Murder of a Sweet Old Lady*. New York: Signet, 2001. Print.
Wait, Lea. *Twisted Threads*. New York: Kensington, 2015. Print.
Wenger, Christine. *It's a Wonderful Knife*. New York: Obsidian, 2016. Print.

Works Cited

"Agatha Awards." *Malice Domestic*. Malice Domestic. N.d. Web. 5 Aug. 2019. http://malicedomestic.org/agathas.html.
Aldridge, Mark. *Agatha Christie on Screen*. London: Palgrave Macmillan, 2016. Print. Crime Files.
"Amanda Flower." *Amanda Flower*. N.d. Web. 5 Aug. 2019. http://www.amandaflower.com/.
"Amanda Flower Books in Order." *Book Series in Order*. N.d. Web. 5 Aug. 2019. https://www.bookseriesinorder.com/amanda-flower/.
The Art of the Mystery Story: A Collection of Critical Essays. Ed. Howard Haycraft. 1946. New York: Carroll and Graf, 1983. Print.
Auden, W. H. "The Guilty Vicarage." *The Dyers Hand and Other Essays* by W. H. Auden. New York: Random, 1948. Rpt. in *Detective Fiction: Crime and Compromise*. 400–10. Print.
Barnard, Robert. *A Talent to Deceive: An Appreciation of Agatha Christie*. New York: Dodd, 1980. Print.
Barzun, Jacques, and Wendell Hertig Taylor. *A Catalogue of Crime: Being a Reader's Guide to the Literature of Mystery, Detection, and Related Genres*. New York: Harper, 1971. Print.
Bedside, Bathtub, and Armchair Companion to Agatha Christie. Ed. Dick Reilly and Pam McAllister. New York: Ungar, 1979. Print.
Bargainnier, Earl F. *The Gentle Art of Murder: The Detective Fiction of Agatha Christie*. Bowling Green, OH: Bowling Green University Popular Press, 1980. Print.
Bernthal, J. C. *Queering Agatha Christie: Revisiting the Golden Age of Detective Fiction*. London: Palgrave Macmillan, 2016. Print. Crime Files.
Binyon, T. J. *Murder Will Out: The Detective in Fiction*. Oxford: Oxford University Press, 1989. Print.
Birns, Nicholas, and Margaret Boe Birns. "Agatha Christie: Modern and Modernist." *The Cunning Craft: Original Essays on Detective Fiction and Contemporary Literary Theory*. Ed. Ronald G. Walker and June M. Frazer. Macomb: Western Illinois University, 1990. Print.
The Black Lizard Anthology of Crime Fiction. Ed. Edward Gorman. Berkeley: Black Lizard Books, 1987. Print.
Bleiler, Richard J. *Reference and Research Guide to Mystery and Detective Fiction*. 2nd ed. Westport, CT: Libraries Unlimited, 2004. Print.

Bridget Jones's Diary. Dir. Sharon Maguire. Perf. Renee Zellweger, Colin Firth, Hugh Grant. Miramax, 2007. Film.

Brownson, Charles. *The Figure of the Detective: A Literary History and Analysis*. Jefferson City, NC: McFarland, 2014. Print.

"Browse the Cozies." *Kensington Cozies: Where Murder Lives!* Kensington Publishing. N.d. Web. 3 July 2019. https://www.kensingtonbooks.com/catalog.aspx/98/Cozy.

Cawelti, John G. *Adventure, Mystery, and Romance: Formula Stories as Art and Popular Culture*. Chicago: University of Chicago Press, 1976. Print.

Chick Lit: The New Woman's Fiction. Ed. Suzanne Ferriss and Mallory Young. New York: Routledge, 2006. Print.

Christie, Agatha. "The Bloodstained Pavement" *Miss Marple: The Complete Short Stories*. New York: Putnam's, 1985. Print.

_____. *The Boomerang Clue*. 1933. New York: Dell, 1966. Print.

_____. *The Man in the Brown Suit*. 1924. New York: Dell, 1974. Print.

_____. *Partners in Crime*. 1929. New York: Dell, 1967. Print.

_____. *The Secret Adversary*. 1922. New York: Bantam, 1974. Print.

_____. *The Secret of Chimneys*. 1925. New York: Dell, 1975. Print.

_____. *The Seven Dials Mystery*. 1929. New York: Bantam, 1971. Print.

_____. *So Many Steps to Death*. 1955. New York: Pocket, 1973. Print.

_____. *There is a Tide*. 1948. New York: Dell, 1965. Print.

_____. *They Came to Baghdad*. 1951. New York: Dell, 1974. Print.

_____. *Three Blind Mice*. *Three Blind Mice and Other Stories*. 1925. New York: Berkley, 1984. Print.

Cohen, Nancy J. *Writing the Cozy Mystery*. 2nd ed. N.p.: Orange Grove Press, 2018. Print.

Collins, Kate. *Moss Hysteria*. New York: Berkley, 2016. Print.

_____. *A Rose from the Dead*. New York: Berkley, 2007. Print.

_____. *Yews with Caution*. New York: Berkley, 2017. Print.

Colloquium on Crime. Ed. Robin W. Winks. New York: Scribner's, 1986. Print.

"Cozy Mystery." *Wikipedia*. 15 July 2018. Web. 16 June 2019. https://en.wikipedia.org/wiki/cozy_mystery.

"Cozy Mystery List." *Cozy-Mystery.com*. 2019. Web. 3 July 2019. https://www.cozy-mystery.com/.

Craig, Patricia, and Mary Cadogan. *The Lady Investigates: Women Detectives and Spies in Fiction*. New York: St. Martin's, 1981. Print.

Crime on Her Mind: Fifteen Stories of Female Sleuths from the Victorian Era to the Forties. Ed. Michele B. Slung. New York: Pantheon, 1975. Print.

Curran, John. "75 Facts About Christie." *The Home of Agatha Christie* [Agatha Christie official website]. N.d. Web. 19 June 2019. https://www.agathachristie.com/about-christie/christie-experts/john-curran-75-facts-about-christie.

Davis, Dorothy Salisbury. "Some of the Truth: Dorothy Salisbury Davis." *Colloquium on Crime*. 63–78. Print.

Davis, Tessa Lanae. "Fanning the Flame: Female User Expectancy of 'Matches' on Tinder." National Popular Culture Assn./American Culture Assn. Conference. 19 Apr. 2019. Speech.

Deadly Women: The Woman Mystery Reader's Indispensable Companion. Ed. Jan Grape, Dean James, and Ellen Nehr. New York: Carroll and Graf, 1998. Print.

DeAndrea, William L. *Encyclopedia Mysteriosa: A Comprehensive Guide to the Art of Detection in Print, Film, Radio, and Television*. New York: Prentice, 1994. Print.

Detective Fiction: A Collection of Critical Essays. Ed. Robin W. Winks. Rev. ed. Woodstock, VT: Foul Play-Countryman, 1988. Print.

Detective Fiction: Crime and Compromise. Ed. Dick Allen and David Chacko. New York: Harcourt, 1974. Print.

Dimensions of Detective Fiction. Ed. Larry N. Landrum, Pat Browne, and Ray B. Browne. Bowling Green, OH: Popular Press, 1976. Print.

Edwards, Martin. *The Golden Age of Murder: The Mystery of the Writers who Invented the Modern Detective Story*. London: Collins Crime Club-HarperCollins, 2015. Print.

Encyclopedia of Mystery and Detection. Ed. Chris Steinbrunner and Otto Penzler. New York: McGraw-Hill, 1976. Print.

Faludi, Susan. *Backlash: The Undeclared War Against American Women.* New York: Three Rivers-Crown, 1991. Print.
Flower, Amanda. *Assaulted Caramel.* New York: Kensington, 2017. Print.
_____. "What Exactly is a Cozy Mystery?" *Publishers Weekly.* Publishers Weekly. 18 May 2018. Web. 16 June 2019. https://www.publishersweekly.com/pw/by-topic/industry-news/tip-sheet/article/76834-the-enduring-appeal-of-the-cozy-mystery.html.
"45 Best Cozy Mystery Novels: Essential 2019 Guide to First Book of a Series. *MysteryTribune.com.* N.d. Web. 16 June 2019. https://www.mysterytribune.com/45-best-cozy-mystery-novels-essential-2019-guide-to-first-book-of-a-series/.
14 Great Detective Stories. Ed. Vincent Starrett. New York: Modern Library, 1928. Print.
Fullerton, Adam. Director, Hickman-Johnson-Furrow Library, Morningside College. Email to author. 27 Aug. 2019.
Gill, Gillian. *Agatha Christie: The Woman and Her Mysteries.* New York: Free Press-Macmillan, 1990. Print.
Great Detectives: A Century of the Best Mysteries from England and America. Ed. David Willis McCullough. New York: Pantheon, 1984. Print.
The Great Detectives. Ed. Otto Penzler. New York: Little, 1978. Print.
Green, Julius. *Curtain Up: Agatha Christie: A Life in the Theatre.* New York: HarperCollins, 2015. Print.
Haining, Peter. *Mystery! An Illustrated History of Crime and Detective Fiction.* New York: Stein and Day, 1977. Print.
Hannah, Sophie. "No One Should Ever Condescend to Agatha Christie—She's a Genius." *TheGuardian.com.* The Guardian. 16 May 2015. Web. 16 June 2019. https://sophiehannah.com/no-one-should-condescend-to-agatha-christie-shes-a-genius/.
Harris, Sherry. "Can We Just Stop?" *The Wickeds: Wicked Good Mysteries.* 9 May 2019. Web. 10 May 2019. https://wickedauthors.com/2019/05/09/can-we-just-stop/.
Hart, Carolyn G. "Why I Don't Write Hard-Boiled." *Deadly Women.* 129–31. Print.
Haycraft, Howard. *Murder for Pleasure: The Life and Times of the Detective Story.* 1941. New York: Carroll and Graf, 1984. Print.
The Home of Agatha Christie [Agatha Christie official website]. N.d. Web. 19 June 2019. https://www.agathachristie.com/.
Hoppenstand, Gary, ed. Introduction. *Popular Fiction: An Anthology.* New York: Longman-Addison, Wesley, Longman, 1998. 1–7. Print.
Houghton, Kristen. "The Immense Popularity of the Cozy Mysteries." *HuffPost.* Huffington Post. 4 Feb. 2016. Web. 16 June 2019. https://www.huffingtonpost.com/entry/the-immense-popularity-of-the-cozy-mysteries_b_9143266.
Ius, Dawn. "Trend Report: The State of the Cozy." *The Big Thrill.* 30 Nov. 2017. Web. 16 June 2019. https://www.thebigthrill.org/2017/11/trend-report-the-state-of-the-cozy/.
Jewett, Robert, and John Shelton Lawrence. *The Myth of the American Superhero.* Grand Rapids, MI: Eerdmans, 2002. Print.
Johnson, Peg. Circulation, Sioux City Public Library. Telephone interview. 22 Aug. 2019.
Keating, H. R. F. *The Bedside Companion to Crime.* New York: Mysterious Press, 1989. Print.
Kinsman, Margaret. *Sara Paretsky: A Companion to the Mystery Fiction.* Jefferson, NC: McFarland, 2016. Print. McFarland Companions to Mystery Fiction.
Klein, Kathleen Gregory. Introduction. *Great Women Mystery Writers: Classic to Contemporary.* Ed. Kathleen Gregory Klein. Westport, CT: Greenwood, 1994. 1–9. Print.
Klein, Naomi. *The Shock Doctrine: The Rise of Disaster Capitalism.* New York: Picador-Holt, 2007. Print.
Klems, Brian M. "4 Things You Should Know about Writing a Cozy Mystery Novel." *Writers-Digest.Com.* Writer's Digest. 22 July 2014. Web. 16 June 2019. https://www.writersdigest.com/online-editor/4-things-you-should-know-about-writing-a-cozy-mystery-novel.
Knepper, Marty S. "Reading Agatha Christie's Miss Marple Series: The Thirteen Problems." *In the Beginning: First Novels in Mystery Series.* Ed. Mary Jean DeMarr. Bowling Green, OH: Bowling Green State University Popular Press, 1995. 33–57. Print.
_____, and John Shelton Lawrence. Introduction. *The Book of Iowa Films.* Berkeley: Book of Iowa Films Press, 2014. 1–40. Print.

Knight, Stephen. *Form and Ideology in Crime Fiction*. Bloomington: Indiana University Press, 1980. Print.
Light, Alison. *Forever England: Femininity, Literature, and Conservatism Between the Wars*. New York: Routledge, 1991. Print.
Lipman, Joanne. *That's What She Said: What Men Need to Know (And Women Need to Tell Them) About Working Together*. New York: Morrow-HarperCollins, 2018. Print.
Makinen, Merja. *Agatha Christie: Investigating Femininity*. New York: Palgrave Macmillan, 2006. Print. Crime Files.
Malice Domestic. "About." *Malice Domestic*. N.d. Web. 16 June 2019. http://malicedomestic.org/about.html.
Mansfield-Kelley, Deane, and Lois A. Marchino, eds. Introduction to Diane Moss Davidson. *The Longman Anthology of Detective Fiction*. New York: Pearson-Longman, 2005. 185–86. Print.
Masterpieces of Mystery and Suspense. Comp. Martin H. Greenberg. Garden City, NY: Doubleday, 1988. Print.
McCaw, Neil. *Adapting Detective Fiction: Crime, Englishness, and the TV Detectives*. New York: Continuum, 2011. Print.
McChesney, Robert W. Introduction. *Profit over People: Neoliberalism and Global Order* by Noam Chomsky. New York: Seven Stories Press, 1999. 7–16. Print.
Munt, Sally R. *Murder by the Book? Feminism and the Crime Novel*. London: Routledge, 1994. Print. Narrative Forms and Social Formations.
Murch, A. E. *Development of the Detective Novel*. 1958. New York: Greenwood, 1968. Print.
Murder Ink: The Mystery Reader's Companion. Ed. Dilys Winn. New York: Workman, 1977. Print.
Murder Is Academic: A Collection of Crime Fiction Course Syllabi. Ed. B. J. Rahn. New York: English Department, Hunter College, 1993. Print.
Murder Most Foul. Ed. Harold Q. Masur. New York: Walker, 1971. Print.
Murderess Ink: The Better Half of the Mystery. Ed. Dilys Winn. New York: Workman, 1979. Print.
A Mystery Reader: Stories of Detection, Adventure, and Horror. Ed. Nancy Ellen Talburt and Lyna Lee Montgomery. New York: Scribner's, 1975. Print.
The Mystery Writer's Art. Ed. Francis M. Nevins, Jr. Bowling Green, OH: Bowling Green University Popular Press, 1970. Print.
Nachbar, Jack, and Kevin Lause. Intoduction. *Popular Culture: An Introductory Text*. Bowling Green, OH: Bowling Green State University Popular Press, 1992. 1–35. Print.
Nehr, Ellen. "Why Do They Call Them Cozies?" *Deadly Women*. 127–28. Print.
The New Mystery. Ed. Jerome Charyn. New York: Dutton, 1993. Print.
Oleksiw, Susan. "Cozy Mystery." *The Oxford Companion to Crime and Mystery Writing*. Ed. Rosemary Herbert et al. New York: Oxford University Press, 1999. 97–98. Print.
———. *A Reader's Guide to the Classic British Mystery*. New York: Mysterious Press, 1988. Print.
Olsen, Tillie. *Silences*. New York: Dell, 1979. Print.
The Omnibus of Crime. Ed. Dorothy L. Sayers. New York: Payson and Clarke, 1929. Print.
100 Great Detectives. Ed. Maxim Jakubowski. New York: Carroll and Graf, 1991. Print.
101 Years' Entertainment: The Great Detective Stories, 1841–1941. Ed. Ellery Queen. Boston: Little, 1943. Print.
Ousby, Ian. *Bloodhounds of Heaven: The Detective in English Fiction from Godwin to Doyle*. Cambridge: Harvard University Press, 1976. Print.
———. *Guilty Parties: A Mystery Lover's Companion*. New York: Thames and Hudson, 1997. Print.
Panek, LeRoy Lad. *An Introduction to the Detective Story*. Bowling Green, OH: Bowling Green State University Popular Press, 1987. Print.
Place, Ali. "IRL Feminism: Bridging Physical and Digital Spaces to Empower Millennial Activists." National Popular Culture Assn./American Culture Assn. Conference. 19 Apr. 2019. Speech.
Plain, Gill. *Literature of the 1940s: War, Postwar, and 'Peace.'* Edinburgh: Edinburgh

University Press, 2013. Print. The Edinburgh History of Twentieth-Century Literature in Britain. Vol. 5.
The Poetics of Murder: Detective Fiction and Literary Theory. Ed. Glenn W. Most and William W. Stowe. New York: Harcourt, 1983. Print.
Poll, Ryan. "Neoliberal Heroes: Clint Eastwood's *Sully* and the Haunting of History." *Journal of Popular Culture* 51.2 (2018): 446–65. Print.
Pronzini, Bill, and Marcia Muller. *1001 Midnights: The Aficionado's Guide to Mystery and Detective Fiction.* New York: Arbor House, 1986. Print.
Radway, Janice A. *Reading the Romance: Women, Patriarchy, and Popular Literature.* Rev. ed. Chapel Hill: University of North Carolina Press, 1991. Print.
Richardson, Maurice. "Crime Ration." *The Observer* 8 Mar. 1953: 11. Newspapers.com. Web. 27 Aug. 2019. https://www.newspapers.com/image/258341832/?terms=the%2Bobserver%2B%22cosy%2Bmurder%2Bmystery%22#.
_____. "Crime Ration." *The Observer* 25 May 1958: 16. Newspapers.com. Web. 27 Aug. 2019. https://www.newspapers.com/image/257877699/?terms=the%2Bobserver%2B%22cosy%2Bmurder%2Bmystery%22.
Rodel, Marie F. *Mystery Fiction: Theory and Technique.* 1943. Rev. ed. New York: Hermitage House, 1952. Print.
Rodgers, Daniel. "The Uses and Abuses of 'Neoliberalism.'" *Dissent* 65.1 (Winter 2018): 78–87. Project Muse. Web. doi:10.1353/dss.2018.0010.
Roerden, Chris. *Don't Murder Your Mystery: 24 Fiction-Writing Techniques to Save Your Manuscript from Turning Up ... D.O.A.* Rock Hill, SC: BellaRosa Books, 2006. Print.
Rogers, Stephen D. "Writing the Cozy Mystery." *Writing-World.Com.* 2013. Web. 16 June 2019. https://www.writing-world.com/mystery/cozy.shtml.
Roots of Detection: The Art of Deduction before Sherlock Holmes. Ed. Bruce Cassiday. New York: Ungar, 1983. Print.
Rosett, Sara. *How to Outline a Cozy Mystery.* 2nd ed. N.p.: McGuffin, Ink, 2018. Print.
Rottenberg, Catherine. *The Rise of Neoliberal Feminism.* New York: Oxford University Press, 2018. Print. Heretical Thought.
Routley, Erik. *The Puritan Pleasures of the Detective Story: From Sherlock Holmes to Van der Valk.* London: Gollancz, 1972. Print.
Rowland, Susan. *From Agatha Christie to Ruth Rendell: British Women Writers in Detective and Crime Fiction.* New York: Palgrave, 2001. Print. Crime Files.
Russ, Joanna. *How to Suppress Women's Writing.* 1983. Austin: University of Texas Press, 2018. Print.
Sanders, Dennis, and Len Lovallo. *The Agatha Christie Companion: The Complete Guide to Agatha Christie's Life and Work.* Rev. ed. New York: Berkley, 1989. Print.
Scaggs, John. *Crime Fiction.* New York: Routledge, 2005. Print. The New Critical Idiom.
Schaub, Melissa. *Middlebrow Feminism in Classic British Detective Fiction: The Female Gentleman.* New York: Palgrave Macmillan, 2013. Print. Crime Files.
Schwartz, Saul. *The Detective Story: An Introduction to the World's Greatest Whodunit Sleuths and Their Creators.* Lincolnwood, IL: National Textbook, 1989. Print.
Stasio, Marilyn. "Crime/Mystery; Murder Least Foul: The Cozy, Soft-Boiled Mystery." *The New York Times.* New York Times. 18 Oct. 1992. Web. 16 June 2019. https://www.nytimes.com/1992/10/18/books/crime-mystery-murder-least-foul-the-cozy-soft-boiled-mystery.html.
Steger, Manfred B., and Ravi K. Roy. *Neoliberalism: A Very Short Introduction.* Oxford: Oxford University Press, 2010. Print.
Symons, Julian. *Mortal Consequences: A History from the Detective Story to the Crime Novel.* New York: Schocken, 1972. Print.
Teel, John. "Whither the Cozy Mystery: Observations on the State of a Sub-Genre." National Popular Culture Assn./American Culture Assn. Conference. Indianapolis. 30 Mar. 2018. Speech.
Thompson, H. Douglas. *Masters of Mystery: A Study of the Detective Story.* 1931. New York: Dover, 1978. Print.
Thorsen, Dag Einer. "The Neoliberal Challenge: What is Neoliberalism?" *Contemporary*

Readings in Law and Social Justice 2.2 (2010): 188–214. Addleton Academic Publishers . 12 Sept. 2019. Web. https://addletonacademicpublishers.com/search-in-crlsj/1365-the-neoliberal-challenge-what-is-neoliberalism.

Tomlinson, Paul. *Mystery: How to Write Traditional and Cozy Whodunits*. N.p.: Paul Tomlinson, 2017. Print.

A Treasury of Great Mysteries. Ed. Howard Haycraft and John Beecroft. Vol 1. Garden City, NY: Nelson Doubleday, 1957. Print.

Trebek, Alex. *Jeopardy*. CBS. KMEG, Sioux City, IA, 22 Nov. 2018. Television.

Turkle, Sherry. *Reclaiming Conversation: The Power of Talk in a Digital Age*. New York: Penguin-Random House, 2015. Print.

Watson, Amy. "Unit Sales of Adult Fiction Books in the United States in 2017, by Category (in Millions)." *Statista*. 22 Jan. 2018. Web. 5 Aug. 2019. https://www.statista.com/statistics/730316/adult-fiction-unit-sales/.

Watson, Colin. *Snobbery and Violence: Crime Stories and Their Audience*. New York: St. Martin's, 1971. Print.

"What Makes a Cozy Just That?" *Cozy Mystery List*. N.d. Web. 16 June 2019. https://www.cozy-mystery.com/definition-of-a-cozy-mystery.html.

White, Teri. "Why I Don't Write Cozies." *Deadly Women*. 133–34. Print.

Wilson, Edmund. "Who Cares Who Killed Roger Ackroyd?" *Classics and Commercials: A Literary Chronicle of the Forties* by Edmund Wilson. New York: Farrar, 1950. Rpt. in *Detective Fiction: A Collection of Critical Essays*. 35–40. Print.

Women of Mystery. Ed. Cynthia Manson. 1992. New York: Castle Books, 2002. Print.

Women's Wiles: An Anthology of Mystery Stories by the Mystery Writers of America. Ed. Michele Slung. New York: Harcourt, 1979. Print.

Yarrow, Allison. *90s Bitch: Media, Culture, and the Failed Promise of Gender Equality*. New York: Perennial-Harper, 2018. Print.

Special thanks for their contributions to this essay go to Jamie Bernthal, Phyllis Betz, Adam Fullerton, John and Nancy Lawrence, the Mystery/Detective Fiction caucus of the Popular Culture Association, Mike Nichols, the Sioux City Booked on Crime group, John Teel, Jeff Zink, and especially my husband, John L. Knepper.

The Cozy from the Margins
The Archetypes of Home and Heroism from Inside and Outside the Modern Cozy

Susan Rowland

Introduction: No Cozy?

Published in 2010, *A Companion to Crime Fiction,* edited by Charles J. Rzepka and Lee Horsley, contains forty-seven essays. None refer to the modern phenomenon that is cozy detective fiction. In the index, a single entry reads, "cozy detection, *see* classical detection" (605). Yet the cozy subgenre is popular, has established antecedents and attracts a complex range of variants and tones. Associated primarily with women writers and readers, the cozy was effectively summed up by Katharina Vester.

> Cozy mysteries developed out of the classic English detective story and, unlike the hard-boiled crime novel, avoid gruesome depictions of violence, gore, and sex. Instead they focus on the puzzle the crime presents and how it can be solved, based on the belief that the world is ruled by causality and can be deciphered through reasoning. The light-hearted texts commonly feature a female amateur sleuth who lives, works, and loves in a tightly knit, small-town community in which everything is in order save the occasional murder upon which the protagonist happens to stumble. The female sleuth is often depicted as nosy, more interested in good relationships and romance than in her career, and more concerned about her family and friends than about herself [31].

Added to this standard definition might be a liberal use of humor and the frequent addition of pets as characters in the story. These tropes occur frequently enough to distinguish a subgenre from the "classical" mystery, also called "clue-puzzle," "golden age" or "traditional mystery." In fact, as author of the classical golden age entry in *A Companion to Crime Fiction,* I can testify that the cozy is not sufficiently covered by exploring the tradition exemplified by Agatha Christie, Dorothy L. Sayers, Margery Allingham and Ngaio Marsh. Only Christie provides an amateur female sleuth, and while

Miss Marple is an inspiration to generations of mystery writers, she does not confront the peculiar modern trials of earning a living, maintaining a family, and sustaining a community. For the cozy detective these are regularly put in peril by murder striking close to home.

Overtly contrasting to the cozy is the development of feminist hardboiled crime from the 1970s and 1980s in the pioneering fiction of Marcia Muller, Sue Grafton and Sara Paretsky. These women writers provided professional detectives who show what it is like for a woman working in a male dominated environment. Private eyes Sharon McCone, Kinsey Millhone and V.I. Warshawski share physical danger with male counterparts compounded by an added layer of sexism and patriarchy. Ostensibly there is nothing cozy about their lives or stories. Do they only share gender with the protagonists and most authors of the modern cozy?

In this essay, I want to look at the contested borders of the cozy subgenre in relation to what might best be called the traditional mystery, in particular with American female pioneers, and to modern crime fiction by women with far from cozy aims. In effect, I will look at this marginal genre from its margins: in specific historical antecedents and contemporary writers using detective fiction for social criticism. Cozies are supposed to be light and comforting so they cannot critique real social oppression, or can they? What marks out the cozy, I suggest, is a tonal quality that makes of a murder story something comforting and restorative. To explore this quality, I will bring in perspectives from myth and Jungian literary criticism. These are particularly suited to working with genres that flower into new modalities while evoking something very ancient. Therefore, first of all, a look at genre, gender and archetype.

The Purest Literature We Have

In *Strong Poison*, Sayers's detective, Lord Peter Wimsey fell inconveniently in love with a woman facing the death penalty for a murder she did not commit. To cap it all, the alleged murderess wrote detective stories for a living. They are "the purest literature we have," retorted Wimsey, asserting mysteries to be the successor to those medieval romances when knights set out to right wrongs (132). Detective fiction is archetypal not just because it grips readers of many ages in different cultures, but also because the detective is a necessary modern hero. Put another way, there are three recognizable prototypes to the modern detective who restores a world to rights. They are the knight errant, the hunter and the trickster. The knight is sent out to aid vulnerable members of the community in an era lacking organized forces of law and order. The hunter is a far older figure, reaching back before settled communities when humans lived hunter-gather lives. There hunters learned to be tricksters in snaring more nimble or larger or elusive prey. Tracking clues brings out the trickster in the hunter. What makes these three figures prototypes of the *cozy* mystery is how far they are oriented to restoring or making a "good place." The cozy contains a recognizable metaphysical dream for safety and justice; a kind of return to Eden without death. I say without death because cozies abolish death by making it unnatural and hence solvable. Cozy narratives are a magic charm against death as inevitable and irreversible. Hence the presence in the cozy of divine archetypes as I shall show below.

According to C.G. Jung, archetypes are not inherited images, forms or ideas. They are rather inborn human potentials for certain sorts of images, behaviors and meaning. Humans have lived for the longest span of time as hunter-gatherers. Perhaps the hunter-trickster archetype became engraved in being. After all, at the root of the hunting archetype is an energy pattern integral to detective fiction as a whole, the ambiguity of the trickster. Found in myth and folktales in many cultures, the trickster is not a reliable savior of the group, but his skills are. Lewis Hyde suggests that trickster energy, in the form of stories, taught ancient humans the skills of hunting and being hunted (1998). In detective fiction, as for our Paleolithic ancestors, humans are both hunters and prey; the detective and criminal frequent both roles. Moreover, the genre itself is a trickster in enticing the reader into a competition to see whodunit.

Hunting was required for the community to survive and thrive while trickster strategies could prevent frail humans from themselves becoming prey. Much later in eras in which justice acquired a social meaning, yet lacked police enforcement, the noble knight could focus desires for a solution to murder that promised a solution to violence and chaos itself. So the fictional detective provides for the modern person the communal hunt where the necessity of tracking ambiguous clues again becomes a matter of life or death.

Hunting for the tribe would be a profoundly collective activity. Unsurprisingly then, it recurs all over the detective genre, not just in the cozy. Hardboiled detective V.I. Warshawski hunts on behalf of her tribe as well as cozy amateur Goldy Schulz. Professional detective and creative caterer each track clues because the social group is threatened. Like the cozy sleuth, V.I. is often called out on behalf of someone considered family, such as the daughter of the single mother living next door in her childhood in *Toxic Shock* (1988). V. I.'s beloved dead mother taught her that they had obligations to this vulnerable family in the neighborhood. Similarly, the cozy woman finds friends and family loyalties propel detecting. Goldy is determined to save her friend and fellow chef, Yolanda Garcia, and irrepressible aunt, Ferdinanda in *Crunch Time* (2011). They are pursued by an arsonist who is also a killer. The sleuth in the feminist hardboiled and the cozy both becomes hunters even if she is also, at times, the hunted.

So far, we have suggested several archetypal energies haunting detective fiction, the knight-hero of good deeds, the hunter and the trickster with the detective having to struggle between them to maintain a savior role. Here appears a significant difference between the classical and cozy mysteries versus the hardboiled: how the story ends. To begin, both the hardboiled and the cozy summon a savior-hero, so invoking aspects of the myth of the holy grail. There must *be* a savior because the world is broken; it is a wasteland while the murder remains unsolved. Indeed, it could get worse. A friend of Yolanda Garcia has been shot dead while the arson attacks continue. Goldy rashly invites Yolanda to stay, so making her own family a target. Therefore, the community is laid waste with its connecting bonds of love and friendship in danger of breaking down. Fortunately, Goldy is the true grail hero, unlike the police, even when represented by her husband, Sheriff Tom. The police mean well, but like many grail seekers, they ask the wrong questions. They have the wrong perspective and miss important emotional and relationship dimensions. Only the cozy woman sleuth will find the grail of the truth, perhaps because she already embodies it. She finds the truth and her family that extends into friends and community— all restored. I suggest that the cozy genre does the best of all mystery subgenres in healing the wasteland; her finding of the grail of truth has the most potency. Here the cozy genre is distinct because healing the wasteland is far more difficult in other detecting subgenres.

For in the traditional or classical genre, the wasteland is restored to its ambivalence, while for the hardboiled, the truth of the grail is far more bitter. What the hardboiled, including feminist hardboiled, detective discovers is that this wasteland cannot be healed. She then becomes not the successful grail knight but rather takes the place of the sick fisher king, whose wounds are those of the corrupt world. V.I. is too appalled to speak when she discovers at the end of *Toxic Shock* that a chemical company has knowingly concealed for decades the diseases it has caused in order to avoid paying compensation. Such moral and legal poison lead eventually to a murder she can solve *and* the revelation that she cannot save those innocent employees.

Christie's detectives also explicitly renounce divine powers of healing. Poirot attributes ultimate justice to God while Miss Marple retains a robust sense of human evil persisting, even in the village of St Mary Mead. The name of the village hints at its role as a community already containing divine powers of renewal in the Virgin Mary. This quality of rebirth is made dynamic in the detection of Miss Marple. On the other hand, Miss Marple's conscious attitude does not correlate with her mythical function. She is far more ambivalent about her capacity to banish evil. In addition to myth in the generic form, there are other powers that tackle chaos in the mystery. There are goddesses in the fictional sleuth, some of whom offer their divine potency to the cozy.

Four Archetypal Story Patterns in Cozies and Feminist Hardboiled

To argue that there are goddesses in detective fiction is not to claim that these authors are pagans. Rather another way of understanding repeated patterns in genre is to see myth as channeling psychological energies. Here Artemis, Hestia, Athena and Aphrodite arise in detective fiction because they are feminine narratives able to surface in this multifaceted genre. In *The Sleuth and the Goddess*, I suggested that these figures range across women's detective fiction rather as they do in the psyche (2015). So instead of regarding the goddess of hearth and home, Hestia, as the sole drive behind the cozy detective, she is actually an emphasis often tempered with other archetypal drives such as Artemis the hunter and protector of young women, Aphrodite sponsoring the pleasures of the erotic body, and Athena of strategies for her community.

The goddesses are complex; so is detective fiction. As patterning energies, rather than fixed ideas, they do not exist alone. Hestia centers individual consciousness and also that of a community. Since the hearth fire she secures was thought also to exist in the center of the planet, Hestia is also a style of ecology. Operating in a relationship with trickster Hermes where one pushes out the other, the custom of the ancient law courts was that at the end of each day an account was placed on the altar of Hestia. Such a centering of meaning in words is equally found in the hardboiled fidelity to the client sealed in a contract. While the cozy most overtly exemplifies Hestia as both hearth fire and its guardian, making house into home, the feminist hardboiled, too, is centered on justice for the client and structures a new family through the detecting. Similar transitions occur with Artemis of the feminine wild who haunts professional P.I.'s like Sharon McCone. She is also to be found caring for young women, for those in childbirth and as a terrifying bringer of death. Artemis appears to shun the cozy except for the important role of pets as integral members of the cozy family. While pets in the cozy are far from wild, they do mark a transition state between humans and nature for the protagonists.

Hence the textual time devoted to the antics of Hannah Swensen's cat, Moishe, as he teaches her loving observation in the gentle wilderness of Lake Eden (Joanne Fluke). Annie Darling, in her rural not-quite-paradise of Broward's Rock, has two cats whose personalities teach her about mystery in the sense of a nature unlike her own, and indomitability (Carolyn Hart). In Aspen Meadow, indefatigable Goldy Schulz has a cat, Scout, who reminds her of the processes of living outside her troubled world (Diane Mott Davidson). She also takes in a bloodhound whose fallibility in tracking echoes her own struggles to detect. In works with a strong cozy flavor set in ancient Rome, Lindsey Davis provides Nux, a stray dog. She earns her place in the Falco family by rescuing the detective from a brutal beating. Her later struggles to give birth to a single pup are watched over anxiously by adults and children in ways that echo their own proximity to natural death in childbirth and unnatural death in a corrupt empire.

Aphrodite takes up residence in the cozy in its affinity with romance. The female amateur frequently gains clues through an erotic attraction to a cop, whether that be the cop boyfriend of Hannah Swensen (along with Norman, the dentist), or Goldy's attentive suitor who becomes her husband, Tom Schulz. Similarly situated is the not quite cozy sleuth Stephanie Plum in the comic, mostly hardboiled, Janet Evanovich series. As a professional bounty hunter with a pet hamster, Stephanie does not quite qualify for cozy membership. As a rather incompetent detective with two incredible lovers, cop Morelli and the enigmatic Ranger, Stephanie is a follower of Aphrodite who develops Artemis determination to succeed in the hunt. She also fulfills Hestia by going home to her mother's house for dinner, at 6 p.m. sharp.

In manifesting her Artemis side, Stephanie still lacks Athena as the goddess of strategy and containment. Not so most cozies in which a sense of community is often pervasive in the relationships between characters. Cozy sleuths, such as Joanne Fluke's Hannah Swensen, are often imposed on by relatives or expected to subordinate running her business to support community efforts such as those of her local church. Here Athena in the protagonist enables her to incorporate her financial needs and still be able to sustain the community hearth as Hestian. Above all, Athena, goddess of weaving and ceramics, *contains*. In the Aeschylus play, *The Eumenides*, it is she who converts the Furies of endless blood and revenge to honored resident aliens by inviting them to live *within* her city, Athens.

So too, I suggest, is detective fiction itself, and the cozy in particular, an artifact of Athena. The cozy contains the utterly disruptive and entirely undefeatable horrors of death converting these into a *solution*. The cozy contains the furies of horror and despair. It fictionalizes death and the ultimate crime against human community, murder, into something that is actually revitalizing. One strategy important to this process is the cozy's metafictional weaving of references to the detecting genre itself. By hinting at the way readers enter into a world they know well, the cozy even more than other detecting genres can metafictionally make death unnatural and *solvable*.

To see how this works in practice, I will explore four texts. Two are pre-modern ancestors of the cozy: *The Leavenworth Case* (1878) by Anna Katherine Green and *The Circular Staircase* (1909) by Mary Roberts Rinehart. Then a modern detective fiction illustrates the social and historical desire for the cozy, *Graveyard Dust* (1999) by Barbara Hambly. Finally, we will consider a contemporary text to Hambly's, the archetypically cozy *Dying for Chocolate* (1992) by Diane Mott Davidson. I begin with earliest detective novel by a woman.

The Leavenworth Case (1878)

In the Collins Crime Club reissue of 2016, John Curran shows how far *The Leavenworth Case* anticipates golden age conventions (2016: vi). A man is shot in his locked library when about to change his will. The book supplies a second murder, floor plans, a secret marriage, a few typical clues such as an initialed handkerchief, and a narrator, Mr. Raymond, in love with a suspect. Green also includes the quietly intelligent detective, Mr. Gryce. What Curran does not explore is the suggestive relationship of this novel to the modern cozy.

Above all, *The Leavenworth Case* centers on feeling. Despite the calm demeanor of Gryce, who tells Raymond to read police reports if he really believes that a woman cannot commit murder, the action is driven by what today seems an excess of sensibility. Cousins Mary and Eleanore Leavenworth are strikingly beautiful young women. However only Mary is Mr. Leavenworth's heir and she risks losing her fortune by marrying an Englishman in secret. She knew that Mr. Leavenworth would prohibit any such alliance because his own dead wife had suffered at the hands of a British brute. Unfortunately, her husband decides to tell the rich uncle the truth, so provoking him to leave his riches elsewhere. Can Mary Leavenworth bear to lose her fortune?

Unaware of the secret marriage, the detective at first finds Eleanor to be a likely suspect to the horror of Mr. Raymond who loves her. Such is her nobility and devotion to the far more selfish Mary, that Eleanore will bear almost any imputation of guilt in order to shield her venal cousin. However, she will protest her innocence and purity at great length. She even goes so far to embrace the corpse in an attempt to prove that she could not have committed the crime: "[w]ould not the body of the outraged dead burst its very shroud and repel me?" (97). Here the novel directly anticipates the cozy where knowledge through love trumps material evidence. When Goldy Schulz's best friend Marla is arrested for murder in

The Main Corpse, Goldy's love and loyalty to Marla as also once the wife of her abusive ex-husband, means that she is *certain* of Marla's innocence. Her new cop husband Tom has to go follow apparently damming evidence. He tells Goldy that the law that does not give way to love and relationship.

Like any true cozy sleuth, Goldy acts on her tried and tested feelings. She stages an unlikely heist to break Marla out of jail. *The Leavenworth Case*, unlike the cozy, does not use comedy to leaven the intensity of the characters' emotions. Rather there is a great deal of Mary (or Eleanore) falling back with a cry "Oh, why were we even born…." (80).

Yet a second characteristic of the cozy is manifest in the blend of the cool detective and the partial feeling-dominated observer. Both are male in *The Leavenworth Case* while the cozy sleuth, typically female, mixes both figures into her questing role. The cozy amateur such as Goldy or Hannah is capable of cool reflection and careful sifting of evidence while being motivated by love for family and/or friends. It is interesting to note that in Isis Crawford's cooking cozies, sisters again divide these roles with Libby supplying the feeling and Bernie the more detached assessments.

In addition to the paramount role of feeling in knowing, what modern cozies gain from *The Leavenworth Case* is the capacity of murder and its solution to renew family or community bonds. Far more than in the golden age or traditional mysteries, the cozy is a genre of rejuvenation by fictionally overcoming death. Death is defeated in the cozy by being solved, dis-solved into nothing. The cozy makes death go away with the successful detection becoming a ritual of discovery and banishment. The core family or community is reborn, rejuvenated by the success of the sleuth driven primarily by love. Hence at the end of *The Leavenworth Case*, the dismembered family is made whole by the discovery of the killer as a member of the household who had not succeeded in gaining a place in the weaving of its affections. He can be removed, leaving the two cousins to reconcile and marry. Each husband is sanctified by making the decision to believe in their beloved's innocence based on the experience of love when gazing on her beauty, rather than actual legal evidence.

The Circular Staircase (1909)

Anna Katherine Green introduced the spinster detective in her Amelia Butterworth, who narrates *That Affair Next Door* in 1897. Twelve years later, Mary Roberts Rinehart's Rachel Innes announces her arrival in the opening of *The Circular Staircase*.

> This is the story of how a middle-aged spinster lost her mind, deserted her domestic gods in the city, took a furnished house for the summer out of town, and found herself

involved in one of those mysterious crimes that keep our newspapers and detective agencies happy and prosperous [Rinehart 1].

Unlike *The Leavenworth Case*, this narrator neither supplies nor fosters a discourse of heightened sensibility around the feminine. Rather, although Rachel is drawn into fiercely protecting her family, niece Gertrude and nephew Halsey, she aims for a cool moderation in facing what begins as disruptive ghosts, then a murder, followed by revelations of financial scandal, more death and even the kidnapping of Halsey. Rachel is both aided and hindered by longtime maid, Biddy who is always threatening to leave. Their familial relationship is a thread of comedy throughout the story. More useful for detecting is the alliance she forms with the lead police detective, Mr. Jamieson.

In fact, *The Circular Staircase* closely anticipates the cozy of a century later in its amateur sleuth who discovers resourcefulness and courage that she never knew she had. Decorous Rachel even scrambles over a roof to find a secret room full of the money stolen from the bank by its owner, who is also owner of the house. The cozy additionally inherits the friendly relationship with the authorities, the Hestian defense of the hearth when Rachel refuses to give up her lease because she is determined to find the truth, and the Artemisian protection of her younger family members.

Halsey and Gertrude have unwisely fallen in love with persons caught up in bank fraud and a faked death, causing Rachel's intimates to act suspiciously in the early part of the story. Naturally those they love prove innocent after spending time as viable suspects. As in the later cozy, detecting motivated more by love of family and less by fidelity to the law proves to re-constitute and rejuvenate the domestic unit. Rachel's success enables two marriages. Her sleuthing invokes suspicion of, and then intense negotiation with, the new partners. Instead of the spinster seeing her younger family members spin off to new households, the story actually expands the Innes family with new relationships that center on Rachel, the savior sleuth.

Also anticipating the cozy is detecting as a kind of death and rebirth for Rachel herself. There are dark days in the rented mansion with mysterious assaults, the murder of the owner's son, horrible suspicion of Gertrude and the ultimate peril for the family when Halsey disappears. However, despite getting locked in the secret room and almost wiped out by a killer, Rachel is sure that the entire mystery has given her a new life: "[t]o be perfectly frank, I never really lived until that summer" (182). Walking through the night to dig up a grave with Mr. Jamieson, Rachel remarks on noticing the beauty of the stars for the first time (159). Clambering over a roof, she likens herself to an animal and ancient warrior.

> Like a dog on the scent, like my bearskin progenitor, with his spear and his wild bow, to me now there was the lust of the chase, the frenzy of pursuit, the dust of battle [170].

The humor of this rhetoric is underlined when she promptly gets stuck in the secret room and has to be rescued. Rachel has found her inner Artemis and also the need for her inner Athena to give her a more strategic approach. Aphrodite is firmly awarded to her nephew and niece as they suffer for love in the suspicions aroused by their beloved.

The Circular Staircase only lacks three ingredients of the modern cozy, pets, the pressure on the sleuth occasioned by having to earn a living and a sense of wider community than the family. Money is an issue in this novel because the bank that has failed due to the malfeasance of its owner, which threatens to ruin many of the characters. Fortunately, Rachel is independently wealthy and does not feel the financial pressures. She can also provide for Halsey and Gertrude if necessary. Not having to work means that Rachel is not dependent upon a community for her living. Murder in *The Circular Staircase* concerns two families: her own while renting Sunnyside and the Armstrongs who own it as well as a bank. And although Rachel does discover a level of natural reality both outside of her (the stars) and inside (the pursuing dog) pets do not become characters.

In fact, the title of *The Circular Staircase* is indicative of the story winding around a very tight knit group of wealthy residents. Naturally for this social class there are servants. Biddy, the maid, has a lot to say for herself. Another servant character is Thomas who is caught up in the Armstrong's deceit and eventually dies. Thomas is African American and is the occasion for Rachel's several racist remarks.

> As for Thomas and his forebodings, it was always my belief that a negro is one-part thief, one-part pigment, and the rest superstition [15].

Today the novel's evident desire that we like and even admire its unlikely protagonist is flawed by such casual racism. There is nothing cozy about it. Therefore, it is worth looking at a mystery from ninety years later that explores the passionate desire for a home in those for whom it is denied by the law of the land. The cozy is dreamed in the impossible longings of African Americans who have known slavery and live in its environs.

Graveyard Dust (1999)

Set amongst the free colored population in 1830s New Orleans, protagonist Benjamin January is a surgeon unable to practice because of his race and so is forced to eke a precarious living as a piano player and teacher. The city is surrounded by plantations worked by slaves. January is forced to carry several copies of his freedom papers lest he be kidnapped back into the condition in which he was born. When he was a child, his mother was purchased to become a placee, a contracted mistress to a wealthy white man. As was customary, her children, January and rebellious sister, Olympe, were also purchased and freed. Now Olympe, a voodoo queen as well as wife and mother, has been arrested for murder, accused of supplying poison to dispatch a son of a placee at the behest of his young wife. Astoundingly the mother of the victim is claiming that he is *her* slave because she can then seize his inheritance from his dead white father.

The book begins with the reminder that slaves are not alone in being at risk of losing everything. It is the summer fever season and people are dying in the jail of what must be yellow fever. The white authorities deny the disease while moving their families out of town. January fears cholera more, remembering the day in Paris when he came home to find his beloved wife dead. Freedom from slavery, however precarious, does not mean freedom from unbearable loss.

> All his life, it seemed to him, he had wanted a home, wanted a place where he knew he was safe [Hambly 1999: 13].

Home is the dream of safety and love, but even in a city with no slavery, Paris, home can be destroyed by death. Therefore, despite the risks, January returns to New Orleans to the only family he knew. There his mother charges him market rent because she, like others, sees money as protection.

January is the avatar of the cozy in this and other, novels. His sleuthing saves Olympe and her enterprising son, Gabriel, later snatched by the killer. Always in Hambly's richly realistic novels, January's quest for the truth is driven by a desire for home defined by security and love. In fact, January's desire for Hestia enables him to become the Hestia for his family. He finds the truth that saves Olympe, rescues Gabriel, and discovers horrible crimes that corrupt families of power, white rich families. Even more, he goes beyond Rachel Innes to become Hestian as well as strategic Athena for his community.

For archetypes are gender fluid as well as innately plural. Hestian January is also Artemis in hunting for truth and protecting the young. In fact, he is more devoted to the Hestian hearth than ally of the wild wet swamps of Louisiana. Only his Artemis drives him into the forest for Gabriel where he watches his companion, Marie Laveau, the most powerful voodoo of all, grab a snake and tell it to inform his friends that she and those she protects are to be safe. January is also Athena in understanding all too well the limitations of his position in this complex hierarchy of race and legal oppression. January's Athena helps him contain the horrors from destroying the fragile home he has with his sisters and a developing relationship with Rose, a free colored teacher who has been reduced to near destitution by prejudice.

January was raised Catholic and in *Graveyard Dust* struggles with his sister's voodoo religion that takes the form of possession by the *loa*, divine personalities. Pursuing a killer who is dragging a wounded Gabriel, January learns the desperation that surrounds the slaves' embrace of this African derived religion.

> Sometimes he thought someone else ran with his legs, someone who carried a sword and whose eyes burned with fire [369].

After his family is safe January finds within himself a reconciliation between his faith and his voodoo. He prays before St. Peter, also worshipped as Papa Legba. What is ultimately cozy in these stories of a far from comfortable existence is that in January, Hambly has desire constitute form. So powerful is January's longing for home and family, that it pervades not only his nuclear family but also the unjust divisions of his city. He has white friends amongst those also regarded as inferior: an uneducated American police officer in a largely French town, Aishbag Shaw, and drunk opium addict Hannibal, afflicted with TB.

Over the novel series, January marries Rose, fathers a child, and becomes involved in the Underground Railroad, helping runaway slaves. Such an activity, of course, imperils his home while it also secures it. He is most truly Hestia when sheltering the stranger, even a fugitive, at his hearth, a sacred task to the ancient Greeks. I am arguing that Hambly's January novels, while they cannot be considered cozy in the typical sense, are cozy archetypically: they incarnate the desire for the cozy world of safety and caring community; one that in the genre itself, can be secured by a ritual of a death and rebirth through solving it in a way that strengthens love.

However, Hamby shows that real social conditions can be far too dark for escape into a private world of small towns and caring families. Her work implicitly argues that the world itself should turn Hestian, implicitly a reminder that she was goddess of community as home, as planet as home. Only when cozy values populate our relationship to the other, only then will this literature of desire become a holy grail that transforms the wasteland. Therefore, it is time to take a look at the cozy itself in its sophisticated treatment by Diane Mott Davidson.

Dying for Chocolate (1992)

What I most admire about Diane Mott Davidson's Goldy cooking cozies is how they fulfill the genre while giving it an edge, mainly through including moving accounts of domestic violence suffered by the sleuth. Over the series, Goldy suffers physical abuse from her ex-husband, charismatic doctor John Richard Korman, aka "the Jerk." Finally, she is accused of his murder. She also marries caring cop Tom Schulz, only to have him kidnapped on their wedding day. Only after a long struggle including financial crises will she find a new happy family with her son, Arch, and new baby, Grace, in *The Whole Enchilada* (2013).

Therefore, the entire series enacts a containing transformation of violence into the emergence of the family as secure Hestian unit. Between *Catering to Nobody* (1990) and *The Whole Enchilada* (2013), the cozy comedy is fulfilled in ways that reach into comedy's roots as a fertility festival of Dionysus. In later Christian terms, one could suggest that the Goldy stories are a Rabelaisian Divine Comedy, where Goldy, who cannot fully escape from her abusive marriage because her son, Arch, wants a relationship with his father, endures hell before achieving rebirth into a new nurturing relationship. Goldy's paradise is signaled by rejuvenated fertility with the birth of a child.

Dionysus is the god of dismemberment and re-membering because he was torn apart at birth and reborn through the thigh of Zeus. Not only does Goldy face physical assaults from the Jerk, she also faces the dismemberment of her containing home because of the fragility of her catering business. Not only do inconvenient murders put off customers, but so do black eyes on the caterer, jealous professional rivals and yes, the threat of new attacks. Gradually Goldy the sleuth emerges to support Goldy the caterer and mother. Earning the respect and then love of Tom, Goldy, her family, and community are re-membered into the Athena containing cozy.

However, this narrative arc is barely visible in *Dying for Chocolate.* Vulnerability and risk beset the cozy account of the mysterious death of Goldy's new beau, Philip, a psychiatrist. So bad are the Jerk's attacks that Goldy has been forced to leave her home and take up residence with retired General Farquhar and his disabled wife. They are also hosting sulky teenager Julian Teller who resents Goldy while making friends with Arch. Notably prescient for a pre–9/11 novel, General Bo, as he is known, is convinced that terrorism is about to become a major problem for the United States. Disbelieved by his superiors, he keeps a huge stash of illegal arms at home and likes to set up explosions, even on a picnic that Goldy is catering.

Indicative of the general's intuition and certainly of his good nature, Bo protects Goldy from the Jerk when he tries to hurt her in the driveway. Bo's house is an impregnable fortress and Goldy is safe there from physical harm. Yet despite the threat of the Jerk, the cozy does not focus on physical violence, and, in fact, the Farquhar residence is about to implode rather than explode. The fortress home is not safe at all. For example, Goldy does suffers emotional harm when she discovers that the murder victim, Philip, regarded her as a case study rather than a potential girlfriend. Julian Teller is not just a needy teenager from Arch's school but, in fact, the son of Bo's troubled wife, Adele, by a local, married philanderer, Brian Harrington. This secret will destroy the Farquhar home from within.

Goldy finds Brian dead in the Farquhar pool. Adele is the killer, having manipulated Julian into her house solely to try to force Brian back into their affair. Meanwhile, Goldy's business has been put at risk by lies in the newspaper from a so-called food critic, Pierre. Almost too late, Goldy realizes that Pierre is Sissy, a girl who wants to make Julian love her and force him into a high paying career. He just wants to cook and learn from Goldy. Like any mother, Goldy rescues Arch from being endangered by crazy Sissy and unmasks Pierre. Her son is safe, and she is making friends with Julian, who will become almost another son and brother to Arch. Her family is able to be renewed, even if at risk. Unfortunately, Bo, deeply devoted to his wife, loses her and his seemingly safe home. Failing as Hestia, his weapons will be confiscated, and he faces prison.

Goldy decides that the horrors of past days, the murders by Adele and reckless endangerment and malice from Sissy, have all been about trying to force love. Even she is guilty of it in coddling Arch, who reacted by asking to live with his father. Fortunately, this cozy suggests that if not forced, love is possible.

> "Mom," Arch said, as if he was reading my mind. He put down his cup. "I'm sorry I said that about going to live with Dad. I'd like to stay with you. I mean, if you want me to."

Tom Schulz, who does not try to force love, has already suggested that Goldy might like to change her name to Schulz. He backs off immediately when it is clear that she is not ready. *Dying for Chocolate* ends with a re-membered family in process. Julian is becoming part of it and even bereft General Bo will re-appear in *The Main Corpse* in a role that makes full use of his military heroism. While authentic in portraying domestic violence and fractured relationships, Mott Davidson's novels are true cozies with a dash of social criticism. They give the genre a dimension of emotional pain that adds to the archetypal reconstruction of the Hestian hearth in the desire for home.

Conclusion: From the Margins

By looking at the marginalized genre of the cozy from its margins, it is possible to see where the definition blurs, from where it might have emerged and how it relates to other styles of mystery, particularly by women authors. I am suggesting that the cozy subgenre is real and yet draws elements from across crime fiction, even in the hardboiled styles which would appear to be so different. V.I. Warshawski, Sharon McCone and Kinsey Millhone all exhibit Hestian features while Goldy takes on one of their more dominant archetypal drives in her Artemisian fierce protection of young Arch. The discourse of feeling and the feminine as a major drive *to know* in *The Leavenworth Case* is tempered by the growing comedy of *The Circular Staircase*, while Barbara Hambly's novels invoke the desire for safety, love as a means of profound social and historical criticism.

Cozy detective fiction is not entirely written by women for women. It is, however, a literature of the marginalized in a crime genre in which male lives and masculine heroism have been more feted. Far from the cozy is the hardboiled fiction that reveals the gritty gore of murder on the streets, whether or not it proves to be part of an intricate plot. Such crime writing inherits the despair and sometimes the catharsis of tragedy. For these hardboiled authors, what is revealed by the sleuth is the indelible stain of the violence and the irretrievable corruption of the community where it occurs over and over again.

The hardboiled detective cannot save his city, unlike the Athenian cozy sleuth. Hardboiled mysteries can be magnificent. So too can the cozy, I suggest, in bringing comedy, rebirth and renewal into the lives of readers. Cozies help readers make peace with death in the way that comedy has always done. Happy endings after the trauma of loss are innate to the cozy; they are an undervalued gift to literature.

Works Cited

Aeschylus. "The Eumenides," in *The Oresteia*, trans. Robert Fagles. New York: Penguin Books, 1966, 227–77. Print.
Curran, John. "Introduction" to *The Leavenworth Case*. By Anna K. Green. London: Collins Crime Club, 1878/2016. Print.
Davidson, Diane Mott. *Dying for Chocolate*. New York: Bantam, 1992. Print.
_____. *The Main Corpse*. New York: Bantam, 1996. Print.
Green, Anna K. *The Leavenworth Case*. London: Collins Crime Club, 1878/2016. Print.
Hambly, Barbara. *Graveyard Dust*. New York: Bantam, 1999. Print.
Hyde, Lewis. *Trickster Makes This World: Mischief, Myth and Art*. New York: Farrar, Straus and Giroux, 1998. Print.
Jung, C. G. "On the Relation of Analytical Psychology to Poetry," in *The Spirit in Man, Art and Literature, CW*15. Trans. R. F. C. Hull. Princeton University Press, 1966.
Knight, Stephen. *Crime Fiction 1800–2000: Detection, Death, Diversity*. Basingstoke and New York: Palgrave, 2004. Print.
Paretsky, Sara. *Toxic Shock*. New York: Delacorte Press, 1988. Print.
Paris, Ginette. *Pagan Meditations: The Worlds of Aphrodite, Artemis and Hestia*. New Orleans: Spring Journal and Books, 1986. Print.
Poe, Edgar Allan. *The Complete Tales and Poems of Edgar Allan Poe*. New York: Barnes & Noble, 2015. Print.
Rinehart, Mary Roberts. *The Circular Staircase*. London and Melbourne: J. M. Dent &Sons, 1909/1986. Print.
Rowland, Susan. "The "Classical Model of the Golden Age," in Rzepka & Horsley, 2010). Print.

_____. *The Sleuth and the Goddess: Hestia, Artemis, Athena and Aphrodite in Women's Detective Fiction.* New Orleans: Spring Journal and Books, 2015. Print.
Rzepka, Charles. J. and Horsley, Lee. eds. *A Companion to Crime Fiction.* Sussex, UK: Wiley-Blackwell, 2010. Print.
Sayers, Dorothy L. *Strong Poison.* New York: Harper Paperbacks reissue, 1930/2012.
Vester, Katherine. "Bodies to Die for: Negotiating the Ideal Female Body in Cozy Mystery Novels." *Journal of Popular Culture,* vol 48; issue 1: 31–43. 2015. Print.

Counterpointing the Cozy
Louise Penny's *Three Pines*
Paula T. Connolly

J'ai rêvé d'un nid où les arbres repoussaient la mort.—Adolphe Shedrow[1]

A "cozy" defines soft mysteries that do more than move sex and violence off page. In many ways, it's what their authors move center page that most recognizably defines the subgenre. Cozy protagonists occupy a world that is insulated but not isolated, often a small town, at times—as in Krista Davis's *Diva* series—a place defined by neighborhood. Here, readers find generally cohesive communities of often companionable characters who know each other as friends, not merely acquaintances, so that the setting is an inviting one even in the midst of murder, a setting further locationally situated in such places as a welcoming home, a bakery, yoga studio, yarn store, and so on. The tangibility of such places—a small town business based in something like crafts or food, or a protagonist with a craft hobby—also emphasizes a sense of remove from a larger, busy world at the same time that it models an activity meant to engage reader interest and identification. Indeed, the centrality of crafts or cooking shapes the genre's promise of comfort in significant ways. As much as one might expect murder to rent social fabric, prompting existential fear and questions of mortality, violence, and loss, the predominant focus on cooking and crafts does not merely de-escalate, but rather offers a substitution for those issues. The creation of the finite object allows a domestication of focus and a means of taming the potential unmanageability of murder.

Such domestication is evident in covers that tonally announce the world of a cozy. Frequently alliterative titles—such as *The Cluttered Corpse* and *Hummus and Homicide*[2]—diminish the sense of death's threat, as do punning titles—such as *State of the Onion* or *The Diva*

Runs out of Thyme[3]—that call upon the reader's game-playing interaction. Because the reader is in on the title's joke, she is already engaged in both meaning-making and the lightheartedness of the genre, the simple puns becoming a type of promise to the reader that these stories will not be frightening ones. The genre holds true to that promise, and part of the comfort for readers is that they "know what they are getting" (Flower), the stability of the genre's narrative patterns articulated through a series of shared tropes.[4] The markers of comfort in cozies are rooted in tangibility and, in addition to location, the genre's psychological comfort most often rests upon food and pet images. In the spirit of coziness, food abounds in a way to make a hobbit happy. It is typically plentiful, omnipresent, and—whether in characters' homes or small businesses—a sign of convivial environments and the centerpiece of welcoming others. Pets (specifically dogs and cats) also offer a repository of comfort and are *de rigueur* companions to protagonists, providing devotion, diversion, and an assurance that the protagonist is both kind and loved. In this way, the inclusion of dogs and cats signals "an extension [and reception] of sympathy and compassion" (Griswold 106) which further redirects emotional focus from the victim to images of comfort. Moreover, pets come with narrative assurance; readers can invest themselves in the stories' dogs and cats with a certainty of good outcome; tangential people may be killed, but one knows that pets will not be.[5]

While the term "cozy murder" presents a startling tension between emotional polar opposites, the genre resolves those tensions by largely sterilizing the murder in both physical and emotional terms and placing it in the narrative background. Since the genre's *raison d'être* is comfort, the murder—which is usually tidily bloodless—is not a source of emotional trauma for the protagonist (nor, usually, for anyone else), and ends up being more a matter of inconvenience. Cozies often feature first-person female narrators who are informal and chatty, as if directly addressing readers who function as implied friends. The murder does not lead the protagonist to grapple with conflicts of morality; she remains upbeat and un-awed by a murder that is typically the result of a flash-point moment rather than a sign of evil[6] which, when it occurs, is ultimately a containable, not metastasizing event. The murder is neatly solved and closure provided by story's end.

Containment, in many ways, lies at the heart of the cozy. It offers a protected world; in Bachelard's terms, what could be described as a nest.[7] The image is layered as a small location (such as a home or shop) is housed within a small geographical area (such as a neighborhood or small town), so that through such sheltered diminutive space a comforting snugness serves as a central trope. In that center protected space, the nest image "knows nothing of the hostility of the world" (Bachelard 103). The snug place is "a refuge and haven associated with sensations of comfort and security, with ease and well-being" (Griswold 6); it offers the promise of an idyllic "felicitous space" (Griswold 25). The settings in cozies do not typically extend to a wider world outside the borders of its specific locale, although murderers and victims may travel into their world to pierce its reverie. The nested space of cozies (as well as the circumference of the protagonist's point of view) remains intact, the genre offering intratextual assurance to readers in an extratextually troubling world.

Assurance is also evident in the closing apparatus of cozies that provides readers everything from knitting to cooking instructions (something reflecting the fictional world), thus offering possibilities of comforting transgressions as readers are encouraged to enact the hobbies or activities of protagonists.[8] Boundaries between fiction and reality are especially blurred when these recipes or craft patterns are narratively voiced by the protagonist directly addressing readers,[9] hence heightening the illusion that cozies are convivial spaces that welcome the reader to actively participate in their world. These final invitations for readers to engage in the life of the book are premised on the cozies' comforting physical "thing-ness" of crafts or cooking or something potentially replicable by readers. As much as the genre offers readers a psychological respite and escape from the complexities of life, the inherent orderliness of activities that come with a set of directions itself provides a promise of comforting order as well as opportunities for play, welcome, and friendship.

While the "thing-ness," the tangibility of comfort and assurance of a protected stability, is a grounding element of cozy mysteries, Louise Penny's Three Pines/Armand Gamache series is defined by its slipperiness. Characters hold secrets, shift course, move along a moral spectrum, become people we didn't know they were in sometimes disquieting ways. The series, which began in 2005 and continues to the present day, is ostensibly divided between two Canadian locations: the small village of Three Pines and everything that isn't Three Pines (still located in Quebec, but including other narrowed locations, ranging from a *manoir* to a monastery).[10] In this series, it is the village of Three Pines that at cursory glance may seem most emblematic of cozy settings, although Penny dispels any such notions within pages of *Still Life*, the first book in the series. It is nonetheless worth exploring the relationship of the cozy form and Penny's series because—and this is a crucial distinction—it is not simply the presence of tropes (such as a focus on a small community, convivial spaces, pets, and the delectability of food) that defines what is or is not a "cozy." *How* those tropes are used and what they come to mean in the context of the overall narrative help to define genres. More specifically, while the depiction of

Three Pines rests upon cozy tropes for narrative emotional relief, particularly in its notions of felicitous space, Penny counterpoints those images as she interrogates the possibilities of "cozy" in terms of location, community, and narrative.

Interestingly, Penny's first book in the series, *Still Life*, echoed cozies in its early packaging by St. Martin's Paperbacks—both through the punning of its title (referring to art and death)[11] and to the lightheartedness of its cover blurb: "Someone is putting the final brushstrokes on a picture-perfect murder." Penny's subsequent book titles dispense with playful punning and announce that cruelty, not cozy, is often at the heart of the mystery, as in *The Brutal Telling* and *Bury Your Dead*. As the series moved from small paperback to the larger trade paperback size, St. Martin's moved away from trying to package the novels as potential cozies. The slightly out-of-focus painting of a small town on *Still Life*'s early St. Martin's Paperbacks cover is exchanged for photographically real shots of nature which evoke the ineffability of the moment, as with the later images of cascaded light in Penny's *A Trick of the Light* and *The Beautiful Mystery*. Rather than the perky promise of "final brushstrokes on a picture-perfect murder" which insinuates, as do cozies, that solving murder is a game-like diversion, cover blurbs for later novels acknowledge the complexity and psychological landscape of Penny's world, as when one reviewer notes that *The Beautiful Mystery* offers "enormous empathy for the troubled human soul."[12]

At their core, cozy spaces exist where "a dialectic of 'inside' and 'outside' is operative" (Griswold 9). In settings that are ultimately unmarred even by murder, the relationship of "inside/outside" in cozies is less a dialectic than a concretized "inside" with a resolute separation from that which is outside. This "felicitous space" of cozies clearly depends upon its isolation from the bigger "outside" world. When readers are introduced to Penny's Three Pines, those distinctions seem in place. Three Pines is a "picturesque village" (*Still Life* 31), so far removed from the outside world that it has no corresponding signage on maps (*Still Life* 27). Indeed, Three Pines is impervious to any system of external navigation, including GPS according to which "no village called Three Pines seemed to exist." Even when a traveler stumbles upon the village, GPS "showed him in the middle of nowhere. Literally. No where. No roads. No community. Not even a forest. Just blank. As though he'd driven off the face of the earth" (*Nature of the Beast* 94).

The village also seems a place out of time, for its "trees, turning breathtaking shades of red and amber, were just about the only things that did change in this venerable village" (*Still Life* 2). A visitor even "had the impression that if he waited long enough the stagecoach would come by" (*Nature of the Beast* 144). In moments like this, the comfort afforded by the village rests upon a sense of a contained, idyllic past. This is a past defined by separate, protected space; the village's origin story describes how loyalists fleeing the American Revolution had "no way of knowing when they were safe. So a code was designed. Three pines in a cluster meant the loyalists would be welcome" (*Still Life* 49). Its still-standing three pines mark the village as a historic and continuing place of "sanctuary" (*Brutal Telling* 15), and newer residents—from Myrna who runs the village bookstore to Gabri and Olivier who run its B&B and Bistro—have moved here seeking refuge from the outside world. As visitors to the area come upon the village unexpectedly, their discovery reveals a welcoming idyll, for here an "old stone mill sat beside a pond, the mid-morning sun warming its fieldstones. Around it the maples and birches and wild cherry trees held their fragile leaves, like thousands of happy hands waving to them upon arrival" (*Still Life* 31).

Removed from the busyness of cities, the village's commercial area is, as Armand Gamache, Chief Inspector for the Sûreté du Québec, notes, "a very short commercial" (*Still Life* 46) with a general store, bakery, bistro, B&B, and bookstore, each connected to the next like a string of beads, a door from one leading into the next. De-commercialization of these businesses heightens the tone of emotional solace and protection, as is typical of cozies. At *Myrna's Livres, Neufs et Usagés*, Myrna "had managed to make it feel more like the library in a cultured and comfortable country home than a store. She'd set up a couple of rocking chairs beside an open fire, with a couch facing it" (*Still Life* 138), and sees her visitors as guests rather than customers. Next door at the Bistro, patrons are also seldom shown paying a bill, and service often seems an expression of the owners' largesse, so that in such spaces hospitality, invitation, and community appear to supplant business. When Gabri describes why he doesn't make his own baked goods at the Bistro, he notes that:

> Sarah's Boulangerie was already here. She'd lived in the village all her life.... All our croissants, and pies, and breads are baked by Sarah.... It'd be cheaper and more fun to bake ourselves but that's not the point.... The point isn't to make a fortune.... The point is to know what's enough. To be happy [*Brutal Telling* 301].

The Bistro, as one might expect, is a place where characters come together for good food and good company. Like the bookstore, the Bistro offers a "lively fire perking in the stone fireplace" (*Still Life* 98). The food served here is comforting, and that one "cups his hands around the mug holding hot, fragrant cider" (*Still Life* 153) becomes its own trope.

In these spaces, food is an invitation for warmth and community, solace and respite. It is typically offered in generous portions and described in comforting terms. When Three Pines resident Clara holds a dinner party, the description of "plates ... piled high with turkey and chestnut stuffing, candied yams and potatoes, peas and gravy" (*Still Life* 23) rivals any cozy.

And the wonder of the village is emphasized when it is redolent with food, as near Thanksgiving, the scent of "woodsmoke and roast turkey" (*Still Life* 14) fills the place. Yet in Three Pines, food is not simply plentiful and positive, but also functions as a moral signifier. When Chief Inspector Gamache is offered a generous tray of "mille feuilles, meringues, slices of pies and little custard tarts with glazed fruit on top" at the Bistro, he chooses one of the "little custard tarts ... covered in tiny wild blueberries," the focus on smallness a sign of discreet indulgence (*Still Life* 104). In contrast, the meal consumed by grasping relatives of the village's first murder victim is described in grotesque terms. In this moment, the specificity of "Black Forest ham" that Gamache had also been offered is exchanged for simple "meat" as Yolanda's husband clutched "a huge sandwich, gushing mayo and meat. Her son Bernard yawned, revealing a mouth full of half-chewed sandwich and strings of mayo glopping down from the roof of his mouth" (*Still Life* 105). Here, simply their interaction with food signals their rapacity and moral vulgarity.

Unlike confident assertions of sheltered space in cozies, the exploration of the tenuousness of seemingly protected space is explored in the series' opening pages when some local boys assault the Bistro—the emotional center of the village—pelting it with duck shit and yelling "'Fags! Queers!'" at Olivier and Gabri (*Still Life* 15). While some of the townspeople soon come together to scrub the Bistro's façade, the Bistro's hominess is also corrupted from inside, where everything—from cups and saucers to tables and lamps—has price tags attached. Although "[e]ach piece looked as though it had been born there" (*Still Life* 51), this has deeper significance than the Bistro doubling as an antiques store and signals a tension between the appearance of companionability and the tallying of everything. While Gabri offers hospitality and food, his partner Olivier cannot quite find his place in such comfort and generosity, and for him both the Bistro and his friends are opportunities for profit. When, at the end of *Still Life*, everyone is invited to take one piece from the victim's home as a remembrance of the woman, Olivier takes not a communal or personal remembrance, but instead "the best thing in the house. He'd tried not to be greedy, but couldn't help it" (308-9). This tension between things as comfort or commercialism, or more properly between one's better nature and one's dirty little secrets, turns the counterpointing of cozy tropes into the psychological interrogations that stand at the heart of Penny's series.

The brutal consequences of Olivier's secret chattering of unmanaged greed are revealed in a later book when he moves the body of a murdered man to a newly-opened business, his translation of a body to a thing and a commercial weapon serving as an outward sign of his corruption. The action is also the culmination of his control of the man whom, for years, he'd exploited, secretly trading him groceries for "near-priceless antiques" (*Brutal Telling* 239). Yet, Olivier is neither a simple foil of Gabri's generosity nor a vapid stereotype of greed; rather, generosity and greed occupy the same person. In this way, the settings of the Bistro and Three Pines become a complex matrix of generosity and greed, comfort and insecurity, love and commodification. Here, even Clara, who seems to be the moral compass of Three Pines in its early books, and is often forgiving, companionable, and generous, has a "nasty little voice that kept her company" (*Still Life* 10); she "secretly held and hugged and would visit [the memory of others' transgressions] in moments when she needed to be comforted by the unkindness of others" (*Still Life* 3). The neat bifurcation of inside/outside space is dissolved here as the complexities of the characters' psychological landscapes are grafted on top of the seeming cozy space of Three Pines.

Even well-honed cozy tropes like the comforting presence of pets are interrogated here. While cozies include cats and dogs as a measure of comfort, Penny's series examines issues of companionability as well as vulnerability. Gamache's dog, Henri, functions as the quintessential loyal companion, both loved and loving. Yet Henri's world is not that of all animals, and Penny explores the vulnerabilities of other dogs, like Gracie and Leo who'd been rescued from a garbage can (*Glass Houses* 19); while Leo is "growing into a very handsome dog," his sibling is a physical "mess" who seems not to be growing, but to have "shrunk" (22). She's loved by her adoptive family nonetheless. In Penny's world, animal companions do not provide a simple deflection from issues of loss; rather they often reveal the ways vulnerability and grief are experienced by animals as well as people. In *Still Life*, the indefatigable and seemingly misanthropic Ruth Zardo takes in the dog of the murder victim, suggesting hope, life, and the companionability at the heart of the cozy paradigm. Yet the two are aged and limping, and their companionability is textured with an acknowledgement of life's accompanying pain. In a later novel, it is perhaps both age and pain that affects the dog of a murdered child's family; he doesn't follow others because he is "either too old to climb, or no longer motivated without the reward of the boy to play with" (*Nature of the Beast* 166). Animals suffer pain both physical and psychological in Penny's world, understanding a grief securely tucked outside the borders of cozy locations. The interaction with animals here does evoke an "extension of sympathy and compassion" (Griswold 106), but pets evince a wider spectrum of emotions and experiences that directs emotional focus *to*, not away from, the stories' victims.

Ruth's connection to Rosa, her duck companion, provides a riff on the expected dog/cat companion, the oddity of their relationship reflecting Ruth's unconventionality. The pairing is used for lighthearted effect, as when the duck is dressed by Ruth in everything from a dress to a rain jacket

(*Brutal Telling* 119, 299), and functions as the irascible poet Ruth's *doppelgänger*, "mutter[ing] 'Fuck, fuck, fuck'" to a recitation of bad poetry (*Glass Houses* 10). The two are inseparable, so much so that Rosa is described as Ruth's "appendage" (*Great Reckoning* 373), but this is an inseparability built from both choice and loss. When Ruth had first rescued some abandoned eggs and realized that one of the ducklings was having a difficult time breaking through its shell, Ruth, "not capable of just watching the little one struggle [had] cracked the shell. Freed little Lilium." But "Lilium's head fell to one side…. Ruth lifted the tiny wings, hoping, maybe, she'd see a flutter. But Lilium was gone. Killed by kindness" (*Cruelest Month* 258). In this series, pets die. Others, like Rosa, leave or return of their own accord in an exploration of the line between love and loss, of finding homes, and of adoptive pairings of otherwise lost creatures in a world where "Love takes all forms" (*Nature of the Beast* 17). The extension of sympathy in Ruth's interaction with Rosa is shown, too, as she adopts the grief-broken mother of a murdered child, offering her a home with "'a broken-down old poet and her duck'" (*Nature of the Beast* 373) and by so doing, rescues the woman from probable suicide.

Rescue is central for many of the characters who see Three Pines as a "sanctuary" (*Brutal Telling* 15). The dialectic of inside/outside is clearly in play here, and characters are keenly aware of the 'outside' as a place they have consciously rejected. Clara, for example, has stopped subscribing to the Montreal papers with their "morose headlines" and accounts of government intrigue, drugs, and loss. Rather, she turns to the local county newspaper with its stories of "Wayne's cow, or Guylaine's visiting grandchildren, or a quilt being auctioned for the seniors' home." Clara wonders if she is "copping out, running away from reality and responsibility. Then she realized she didn't care. Besides, she learned everything she really needed to survive right here at Olivier's Bistro, in the heart of Three Pines" (*Still Life* 3). Here, news is not the anonymity of what happens to others in a vast metropolis; rather, it is the daily events of a small community of people Clara knows. In psychological terms, "snugness is a remedy sought for the existential discomfort with expansiveness, and the snug place is an enclosed locale where that vulnerability is exchanged for feelings of comfort and security" (Griswold 29); it is "a safe anchorage where the soul's calmness can be restored and well-being enclosed" (Griswold 30). As the series progresses, the hope for safe anchorage is perhaps most true for Chief Inspector Armand Gamache who sees in Three Pines "a shore. A place where the shipwrecked could finally rest" (*Nature of the Beast* 8).

As much as Three Pines may seem at an inattentive glance to be a model of coziness in the sense of a separate, symbolically walled and protected convivial space, Penny examines the many ways in which even ostensibly protected space cannot be so fully separated from the larger world. Neither can location offer an easy corrective or cure to its residents. The journey of characters, like Gamache (who eventually moves to Three Pines), is inflected with a recognition of trauma that denies the possibility of emotional tidiness or the assurance of borders that hold a neat separation between inside/outside or sanctuary and pain. Trauma, in particular, shows the superficiality of assuming either easy recovery or containment. Gamache, who "staggered under the emotional burden" of his work, had "had enough of death ... but the memories remained, embedded" (*Nature of the Beast* 8). While serving as a representative witness of a serial murderer's trial, he had "absorbed the horror ... so that the rest of the population didn't have to. One person sacrificed for the common good" (*Nature of the Beast* 34). Years later, he felt "the weight of memory.... It came crashing, crushing, down" (*Nature of the Beast* 118). Trauma holds its own type of "inside" space, and that "'trauma time'" functions in a different way from "'linear time'" (Andrews 155)[13] shows how it can be an eternal present, a locked, contained environment which can be self-consuming. Linear time becomes porous, with one time linking to another as "memory [comes] crashing, crushing down." Yet even this horror that Gamache recalls is only one of many. He has had people die under his command and made decisions that would hurt and kill many more. Kind, generous, brilliant, and lethal, that Gamache suffers ongoing trauma show how the individual's psychological canvas becomes strafed from a world of violence. While Three Pines offers the promise of respite, this is a place where people seeking solace acknowledge the pain they bring with them. In this pain, Penny's series shows the ways in which life—and murder—matter. Those killed are not always tangential characters, as is typical of the emotional containment offered in cozies. In Penny's world, central characters serve as both victims and suspected perpetrators.

Others have committed what may be even worse crimes; Ruth Zardo suffers years of grief over what was ostensibly a simple matter of referring a business contract to another resident. But simple matters in Penny's world are not so simple; Ruth recognized evil and had "saved herself by betraying someone else." Gamache reflects on this that "She'd have named names to McCarthy. She'd have pointed out heretics to the Inquisition, to avoid the flames and save herself.... And then she'd have sat down and wept" (*Nature of the Beast* 343). There is a recognition here that seemingly small decisions have enormous consequences—and a recognition, as well, that the individual is always linked to a wider world in both geography and time. Moments are rarely tidily contained and in this world the grief of loss seems unbounded. When a young boy is killed in *The Nature of the Beast*, Gamache realizes that what "the autopsy couldn't show was the ongoing trauma to everyone who loved the child" (57). Here, grief is deep and the pain is on-page. When the boy's mother says of her grief that she feels "'like my bones are dissolving,'" Clara realizes there "wasn't just a wound where Laurent had once been. This was a vacuum into which everything tumbled. A great gaping black hole that sucked all the light, all the matter, all that mattered, into it" (*Nature of the Beast* 166). Clara knows from experience that

> grief took a terrible toll. It was paid at every birthday, every holiday, each Christmas. It was paid when glimpsing the familiar handwriting, or a hat, or a balled-up sock. Or hearing a creak that could have been, should have been, a footstep. Grief took its toll each morning, each evening, every noon hour as those who were left behind struggled forward [*Nature of the Beast* 168].

Unbounded by time and location, grief rips the veneer from cozy images—of birthdays and holidays, of everyday items of warmth in hats and socks. In this way, Penny's series acknowledges the lack of easy repair and the way damaged people survive by forgiving, loving, and negotiating the sometimes fraught connections with others.

Several characters also negotiate pain and hope through art, and in this Three Pines offers solace and yet is not so very separated from the larger world. Artist Clara and poet Ruth both create their art in Three Pines and show the ways in which art (unlike representations of crafts in cozies) is not neatly definable. In cozies, crafts—and art, when it appears—offer a means for a contained, ordered, and comforting world, one that produces tangible, finite, and understood things. In Penny's world, art is principally dangerous.[14] Ruth, for example, argues that "'Poetry scares most people.... I know mine does'" (*Nature of the Beast* 18). Here, poems and paintings serve as landscapes of the psyche; a line from Ruth's poem—"'Who hurt you once/so far beyond repair?'" (*Nature of the Beast* 372)—is both an expression of grief and a challenge for uncomfortable self-exploration. That art is not so much a thing as meaning itself is inherent in the description of it functioning as a "long house" where "every one, every event, every thing, every emotion is present" (*Still Life* 251), yet at times still ineffable. Viewing Clara's art, for example, requires an engagement of meaning-making, an investment in seeing details that others may miss. Art is difficult to fully grasp at times here and is about exploring the outlandish and the meaningful—and how at times the two may be the same thing. Here, art, like life, is infinitely explorative. The breadth of effect is evident, too, in that while Clara and Ruth's art is constructed in the nest of Three Pines, it moves into conversation in the larger world where the work of both artists is well known.

Countering images of Three Pine's insularity also underpin the forest that rims the village. As untamed wilderness, forests represent wild space where one's soul meets its test— it's where Hawthorne's Young Goodman Brown goes to meet the devil and where Hester Prynne travels. Such space is neither cozy nor capable of domestication. A "living, metamorphosing being" (Thomas 127), forest space often provides a "symbol of the unknown and the unconscious," a place where "[a]nything might happen" (Thomas 128). The forest sitting upon the doorstep of Three Pines is no exception. While the village's namesake stands as three trees in protected isolation, the surrounding landscape is dense forest that "had taken root thousands of years ago" (*Nature of the Beast* 176). This is the place where Olivier's greed comes alive, as if the forest magically breathes form into it. Here, in the secret of the forest and late at night, Olivier races and "the more he hurried the more frightened he became, and the more fearful he grew the faster he ran until he was stumbling, chased by dark words through the dark woods" (*Brutal Telling* 4). The forest and the darker impulses of his psyche become symbiotically entwined and Olivier runs "feeling his fear growing and feeding the rage" (*Brutal Telling* 5) with "the dark forest closing in" (*Brutal Telling* 179). He races to terrify an old man from whom he recovers art objects, Olivier's journey an expression of his greed. He, himself, is a beast of the forest, the "Chaos" that descends on Three Pines (*Brutal Telling* 5).

The forest that hems Three Pines does not provide the village with nested space as much as it serves as liminal space, grafted upon by human design. It is what happens in the night or when no one is watching. Even when it could serve as positive space—when it is the site for a boy's imaginative play, as he goes "running, stumbling, running" (*Nature of the Beast* 1)—it remains deadly. The child's play is so fraught with danger that the forest becomes the place of his murder. The forest bespeaks psychological terrain of what is hidden and, in the eventual resolution of Penny's mysteries, what must be revealed. Secrets and the forest go hand-in-hand, and Gamache's investigation reveals the ways the forest and village exist in a sometimes symbiotic relationship. For all its seeming idyll, Three Pines is a place of both respite and conflict, not as shut off from the world as it might initially appear. An early description of Three Pines describes how "Like Narnia, [Three Pines] was generally found unexpectedly and with a degree of surprise that such an elderly village should have been hiding in this valley all along" (*Still Life* 14). The simile is telling: C. S. Lewis's Narnia is a place both magical and devastating, one where the battle between good and evil is fought upon vast landscapes but is ultimately a matter of individual choice and responsibility. One of the most comforting features of cozies is that the evil is contained; it is "other" and the other is identified, captured, and neatly expelled. Yet in her presentation of crime, Penny argues that the process is "Facing the monster. And recognizing it. Knowing that it was not a vile few. It wasn't 'them.' It was us. The banality of evil ... wasn't the frothing madman. It was the conscientious us" (*Glass Houses* 247).

As much as it may seem that the forest provides a metaphor for the Jungian shadow of the other, its danger and psychological resonance is echoed in Three Pines, a place whose picturesque insularity—the very fact that it cannot be located on maps—makes it an enticement not only to city refugees like Myrna and Gamache, but also to those "'trying to hide something'" (*Nature of the Beast* 176). The threat of such isolation to the residents of Three Pines is especially evident in the discovery of a weapon of mass destruction in the forest nearby and, in *Glass Houses*, because the village has "no police force, no traffic lights, no sidewalks, no mayor" (*Brutal Telling* 24), it later becomes the chosen meeting place of a drug cartel. It is the Bistro— the otherwise comforting nest within the nest of Three Pines, with Gamache's family and friends present—that comes under assault by the cartel so that "the safest place in the world was not safe after all" (*Glass Houses* 355). Following the assault, one of Gamache's long-time colleagues who suffers life-threatening wounds is taken out of the Bistro and placed in an ambulance; she lies in the gurney as if wrapped up "like a nest" (*Glass Houses* 387)—but this nest, like others here, is no promise of protection or recovery.

In Penny's series, the appreciation of what is dear is emphasized by the understanding of what can be lost. The distinction of inside/outside thus requires an appreciation of that dialectic and a grasp of the preciousness of protected space particularly *because* of its vulnerability. A nest, after all, offers "a sort of paradox of sensibility." It is "a precarious thing," although the idea of it "sets us to *daydreaming of security*" (Bachelard 102, italics in original). Although Bachelard argues that "the nest ... knows nothing of the hostility of the world" (103), in Penny's series, it is precisely this knowledge of the world's dangers that heightens the hope of Three Pines as sanctuary space. As Gamache plans for the arrival of the U.S. drug cartel, the "village had never looked more beautiful. More at peace with itself. The gardens in full bloom. The children, having eaten dinner, were playing on the village green. Squeezing out every last moment of a perfect summer day" (*Glass Houses* 341). The beauty, peace, gardens, children playing—the "perfect summer day"—are balanced with intimations of the fragility that is Three Pines, hence the need of "squeezing out every last moment" of its wonder. Gamache had expected to confront the cartel "in the woods that night, not in the bistro" (*Glass Houses* 323), but here, evil doesn't wait for the night nor is it circumscribed to outside places. Drugs, "a modern-day Black Death" (*Glass Houses* 371) bound for Canada and the United States, and the weapon of mass destruction which was constructed to destroy entire cities show the impossibility of truly removed, unconnected space. In both expressions of art and evil, Three Pines cannot fully stand in concretized, separate space.

Loss, grief, guilt, and trauma matter in this series, and they are not easily resolved by setting, no matter how picturesque. Yet there are ways in which characters find hope through moments of forgiveness and kindness. Despite his burdens, Gamache is, in Three Pines, "'Happier than [he] ever thought possible'" (*Nature of the Beast* 175).

> He looked down at the village and his heart soared. ... People were walking their dogs ... racing the gently falling snow. They were shopping at M. Beliveau's general store and buying baguettes from Sarah's boulangerie. Olivier stood at the Bistro doorway and shook out a tablecloth. Life was far from harried here. But neither was it still [*Still Life* 312].

"'It's so beautiful,' he said, almost under his breath" (*Nature of the Beast* 175). The nest of Three Pines may be a dream of protection, but it is a beautiful one, all the same.

Notes

1. "I dreamed of a nest in which the trees repulsed death." From Adolphe Shedrow, *Berceau sans promesses*. Cited in Bachelard, 103.
2. See Maffini and Kashian.
3. See Hyzy and Davis.
4. In *Writing the Cozy Mystery*, Cohen lists "The Eight C's of Cozy Mysteries": Crime, Clues, Characters, Canines, Cooking, Crafts, Cats, Chuckles (5).
5. In some cozy series, the animals are anthropomorphized enough to solve crimes on their own. See, for example, Albert whose series is fictionally set on Beatrix Potter's farm.
6. Amanda Flower notes that cozies typically present "a killer who isn't an evil person, just a person who made a gigantic mistake when he or she decides that the only answer is murder." Also see Vester who describes the "utopian space" of cozies (31).
7. In his discussion of space, Bachelard reflects, "so when we examine a nest, we place ourselves at the origin of confidence in the world, [with] an urge toward cosmic confidence" (103).
8. This provides important marketing outlets to publishers. As Kensington Publishers point out, as much as cozies "encourage readers to engage with beloved pastimes ... the range of topics enables Kensington to do promotion well beyond the traditional book-related channels, including knitting publications." Kensington also sends stores a "'CozyBowl' gift pack 'filled with all kinds of things that make cozies so much fun, from baking utensils to adorabowl toy dogs and cats, to puzzles, crafts, candy and more'" (see Kensington).
9. One sees this, for example, in *State of the Onion* when the protagonist offers readers recipes for "A Presidential Menu," providing "some representative foods I serve to the First Family in the current White House" (Hyzy 305).
10. *A Rule Against Murder* and *The Beautiful Mystery*, respectively. As of 2019, there are fifteen books in the series proper, plus *The Hangman* which was published as a stand-alone for the Good Reads series.
11. The title also reflects a character's comments that "'Life is change. If you aren't growing and evolving you're standing still, and the rest of the world is surging ahead. Most of these people are very immature. They lead 'still' lives, waiting.'" (*Still Life* 139).
12. This reflects Penny's own description of her novels as "psychological." (See her interview with MacDonald). The reissue of *Still Life* in larger trade size removed the punning blurb and offered new, more evocative visuals.

13. Andrews here discusses J. Edkins's contributions to trauma theory. I am grateful to my colleague, Dr. Maya Socolovsky, for her discussions with me about trauma. Also see Gillies's essay about other traumatized characters in crime series.

14. In several novels of the series, art also serves as motive and answer to a murder, as well as a means of psychological exploration. See, for example, *Still Life, A Trick of the Light,* and *The Long Way Home.*

Works Cited

Albert, Susan Wittig. *The Tale of Hill Top Farm.* New York: Berkley, 2004.
Andrews, Molly. "Beyond Narrative: The Shape of Traumatic Testimony" in *Beyond Narrative Coherence.* Ed. Matti Hyvärinen, Lars-Christer Hydén, Marja Saarenheimo, and Maria Tamboukou. Philadelphia: John Benjamins Pub, 2010. 147-166.
Bachelard, Gaston. *The Poetics of Space.* 1958. Translated by Maria Jolas. Foreword by Etienne Gilson. Boston: Beacon Press, 1969.
Cohen, Nancy J. *Writing the Cozy Mystery.* Second Edition. Orange Grove Press, 2018.
Davis, Krista. *The Diva Runs Out of Thyme.* New York: Berkley-Penguin, 2008.
Flower, Amanda. "What Exactly is a Cozy Mystery?" *PW [Publisher's Weekly].* May 18, 2018.
Gillies, Mary Ann. "Trauma and Contemporary Crime Fiction." *Clues* 37.1 (Spring 2019): 40-50.
Griswold, Jerry. *Feeling Like a Kid: Childhood and Children's Literature.* Baltimore: The Johns Hopkins University Press, 2006.
Hyzy, Julie. *State of the Onion.* New York: Berkley-Penguin, 2008.
Kashian, Tina. *Hummus and Homicide.* New York: Kensington Books, 2018.
Kensington. "A Cozy Homes for Cozies at Kensington" [release]. *Publishers Weekly.* 265.10 (5 March 2018): 41.
Lewis, C. S. *The Lion, the Witch and the Wardrobe.* 1950. New York: Harper Collins, 2000.
MacDonald, Jay. "Transcending the Cozy Village Mystery." *BookPage* (September 2015): 14+. *Literature Resource Center,* https://go.gale.com/ps/i.do?id=GALE%7CA427301988&v=2.1&u=char69915&it=r&p=LitRC&sw=w.
Maffini, Mary Jane. *The Cluttered Corpse.* New York: Berkley-Penguin, 2008.
Penny, Louise. *The Beautiful Mystery.* New York: St. Martin's-Minotaur, 2012.
_____. *A Better Man.* New York: St. Martin's-Minotaur, 2019.
_____. *The Brutal Telling.* New York: St. Martin's-Minotaur, 2009.
_____. *Bury Your Dead.* New York: St. Martin's-Minotaur, 2010.
_____. *The Cruelest Month.* New York: St. Martin's-Minotaur, 2007.
_____. *A Fatal Grace.* New York: St. Martin's-Minotaur, 2006.
_____. *Glass Houses.* New York: St. Martin's-Minotaur, 2017.
_____. *A Great Reckoning.* New York: St. Martin's-Minotaur, 2016.
_____. *The Hangman.* Edmonton, Alta.: Grass Roots Press, 2010.
_____. *How the Light Gets In.* New York: St. Martin's-Minotaur, 2013.
_____. *Kingdom of the Blind.* New York: St. Martin's-Minotaur, 2018.
_____. *The Long Way Home.* New York: St. Martin's-Minotaur, 2014.
_____. *The Nature of the Beast.* New York: St. Martin's-Minotaur, 2015.
_____. *A Rule Against Murder.* New York: St. Martin's-Minotaur, 2008.
_____. *Still Life.* 2005. New York: St. Martin's Paperbacks-Minotaur, 2007.
_____. *A Trick of the Light.* New York: St. Martin's-Minotaur, 2011.
Thomas, Joyce. "Woods and Castles, Towers and Huts: Aspects of Setting in the Fairytale." *Children's Literature in Education.*17.2 (Summer 1986): 126-34.
Vester, Katharina. "Bodies to Die for: Negotiating the Ideal Female Body in Cozy Mystery Novels." *The Journal of Popular Culture* 48.1 (2015): 31-43.

Is the Cozy a Tailor-Made Style for Historical Crime Set in the 1920s and 1930s?

Jennifer S. Palmer

The genres of Historical Crime and Cozy Crime are both very popular as crime fiction continues to expand. Borders between different styles seem to be blurring—horror, supernatural, psychological, thriller, police procedural, amateur detectives, to name just some, can be combined, or at least a small number of them can, into one book! My contention is that Historical Crime, when it is set in the 1920s and 1930s, can make a very good home for a Cozy Crime tale. I am not suggesting that all mysteries set in the 1920s and 1930s are cozy; that is patently untrue. To paraphrase Thomas Hobbes, historical crime stories are frequently about lives that are "solitary, poor, nasty, brutish and short!" (Hobbes, 143). Nor I am suggesting that only the 1920s and 1930s is a suitable historical period for cozy historicals.

The ending of the First World War introduced a new world as four empires fell (German, Astro-Hungarian, Turkish and Russian), new political ideas blossomed, and revolutions broke out. The era between the wars was one of very real violence as Communism and Fascism rose up throughout the world. Old people were crushed by the war's effects; young people were freed from the shackles of correct behavior, while those who fought the War sought to forget it. By the 1930s people were also trying to forget the hardships of the Depression and were starting to realize that hopes of a new co-operation in the League of Nations and disarmament were to be destroyed. Despite those grim realities the plethora of cozy historical crime examples in the '20s and '30s is what occasioned my title statement. Cozy historical crime books can build on the desire of that era to forget. In the Dorothy Parker mystery *The Broadway Murders*, author Agata Stanford has Dorothy Parker in 1924 musing, "Senseless death inspires in some people a quest for meaningful living: for others, senseless death gives rise to senseless living" (Stanford 5.)

I have limited my survey to this particular period because with so many historical crime books on all periods available I would need to write a book, not an essay! Secondly, the era from 1918 to 1939 is a growing and expanding area for crime writers. The popularity of the era online is enormous with, for example, Amazon advertising "a cozy historical 1920s mystery" (Lee Strauss' *Murder on Eaton Square*, which is 10th in a series), and "1920s historical cozy mystery" (Sonia Parin's *Murder in the Cards*, 4th in a series). Thirdly, despite the grim aspects of the era as delineated above, it does often have suitably cozy features. Fourthly, the era has a more easily understood history than say the sixteenth century; however, it retains a different morality to our own and a harsher legal system. Finally, the real era of the 1920s and 1930s was the one in which the first "cozies" were written. It seems fitting that many writers of historical crime want to return to this "Golden Age" setting.

What does a historical crime novel involve? There are two distinct elements here—crime and history. Let's take crime first. Any traditional crime novel to succeed must have the proper elements of a detective story. As Margery Allingham expressed it, "The Mystery remains box-shaped, at once a prison and a refuge. Its four walls are roughly, a Crime, a mystery, an Enquiry and a Conclusion with an element of Satisfaction in it." (This definition is given on the CWA site advertising the Margery Allingham Short Story Competition and comes from Margery's own words). A historical novel, however, must present a story which is steeped in the history of the era chosen; the elements of the tale—the motives, the actions, the relationships, the social conditions must resonate with that era. The Britannica definition is "a novel that has as its setting a period of history and that attempts to convey the spirit, manners, and social conditions of a past age with realistic detail and fidelity ... to historical fact" (britannica.com). Historical novels can deal with actual historical figures or mix historical and fictional characters; often the intention is to show how great events are reflected in their impact on real or fictional figures.

Does the existence of crime books genuinely written in the era have any influence? Any study of the Golden Age of crime writing, 1920–1939, shows the enormous variety of approaches used at that time making cozy an inadequate overall label. Obviously, the original books from the era do provide helpful background information though a contemporary 1920s and 1930s writer never gives the full background that a modern writer trying to recreate the era does. It is the difference between an insider and an outsider.

Turning to cozy crime—many definitions of the cozy are pejorative, suggesting that it is unreal because it lacks graphic violence and sex and fails to evoke a feeling of evil. I paraphrase Bruce Murphy in the *Encyclopedia of Murder and Mystery* here; he continues, "at its worst, the cozy mystery deteriorates into the cutesy mystery, presenting a world in which CATS [*sic*] show preternatural ability to solve crimes, romance submerges detection and realism is ignored" (Murphy 114). Maxim Jakubowski, crime expert and founder of the Murder One bookshop in London (now closed), says so-called "cozy" crime, is set in "an idealistic world where nothing really bad happens and everyone can gather in the living room to discuss the culprit" (Flood 3 August 2015 *The Guardian*, UK). In *Murder Ink* Dilys Winn suggests that "the Cozies surfaced in England in the mad Twenties, and their work featured a small village setting, a hero with faintly aristocratic family connections, a plethora of Red Herrings and a tendency to commit murder with sterling silver letter openers and poisons imported from Paraguay" (Winn 3–4).

What must a cozy have? It can be seen as the opposite of the hard-boiled genre which was also established in the 1920s. The classic hard boiled is graphic, violent, unsentimental and sordid, with an urban background, and fast paced dialogue, usually set in the USA. Chandler wrote in the "Simple Art of Murder": "Fiction in any form has always intended to be realistic" (Chandler 1). The frequently repeated phrase "gritty reality" is one that hard-boiled exponents use to describe their work though I doubt that many of them have experienced such a level of violence! It is hard to date the first use of the term cozy: in the *Oxford Companion to Crime and Mystery Writing* Susan Oleksiw states that Cozy was " a term first used in a review in *The Observer*, 25 May 1958"; so it is comparatively recent as a description (Herbert 97). In Marilyn Stasio's article in the *New York Times* in 1992, she comments on a new wave of cozies being produced after the "homicidal maniacs who tracked blood all over the genre for the last few seasons" (Stasio October 18, 1992, *New York Times*). Since cozy is defined as the opposite of hard-boiled, it lacks graphic sex and violence, is romantic, amusing, and is situated in a comfortable middle-class setting in a small place. The hard-boiled protagonist is usually male and carries a gun; the cozy equivalent is usually female and without a gun.

I propose to break the cozy down into various features and to see how they work for historical crime set in the 1920s/1930s. There must be a protagonist, usually female and amateur, who investigates a crime; a place setting (usually a village, small town or city suburb); and a time setting, usually the present day, which is almost static or develops over years. There must, at some point, be police involvement so that the villain can be dealt with by the law. The victory of good over evil and the punishment of the guilty is a core element of all traditional crime fiction. In modern cozies the relationship between the amateur detective and the police is variable on a scale from hostile to romantic. The accretion of recurring individuals around the central protagonist provides a cast of characters who illuminate the stories. Avoidance of scenes of graphic sex and violence has been a hallmark of cozy crime as has the omission of profanity. My final feature concerns the light-hearted approach that is seen frequently in cozies including a touch of humor even in a dreadful situation; using a protagonist who is cack-handed or even totally incompetent; or in a rather different vein, using a punning title.

I shall consider four authors whose work fit my definition of the historical cozy crime: for the 1920s there are Carola Dunn (23 books on Daisy Fletcher) and Kerry Greenwood's 20 novels about Phryne Fisher. For the 1930s, Rhys Bowen's adventures for Her Royal Spyness (whose 13th novel was published in August 2019) and Susan Wittig Albert's Darling Dahlias series with 8 books so far. The four do illustrate somewhat different aspects of historical cozy crime. In the Darling Dahlia books, we have several protagonists and a wholly different scenario of small-town working women in the Depression; more on that later.

Daisy Dalrymple, in the series by Carola Dunn, is the daughter of a deceased viscount in England; she has decided to work in the aftermath of the Great War writing articles for illustrated magazines. She is introduced in the first book *Death at Wentworth Court* as she starts her journalistic career in 1923 by visiting this house to write about its style and history and to take photographs (Dunn 11). Daisy is the type of cozy heroine who accidentally becomes embroiled in murder cases (regularly!) and has no professional status as investigator. She matures through the series, and by the one most recently published, *The Corpse at Crystal Palace*, which takes place in 1928, Daisy has married a police detective, had children, and lives a suburban life in a comfortable middle-class villa with servants in London.

The Honorable Phryne Fisher arrives in Melbourne, Australia, in the first book of the series, *Death by Misadventure* (also entitled *Cocaine Blues*), in 1928 to investigate a family issue at the request of an English colonel; she finds that she likes such investigating and sets up as a professional. Phryne is wealthy, so she sometimes gets clients to give money to good causes or asks for unusual payments such as the invitation to sit at High Table from an academic in the short story "The Hours of Juana the Mad," in *A Question of Death: An Illustrated Phryne Fisher Treasury* (Greenwood 173). Her adventures take place mainly in Australia during 1928–1929.

A second amateur investigator between 1932 and 1935 is Lady Victoria Georgiana Charlotte Eugenie Rannock, 34th in line to the British throne, but from a very impoverished Scottish branch of the family. Georgie becomes an emissary of Queen Mary in what seem at first to be simple missions but end up as complex, nefarious affairs. In *Her Royal Spyness*, the first of the series, Georgie is ordered by the Queen to spy on the Prince of Wales, but things develop to a point where Georgie must investigate a murder to save her brother, Binkie, the Duke, from being found guilty of the crime. Whilst she does succeed somehow in her missions, Georgie is an example of what I call the Hapless Heroine who is surrounded by eccentric fools and has disadvantages such as poverty, clumsiness, and naïveté, but still fights her way through to success, often through happenstance.

Circumstances of class, wealth and education in the 1920s and 1930s mean that detectives are frequently members of the upper classes and/or independently wealthy thus enabling them to indulge a hobby of detection. Dorothy Sayers led the way in 1920 with Lord Peter Wimsey in *Whose Body?* and Margery Allingham followed in 1929 with a suitably silly ass aristocrat called Albert Campion in *The Crime at Black Dudley*. Dorothy L. Sayers wrote in an article quoted in Barbara Reynolds' biography of Dorothy that "Lord Peter's large income.... I deliberately gave him ... at the time I was particularly hard up and it gave me pleasure to spend his fortune for him" (Reynolds, 263). Phryne Fisher is certainly the most glamorous of the protagonists. She is rich, wears beautiful clothes, eats delicious food, flies her own plane, and drives a Hispano-Suiza; it all gives the reader pleasure when reading the books. Daisy is financially secure after her marriage, but not before that; she refers to "her less than affluent days" in *Superfluous Women* (Dunn 292). Georgie is dependent on her financially strapped brother and his cheese paring wife (reminds me of the beginning of *Sense and Sensibility*!). These upper-class protagonists can use their status when detecting, particularly in the class ridden society of 1920s and '30s Britain. It is a given that cozy protagonists must be able to deduce from evidence and read human behavior. They can get people to talk freely; Daisy Dalrymple in *Death at Wentworth Court* comments that she was "constantly amazed at the way total strangers insisted on regaling her with their life stories, their marital misfortunes, or their children's misdeeds" (Dunn 3). She adds, in *Murder on the Flying Scotsman*, a comment on the willingness of a lady to cooperate when she hears that Daisy is the Honorable: "Daisy had never understood why her courtesy title should be regarded as a guarantee of respectability" (Dunn 45). Phryne can overawe her interlocutors, but also uses the truculent Communist dock workers, Bert and Cec, to question people when necessary. Georgie manages with careful listening to people around her rather than direct questioning.

In some newer historicals authors use a servant as protagonist. In Jessica Fellowes's *The Mitford Murders* a nursery maid who is confidante to the Mitford sisters is the detective while in Dorothy Cannell's "Florence Norris Mysteries," *Murder at Mullings*, a housekeeper is the protagonist. *Murder Most Malicious* by Alyssa Maxwell is described on the cover as "A

Lady and Lady's Maid Mystery," and it does a sort of Downton Abbey contrasting the world of above and below stairs as Lady Phoebe and Eva, her maid, try to discover a murderer. It is rare in Golden Age fiction that "the Butler did it!," and the idea of a menial murderer is considered unlikely; however, in *Superfluous Women* it happens, despite the remark made, "A cleaning woman bumping off her employer? Unheard of and an unsettling idea" (Dunn, 294).

The connection to a craft shop or small business that exists in many modern cozies does not fit with the 1920s/1930s, especially at the society level. There is a disapproving attitude to women working outside the home, and the stigma for an upper-class family of having an independently minded woman member is strong. The flappers, like the ones who appear in Christie's 1920s thrillers, wanted to shock and certainly succeeded with their short hair, short skirts, smoking, made up faces, and, sometimes, their drinking and drug taking. Those who really flaunted themselves were the "Bright Young Things" who held famous fancy-dress parties such as the Second Childhood Party of 1929 and the Mozart Party in 1930 in London. There are photos of these in D.J. Taylor's *Bright Young People: The Rise and Fall of a Generation, 1918–1940*. Similar Bright Young Things move to Australia where Phryne Fisher solves a complex and rather nasty series of disappearances from their decadent party in *Murder in the Dark*. Phryne Fisher is not a Bright Young Thing: she is too independent and too mature, but she is a perfect flapper on her own terms—sophisticated with magnificent designer clothes, a perfect black bob, and a slender figure. She smokes, drinks strong cocktails, and is sexually voracious. The first description of her clothes in *Cocaine Blues* is "a fetching sailor suit in dark blue with white piping and a pique collar. The waist dropped below her hips, leaving five inches of pleated skirt" (Greenwood, 8).

Daisy Dalrymple bemoans her unfashionably full figure though Detective Chief Inspector Fletcher (later to be her husband) enjoys watching her walk up the stairs and thinks to himself that she is "cuddlesome" (*Death at Wentworth Court*). In the same book Marjorie is designated as a "quintessential flapper" with "cherry red ... coat and skirt," "bobbed hair set in Marcel waves," "a fashionably boyish figure," plucked and darkened eyebrows and lashes and "Cupid's bow" scarlet lipstick. Daisy cannot really behave as outrageously as Phryne since she is young and not wealthy; she has to consider a formidable mother who is opposed to her daughter working, and her employment as a writer for magazines would end if she behaved outrageously. Daisy does not bob her hair until away from her mother. Daisy Dalrymple's Honorable status opens doors for her but also limits her, and when she eventually marries her middle-class policeman and becomes Daisy Fletcher, she needs to propitiate his mother as well as her own! Georgie's penury prevents her being much of a flapper, and she must also wrestle with the problems of appalling marriage suitors being suggested for her like Prince Siegfried of Rumania, "a cold fish with staring eyes, a limp handshake and a look that indicated a perpetual bad smell under his nose" (Bowen, *Her Royal Spyness*, 11).

London is the base setting for Daisy and Georgie as Melbourne is for Phryne, but these protagonists do not need to stay mainly in one place like an owner of a shop or a librarian in a modern cozy must. A professional detective must travel as the case dictates. So, Phryne goes outside Melbourne to other parts of Australia including flying alone in her plane to a very remote mountainous area (*The Green Mill Murder*). Daisy Dalrymple, in pursuit of her articles, goes all over Britain to suitable castles or large houses. In modern settings of cozies a protagonist begins by moving to a new town, village, job, or business because of a traumatic event such as the death of a relative, the ending of a love affair, or the loss of a job. In historical crime novels of the 1920s there is the omnipresent shadow of World War I to provide such reasons for becoming a detective. Both the 1920s protagonists have personal experiences of World War I: Phryne has spent time as a nurse on the Western Front. The flapper of the 1920s who makes a perfect female detective, as personified by Phryne, is confident, willing to shock, and tough: the product of the effects of the war in loosening traditional norms of behavior. Phryne remembers her wartime experiences (*Murder in Montparnasse*) when she becomes involved in the case of Aussie soldiers from the war being murdered. The Honorable Daisy Dalrymple enjoys working as a journalist, but she works since she lost both her brother and fiancé in the War and her home passed to the next in line, a cousin, when her father died of the "Spanish flu." In *Superfluous Women* there is a reference to many women as "victims like the boys that should have lived to marry them" (Dunn 233). By the 1930s the relevance of World War I may have lessened, but fears continue for the future as Fascism and Communism are established while domestic life is blighted by the effects of the Great Depression. Georgiana Rannock's father killed himself when the Wall Street Crash took his remaining money, leaving his family to pay crippling death duties. *Naughty in Nice* begins with Georgie helping at a soup kitchen in Victoria Station: "It was a bitter and bleak January day, and I felt as cold and miserable as those poor wretches who shuffled past me" (Bowen 1).

To move on to my fourth example which is also in the 1930s: The Darling Dahlias is the name of a gardening club in Darling, Alabama, a community of 907 people. In 1930 these ladies face the serious problems of the Depression and the traditional attitudes to women's place in society, whether married or not. The problems faced by these women include the lingering effects of World War I; there is a reference to Liz's fiancé having been killed in the war. Other problems will follow: the Wall Street Crash has affected many; Liz's mother "had put up her small annuity and her paid-for house as collateral against a bank loan to buy stocks ... when the bubble burst and Wall Street crashed she lost everything" (Albert, *Darling Dahlias and the Eleven O'Clock* Ladies, 131). All the ladies have the status of respected members of a small town, nearly all of them have jobs, and they work together as women against a male dominated society. The Darling Dahlias Garden club grows vegetables for these who need help in the community. The women in Darling must behave correctly in a small society where transgressions will be noticed. They earn money in various ways, as a cafe owner, secretary, linotype operator for the newspaper, or telephonist while still working to look after their homes and families. Husbands during the Depression are like Jed in *The Darling Dahlias and the Eleven O' Clock Lady* who tells his wife, a woman "should stay home where God put her," although he shows no reluctance when she gives him her paycheck (Albert, 151, 155). The books have now reached Christmas 1934 and the period of the New Deal, so there are some improvements coming.

A further feature of contemporary cozies is an interest in clothes, and many of these historical protagonists have this. The Darling women weren't well paid, but they could buy copies of fashionable clothes or make them. Liz wears serviceable, cheap rayon stockings all week, but she has a pair of filmy stockings for Saturday evenings. One thing that the Darling Dahlia books have and the other three do not is the provision of recipes (another interest in modern cozies). These are, of course, period Southern recipes as mentioned in the text. (Southern corn pudding and Jefferson Davis pie feature at the end of *The Darling Dahlias and the Eleven O'Clock Ladies*.)

As historical crime novels these books have a mixture of fictional and real characters and fictional and real events. Phryne encounters the famous madam, Tillie Devine, in Sidney and a fictional and rather nasty exponent of Black Magic, Marrin (he has filed his teeth to points), who follows the ideas of Fraser's Golden Bough; she dresses in a daring costume like the real Dulcie Deamer in 1924 for the Sidney Artists Ball in *Death Before Wicket*. Daisy, as mentioned earlier, has friends who are unmarried women after World War I, and she visits contemporary buildings like the Crystal Palace but the stately homes she visits are imaginary. Rhys Bowen surrounds her imaginary royal with real characters like Queen Mary, David, the Prince of Wales, Mrs. Simpson, and Coco Chanel. There is a New Deal Civilian Conservation Corps camp near Darling (an imaginary town) which features in *The Darling Dahlias and the Eleven O' Clock Lady*; not surprisingly the ideas of FDR are discussed as are the promises of social reforms by Huey Long, the Governor in Louisiana. The CCC setup is commented on as "look(ing) like a Fascist militia like what that fellow Hitler was cooking up in Europe"(Albert, 194). Authors try to incorporate attitudes, events, and enthusiasms of the day: Phryne is present in a dance hall when one of the final two couples in a dance marathon is murdered (*The Green Mill Murder*); Daisy Fletcher visits a group of female friends who have bought a house together as *Superfluous Women* who could not find husbands after World War I. Georgiana is in Nice when Coco Chanel is staying there and briefly becomes a model for her in *Naughty in Nice*.

In the 1920s and 1930s blackmail for homosexuality or the threat of social exclusion is quite possible. Conditions of arrest and imprisonment especially for the poor are harsh, and the threat of execution hangs over this period: however, cozies can gloss over such realities as they wish. The Daisy books often feature the sort of secrets that the upper classes might kill over—the besmirching of the family name—as in the first book, *Death at Wentworth Court*. Several Phryne Fisher books show Phryne helping homosexuals avoid blackmail. Georgie's objections to Prince Siegfried of Rumania as a suitor also relate to his gayness. In Darling the ladies do not discuss such matters though the closeness of Myra May and Violet at the diner is noticed. A potent local issue of law breaking is the production of moonshine during the Prohibition period and after.

There is the connection between sleuth and police which can, in modern cozies, reflect a relationship of some kind either enabling the sleuth to get confidential information or showing a mistrust by the authorities of the amateur "busybody." Romance can eventually ensue as antagonism melts into love. Detectives in these 1920s and 30s books can be in such situations. In the Daisy Dalrymple books we have the classic relationship as Daisy and Chief Inspector Alec Fletcher, CID, meet in book 1 (*Death at Wentworth Court*) when she is a witness to a murder; by book 6 (*Dead in the Water*) they are engaged; they marry before the opening of book 9 (*To Davy Jones Below*) and after several books work their way through her pregnancy, she has twins two months before the opening of book 16 (*The Bloody Tower*). Alec's superior is always annoyed by Daisy's propensity for getting involved with murders but has to accept her sleuthing abilities do help to solve crimes. He tells Alec in *Superfluous Women*, "It's the devil of a mess your wife's dragged you into now!" (Dunn, 135). Phryne Fisher in Melbourne is not swayed by romance but by lust! She is not, however, involved in that way with the police. She has quickly proved her abilities to the elderly Inspector Jack Robinson. (Note that the TV series *Miss Fisher's Murder Mysteries* changes the placid relationship of the books with the elderly inspector to a more sexually fraught one with a younger man as Inspector). Fortunately for the comfort of Phryne and her family, the Butlers, who cook and keep the house in order, do not decide to leave because of what Dot describes as "Phryne's habit of strewing her boudoir with beautiful naked young men" (Greenwood *Flying Too High*, 29–30). Dot's concerns prove groundless when Mr. Butler and his wife decide that Phryne is "a vamp" and that "Young men are clean about the house. It's better than the old gentlemen's [their previous employer] greyhounds." Thereafter Phryne's household always refer to her lovers as "the pets" (163).

The Darling Dahlias are all amateurs, but they are not ignored by the sheriff. Verna has a great deal of status after she becomes the county treasurer. The sheriff might say "That damned Tideswell woman again," but he is forced to listen to her and to thank her once or twice (Albert *The Darling Dahlias and the Eleven O'Clock Lady*, 113). In *Her Royal Spyness* the Police Inspector is suspicious of Georgie. The fear that one of the nobs is trying to influence police actions is rather a prevalent one in this era. *Naughty in Nice* has a bumbling French police inspector who suspects Georgie of a jewel theft. Fortunately, she can bring a police inspector from the Surete and her grandfather, a retired British policeman, to her aid. So, Georgie is a suspect to the police, but the others are accepted, if reluctantly, though busybody might be the term police would use to describe the ladies!

A cast of recurring characters around the protagonist relatives, friends, employees, and even pets, matter in cozies. Kerry Greenwood's Phryne does rather specialize in rescuing young women from bad treatment at male hands. Dot, her companion, was turned off without a character when she rejected the attentions of the young man in whose house she was working (*Cocaine Blues*); later Phryne rescues two young girls and adopts them, and they, like Dot, continue as regular characters in the series. The Fisher household has Dot, the two adopted girls and the cat, Ember, and dog, Molly, with all home comforts including delicious food and cocktails provided by the Butlers. Daisy's family is dealt with earlier; she also has numerous friends who can be in one story or several. Other characters around Georgie include Georgie's mother who is, in 1920s parlance, a "bolter," who left her husband for another man when Georgie was two; Georgie's old schoolfriend Belinda who offers an opposite view of life in the 1930s to Georgie's; and Georgie's useless clumsy maid, Queenie. In a rather different milieu the Garden Club members in Darling, Alabama, provide a loose grouping of women who form the background to each tale together with other female characters in their small town. The solid background here is always the Depression and the struggle to survive. Each book begins with a bulletin from the Darling Dahlias Garden Club, which is very much in the style of that era with a roster of Club members. This crucial build-up of supporting characters in a series of books really helps to make them into cozies.

Avoidance of graphic violence, detailed sex scenes, and profanity can carry through both cozy and historical genres; in the early years of historical crime books this was partly as a distinguishing feature from the sex in the Bodice Rippers. Such avoidance of graphic portrayals is becoming rarer in both genres. Now there can be more graphic sex scenes. In the Phryne Fisher series Phryne's lovers can change from book to book; there is often some description of the erotic tension of her encounters. Phryne's light-hearted liaisons contrast with the conventional route of marriage and children in the Daisy books. Romance can feature in the Darling Dahlias series, but, more seriously, Liz has to deal with her apparent longtime suitor Grady having made another woman pregnant; by *The Darling Dahlias and the Eleven O' Clock Lady* she has come to terms with this. A recurring love theme is part of the Her Royal Spyness books; a character, Darcy O'Mara, re-appears in each book. There is an interesting quote on Amazon from the publishers of the Daisy Gumm books (another 1920s cozy series in the U.S.): "The Daisy Gumm Majesty Cozy Mystery Series is a light-hearted Mystery in a historical setting. There are no explicit sexual scenes and minimal cursing and will be enjoyed by readers who appreciate clean and wholesome reads" (*Strong Spirits*).

We are told that in cozies although violence is necessary to fuel the plots it is simply described and there is no gloating over it. However, in actuality violence can be shown much more extensively now, and the cozy protagonists are frequently put into highly threatening situations particularly at the climaxes of their stories. Phryne carries a pistol which she is prepared to use, and she faces death several times. (*The Green Mill Murder* and *Cocaine Blues* are just two books where she is in danger). Violence is rather more at arm's length for Daisy; in *Superfluous Women* she is locked in a cellar with a friend but without other overt violence. Georgie is next to a woman who is shot dead in *Naughty in Nice* and falls down an oubliette in *Royal Blood*, but again is not attacked directly. In Darling direct violence is never offered to a Darling Dahlia though there are, of course, murders, often of women. The protagonists in my four examples are of an era and class in Great Britain and the USA when swearing was not common for women. When Georgie uses the word "bloody" in *Her Royal Spyness*, she attributes its use to the loosening effects on her tongue of a strong cocktail; her more usual expletive is "golly." The slang of the era can also be used where swearwords might otherwise fit; Daisy is fond of words like "spiffing." In Darling the mores of a small country town are such that the local newspaper proprietor knows that he cannot print the sordid details of a murder and can never put photos of the body in the paper.

The light heartedness that pervades many cozies can be found in historical cozies—back to Phryne Fisher and her insouciance when faced with attacks on her person. In *Cocaine Blues* Phryne returns to the best hotel in

Melbourne where "The apparition of Miss Fisher, clad in rags, escorted up to the front door by a shirtless dancer ... made a lasting impression on the doorman" (Greenwood 178). Humor appears in cozies in different forms. Consider the genuine financial problems of Lady Georgie in *Her Royal Spyness* which lead her to take menial jobs and then to have to disguise what she is doing. She is always in danger of her two roles being revealed, though the inability of aristocrats to recognize servants is helpful! The habit of nicknames is very much of the era. Young men in the series of *Royal Spyness* novels are called Binky (George's brother), Roly, Whiffy, and a man with trouble pronouncing his R's is named Tristram. The use of punning titles is enormously prevalent in cozies, and Rhys Bowen uses it in the Royal Spyness series: *Naughty in Nice* and *On Her Majesty's Frightfully Secret Service* are two. Daisy is a cheerful individual throughout. I assume the choice of the name Darling for the town of the Dahlias Garden Club reflects humor too.

In conclusion, out of the defining characteristics of the cozy I see as most important the central protagonist, whether an amateur or professional investigator; the clearly delineated settings in place and time; the cast of surrounding characters; the essentially parochial involvement with events; the avoidance of much sex, violence or swearing; and the light-heartedness. Can a cozy historical work without one or more of these features, since my definition of "tailor" made suggests that the clothes (historical crime) fit the body (the cozy), but that if they don't, they are altered to fit perfectly? Such alterations might involve the omission or limitation of one or more of these features. Taking the books I have considered, Phryne's professional status, sexual voracity, and ability to use a gun differentiate her from the other protagonists, but, to me, she remains a cozy historical figure. She can deal with a potentially dangerous subject like a kidnapping by using her two adopted girls to assist in following a suspect (*Murder in Montparnasse*). In the case of Daisy Dalrymple a serious theme such as that of *Anthem for Doomed Youth*, which involves the deaths of several ex–World War I soldiers who have been buried in an English forest, is not a cozy topic, but the investigator, her friends, and husband maintain the cozy atmosphere, just! I do see Georgie as a very traditional cozy heroine except for her remarkable pedigree. That is what enables her to do the sort of investigations that she does; a royal outsider could not gain such access. The Darling Dahlias differ from conventional cozy crime fiction only in their numbers, but they also tread a very normal cozy path in their very small rural 1930s town.

The four examples I chose do not have major problems fitting into the format, but, of course, the incorporation of history into a cozy could be problematic. While the ending of World War I meant many women losing jobs, it was accompanied by the vote (for Americans in 1919 and for British women over 30 in 1918 and over 21 in 1928). In practice there was little difference in the ways women were treated in the world of work and limits of etiquette differentiate the 1920s/1930s from modern life. Female professionals in all fields are regarded with, at best, some tolerance and, at worst, contempt. For cozies this era fits the idea of a female investigator, who, even in a modern era, can be denigrated as a meddling female. As in modern cozies, the amateur detectives of the era are working for a living at least part of the time (Daisy Fletcher and the Darling Dahlias) or struggling to make ends meet and keep up appearances like Lady Georgiana or a professional part-time investigator like Phryne Fisher. Lower class workers have little leisure time like the nursery maid in *The Mitford Murders,* which is one reason for the preference for independent women and upper-class protagonists. Interesting new writers include Sujata Massey, who writes of the Raj; she has started a series which fits the cozy without going outside the 1920s parameters for female behavior in India. Perveen Mistry, a female lawyer, is perfectly suited to work with women who are in purdah and who cannot interact with a male (*The Widows of Malabar Hill*). Perveen qualified in London and now works in her father's Indian law firm. Ovidia Yu has the Chinese girl, Su Lin, avoiding an arranged marriage by acting as nanny for the Acting Governor's daughter in Singapore in the 1930s and trying to solve the mystery of the death of her predecessor in *The Frangipani Tree Mystery*. Note, however, that both these protagonists have opportunities few others would achieve in their societies then. The historical background in these cozies, therefore, does not detract from the establishment of a female protagonist as a suitable detective.

Because of the desire to present an era accurately in all aspects, the writer faces the twin fears of producing widespread anachronisms and of boring the reader with excessive historical detail. I think most readers like interesting details of the era, however. These writers use notes at the end or beginning of the books to explain why they have used certain characters, phrases, or ideas and where to find more information. Kerry Greenwood always has a bibliography. Rhys Bowen explains the historical reasons for including certain well-known people in notes. Carola Dunn's acknowledgments indicate the lines of her research. Susan Wittig Albert writes about the 1930s world and the research needed: she also adds a note to each book: "Writing about the rural South in the 1930s requires the use of images and language that may be offensive to some readers, especially words that refer to African Americans such as 'colored folk' and 'Negro.'" Another small difference with the modern era in all these books is the frequent smoking by all characters including females, but as Susan puts it, the era must be accurately reflected even if it does not suit modern taste. The success of these historical cozies in establishing a firm period background—in this case in the 1920s/1930s—adds a further and fascinating layer to the books.

These cozy, historical mysteries have deaths in them, hopefully without too much blood; there is an investigation by the protagonists in which clues emerge to titillate the reader and help them to predict the denouement in which the murderer is identified. At the same time the 1920s/1930s era provides a rich background of period crimes. In *The Darling Dahlias and the Eleven O'Clock Lady* the victim is a blackmailing telephonist who gained her scurrilous information by illegally listening in to the calls that she had connected through the local exchange. Not the form of a crime to be committed today! These are only four of the many series about the 1920s and 1930s, but they do fit the mold extremely well as I hope I have shown.

Note on Other Authors

Many other series fit totally or partially the cozy historical framework. For the 1920s we have Frances Brody with Kate Shackleton in Yorkshire, Alice Duncan with Daisy Gumm Majesty in the USA, Dolores Gordon-Smith (male protagonist Jack Haldean), Simon Brett (Blotto and Twinks humorous series), Catriona McPherson (Dandy Gilver in Scotland), and Barbara Cleverly has another male protagonist, who is also a high ranking policeman with Joe Sandilands, first in India then in London (the two last mentioned series go on into the 1930s),

For the 1930s, authors include Sulari Gentill (Rowland Sinclair in Australia), Jill Churchill in the USA, and David Roberts who combines Lord Edward Corinth and Communist Verity Brown in the 1930s buildup to World War II.

Jacqueline Winspear now covers from 1929 to 1940 with Maisie Dobbs.

Works Cited

Albert, Susan Wittig. *The Darling Dahlias and the Cucumber Tree*. New York: Berkeley Prime Crime. 2010.
_____. *The Darling Dahlias and the Eleven O'Clock Lady*. New York: Berkeley Prime Crime. 2015.
Allingham, Margery. *The Crime at Black Dudley*. 1st ed. 1929. London: Penguin. 1977.
Bowen, Rhys. *Her Royal Spyness*. New York: Berkeley Prime Crime. 2007.
_____. *Naughty in Nice*. New York: Berkeley Prime Crime. 2012.
_____. *On Her Majesty's Frightfully Secret Service*. New York: Berkeley Prime Crime. 2018.
_____. *Royal Blood*. London: Constable. 2016.
Cannell, Dorothy. *Murder at Mullings*. London: Severn House. 2014.
Chandler, Raymond. *The Simple Art of Murder*. Original publication 1950 New York: Vintage Books. 1988.
Duncan, Alice, *Strong Spirits*. New York: Zebra Books. 2003.
Dunn, Carola. *Anthem for Doomed Youth*. London: Constable & Robinson. 2011.

_____. *The Bloody Tower.* New York: Kensington Books. 2007.
_____. *The Corpse at Crystal Palace.* London: Constable. 2018.
_____. *Dead in the Water.* New York: St. Martin's Press. 1998.
_____. *Death at Wentworth Court.* New York: St. Martin's Press 1994.
_____. *Murder on the Flying Scotsman.* New York: St. Martin's Press. 1997.
_____. *Superfluous Women.* London: Constable. 2015.
_____. *To Davy Jones Below.* New York: St. Martin's Press. 2001.
Fellows, Jessica, *The Mitford Murders.* London: Sphere. 2017.
Flood, Alison, "Murders Most Cosy: Why Mystery Novels Involving Quilts and Cats Are Big Business" *The Guardian*, 3 August 2015.
Greenwood, Kerry, *Death Before Wicket.* 1st ed. 2003. Scottsdale: Poisoned Pen Press. 2008.
_____. *Death by Misadventure.* New York: Ballantyne Books. 1989. Original title *Cocaine Blues* now used in the US.
_____. *The Green Mill Murder.* 1st ed. 1997. Scottsdale: Poisoned Pen Press. 2007.
_____. *Murder in the Dark.* NSW: Allen & Unwin. 2006.
_____. *Murder in Montparnasse.* NSW: Allen & Unwin. 2002.
_____. *A Question of Death, an illustrated Phryne Fisher Treasury.* NSW: Allen & Unwin. 2007.
Harris, Rosemary, ed. *Oxford Companion to Crime and Mystery Writing.* New York: Oxford University Press. 1999.
Hobbes, Thomas. *Leviathan.* Original publication 1651. London: Fontana Library. 1962.
Massey, Sujata, *The Widows of Malabar Hill.* New York: Soho Press. 2018.
Maxwell, Alyssa, *Murder Most Malicious.* New York: Kensington Books. 2016.
Murphy, Bruce. *Encyclopedia of Murder and Mystery.* 2nd ed. Palgrave New York: Palgrave. 2001.
Parin, Sonia, *Murder in the Cards.* Kindle Edition.
Reynolds, Barbara. *Dorothy L. Sayers: Her Life and Soul.* 1st ed. 1993. London: Hodder & Stoughton. 1998.
Sayers D. l. *Whose Body?* 1st ed. 1923. London: Victor Gollantz. 1954.
Stanford, Agata. *The Broadway Murders.* 2nd ed. New York: Jenavacris Press. 2011.
Stasio, Marilyn. "Murder Least Foul, the Cozy, Soft Boiled Mystery." *The New York Times* October 18, 1992.
Strauss, Lee, *Murder in Eaton Square.* Kindle edition. La Plume Press. 2019.
Taylor, D. J. *Bright Young People: The Rise and Fall of a Generation; 1918–1940.* London: Chatto & Windus. 2007.
Winn, Dilys. *Murder Ink.* UK edition. Newton Abbot: Westbridge Books. 1978.
Yu, Ovidia, *The Frangipani Tree Mystery.* London: Constable. 2017.

Displaced Controversies
The Paradoxes of the Cozy Setting
Phyllis M. Betz

> "Crime must always be contextualized by a robust geographic imagination."
> Ryan Roll, "The Rising Tide of Neoliberalism: Attica Locke's *Black Water Rising* and 'The New Jim Crow'"

The importance of place in the detective novel is beyond question; the scene of the crime is the literal starting point for any investigation. The body is situated within a particular space that delineates who will become involved in the pursuit of the crime's resolution: from victim to witnesses and suspects, to perpetrator and detective. The scene of the crime often becomes the dominant focus of the crime narrative determining the interactions between characters; at various times over the course of the novel characters will return to the scene either to add to the information already gathered or to disrupt the investigative process. The location also shapes the nature of an individual's engagement with the setting particularly the detective's search for clues, from Sherlock Holmes and his magnifying glass to Temperance Brennan's detailed forensic examinations. Place determines the status and acceptance of the participants within the development of the novel, and characters' behavior within these spaces illustrate the complexities of knowing whom to trust and understanding how to achieve a positive outcome. The places where crime occurs not only provide the concrete location for the action, but also suggest how the crime will be solved as the detective works through the sorting out of the details of the crime. In addition, the detective becomes identified with a specific place— Miss Marple and St. Mary Mead, Joe Leaphorn and Jim Chee and Navajo country, or Dave Robicheaux and New Orleans. The close connections between geography and character, especially as developed over a series, add texture and nuance to the physicality of the place and the ethos of its people.

But the setting of the crime serves a much deeper and more complex purpose in the crime novel. Place acts as the arbitrator of a range of meanings including the delineation of private and public identities, as well as how social relationships are defined. Depending on the type of geographic location, the crime scene becomes more than the place where the body may be found; it becomes not merely the site for an interrogation of suspects or witnesses, but the place where the markers of a society's sense of itself are created and challenged. The urban space of the hard-boiled detective story contextualizes the private eye and the crime in very specific ways; the city with its diverse populations of race, class, and ethnicities emphasizes the complexity that often drives the detective narrative. The traditional mystery's isolated manor house, whether set in an isolated environment or positioned within the confines of a small town, is specific to the rational detective's approach. The boundaries of the crime scene determine who is included not just as participants in the mystery, but as representatives of a particular place and time. Setting establishes the boundaries for how the various ideologies of race, class, and gender are interpreted and integrated into the narrative. Explicit as well as implicit biases, which exert tacitly accepted ideas of what will and will not be seen as acceptable behavior, are frequently expressed through the spaces the characters inhabit.

The spaces described in the detective novel extend beyond the physical attributes of the crime scene; often intangible issues of history, economics, politics, race, and gender also shape the contours of the particular environment which, in turn, contribute to the way the crime and its investigation will be presented. The motives behind the commission of the crime tend to be tied to the perpetrator's and victim's lives being intertwined with their allegiances to social beliefs and expectations. Even though these influences remain in the background of a novel, they exert pressure on the narrative as characters often unknowingly respond to the crime because of how they have been shaped by the places where they have previously lived and currently reside. How often is the murder the result of thwarted ambitions or uncovered secrets that threaten the social status of both the killer and the victim? How often does the location of the crime itself or the suspects feed into the investigator's preconceptions of guilt or innocence? How often will an individual's expression of identity influence their treatment by the authorities? Over the course of the narrative such influences can explicitly impact the development of the investigation, but their impact can be more insidious by *not* be concretely articulated.

The scene of the crime, then, becomes the locus for examining how the society and its inhabitants depicted in a novel work to reconcile the real and perceived threats to the community's sense of itself. Not surprisingly, the first reaction of the town's inhabitants recorded in a novel is often the standard shocked response that such a crime, like murder, could never happen here. This refusal to recognize that crime can occur even in these particular places lays out the first of several paradoxes that can be discerned when looking closely at setting in the detective novel. Crime must occur somewhere, but the perception of many characters, particularly in the cozy mystery, is that theirs is not that place. Violence, especially extreme violence, also belongs in some other place; accompanying this assertion is the declaration that the people in our town could not possibly encourage or participate in such behavior. Bad people who commit evil deeds are seen to come from somewhere else; they are not like us in any way. Only someone not from the community would be capable of committing such acts, despite the fact that perpetrators are often revealed to be intimately connected to the community. The obvious range of biases underpinning these statements may be incorporated in the plot—the hate crime detailed in many lesbian detective novels, for example, or more often are glossed over. However, as soon as race or ethnicity becomes explicit, the mechanics of the investigation take over the narrative and push the deeper questions raised by such statements to the margins. Yet, the raising of these implicit biases offers a possible open space for engaging with how they have shaped the community's conceptions of others and otherness, but at the same time closes off this opportunity.

Certain sub-genres of detective fiction use this tension of the community's idealized vision of itself with the brutal reality of the dead body; perhaps the hard-boiled detective novel and the noir crime novel are the only narratives where crime and violence are not unexpected. In these texts the setting and its representations are clear-cut; the seedy side of town embodies the loss of social restraints, thus defining its inhabitants as outsiders and allowing violence to occur. The economic elites have positioned themselves literally and figuratively above these places, but their manipulation of the social institutions of the city have guaranteed its moral collapse. In other detective narratives this same situation infiltrates the overt configuration of the crime scene, although its expression is underplayed by the demands of the particular narrative development, to reinforce a set of shared ideological constructs. For example, the insular setting of many country house murders tends to place the commission of the crime on those who are defined as outsiders to the community, whether by an affront to a moral code or racial or class animus. Once the idea penetrates that a crime has indeed occurred, all of the characters, whether actively involved in the investigation or not, begin a process of confronting the meaning of the event and, more importantly, the implications once the investigation has concluded.

Often the resolution to the crime simply reinforces the community's idea of itself and those who inhabit it, even though the villain in the traditional crime novel is more likely to be a member of the very same community. At times, though, the crime itself and the subsequent investigation open fissures that may be papered over in an attempt to return the community to its previous beliefs; even though the ending of the novel may present such a return to normalcy, there can really never be a total recuperation of former beliefs.

The one setting that particularly embodies this range of contradictory responses is the small town; it is the place that effectively illustrates the competing impulses that contribute to the crime and interfere with or facilitate the detective's investigation. The town's inhabitants are more likely to share concepts of community, including what is appropriate behavior—both civil and personal—and to determine how they will respond to the disruption of daily life because of the crime. The dominant image of the small town is of a space that is self-sufficient: there is enough room for numerous entrepreneurial efforts to be successful. Most of the lead characters in cozies, for example, are able to establish businesses that both support themselves and help maintain the town's unique identity. There is a comity among its inhabitants which enables the smooth functioning of public and personal relationships. This intimacy is reflected in how the main character manages the investigation by depending on these various social and personal connections. There is an acceptance of an implicit idea of what behaviors are acceptable. This image of the small town has been framed and developed through a wide range of popular forms, from television shows like *Mayberry R.F.D.*, to Disney World's Main Street.

Traditional detective fiction utilizes these accepted ideas of the small town and constructs a range of narratives that ask readers to engage with how the intrusion of a crime into this space challenges theirs and the characters' expectations. While urban based crime forms a large percentage of detective narratives, the small town has become an increasingly popular setting for traditional as well as cozy mysteries. David Geherin identifies several reasons for the use of small towns as the location for crime, including a writer's own connection to such a place, the way a small environment shapes characters, or using these sites as a way to comment on ecological, social, and moral issues. His assertion that the "movement away from big cities to locations where crime is less common is that it can be humanized again" represents, perhaps, the most compelling value of the small town as the setting for crime and its detection (7). Geherin's study selects ten authors whose work describes the disruptions crime brings to the small towns in which their detectives reside. Although his analysis provides concrete examples of how the small-town setting functions, Geherin is dismissive of the cozy detective novel's reliance on a small community as the scene of the crime:

> Cozies are, as the name suggests, comforting novels—no graphic violence, no sex, no profanity. Murders are usually antiseptic affairs.... Characterization is often reduced to stock figures.... The amateur sleuth is seldom placed in any physically threatening situation. Everything is infused with a strong dose of nostalgia as these novels portray a quiet, peaceful world temporarily inconvenienced by the intrusion of an unpleasant crime by the resident crime solver. No sense of the presence of evil in the world lingers as life reassuringly returns to normal at the end [4].

Cozy mysteries settings do frequently embody Geherin's criticism. The typical novel presents a self-contained community that offers strikingly homogeneous settings and characters. Usually, the story takes place in a suburban or semi-rural town, full of charming houses, quaint shops, and like-minded people. The overwhelming majority of the characters in these novels tend to be white and middle to upper middle-class. Working class inhabitants or people of color are often absent or marginalized, typically serving as narrative filler for the main story and characters. Even ethnic diversity, when referenced at all, is pushed into a secondary position, often serving as a source for comic relief or as a reference for the particular geographic situation of the story. The main characters reflect the ethos of the community and, when confronted by the crime, become involved in the investigation as a way to restore order. However, simply condemning the cozy for its setting diminishes the cozy's ability to problematize and add complexity to a seemingly straightforward characteristic of the form. More often they continually engage with the meanings evoked by characters' awareness of the situation and how its influences the pursuit of the investigation.

In the Merriam-Webster dictionary the word situation carries two distinct meanings that play off one another in the cozy narrative—location and condition or circumstance: in other words, the geographic place in which events transpire, but just as important to the story, the unwritten codes of conduct that compel both the crime and the investigation. The criminal has chosen to commit a crime in the setting of the cozy and, as a result, enters into and challenges the socially constructed ideas that have shaped that place. While not all cozies develop this connection deeply, others fully use setting as a way to interrogate the ways the characters' sense of self is tied to the places they inhabit. However, while the dominant outcome of the cozy is to reinforce a standardized idea of the people and the place, the very same actions undercuts this sense of complacency. The limited series by Shelley Costa and Susan Goodwill and the first two Garage Sale Mystery novels by Sherry Harris will be used to examine how the paradoxical use and avoidance of race, class, and ethnicity impact the small town in the cozy mystery.

Setting the Scene

Shelley Costa's Eve Angelotta mysteries adhere most closely to the typical cozy framework. The novels are set in the fictional suburban community of Quaker Hills, PA, located about forty miles north of Philadelphia; this places Quaker Hills in Bucks County, which is made up of historic, blue collar and well-to-do towns. This area of Pennsylvania has a history that stretches back to William Penn, the founder of Pennsylvania, and whose original inhabitants were predominantly English settlers.[1] While the racial and ethnic make-up of many Bucks County towns today has expanded beyond that of the first settlers, the majority of these communities is still made up of white, middle and upper-middle class people. Costa's creation of Quaker Hills relies on commonplace features typical of such places. In fact, her description of the town includes a number of clichés: Market Square, the commercial center of the town, contains a small park surrounded by a vegetarian restaurant, an authentic British pub, a few boutiques, and professional offices. Also located in Market square is Miracolo, the Italian restaurant where Eve is head chef and where the central crime that forms that plotline of both novels is committed.

In spite of the detailed description of Market Square, the rest of Quaker Hills receives little attention, particularly in *You Cannoli Die Once*, the first novel. Other areas of the town receive cursory, almost generic descriptions; readers may imagine quaintly named developments full of McMansions and winding roads that meander through other similar communities. In Costa's second novel, *Basil Instinct*, readers learn that Quaker Hills does include a facility for troubled youth and a community college within its environs. However, beyond the detailed depiction of Market Square in the first novel and a fuller depiction of the home of Fina Parisi in the second, Costa's narratives lack a sense of Quaker Hills as a distinct place. Even Miracolo, the central location of both novels, receives only minimal descriptive attention; readers learn that the dining room seems large enough for a bar and a piano and able to serve a reasonable number of tables. Only the kitchen, the actual scene of both murders, is presented in some detail. What readers do discover about the restaurant's decor is Eve's determination to prevent it from becoming just another stereotypic illustration of an Italian restaurant: Eve has used the interior of the restaurant to highlight her collection of antique opera memorabilia, including rare recordings of Caruso. At one point in the novel, Eve has realized that her grandmother, Maria Pia Angelotta, has planned to renovate Miracolo's interior to reflect that stereotypical image of an Italian eatery: "red-flocked wallpaper ... and paintings of Mount Vesuvius, with maybe a *fontana* up front near the cash register" (*Cannoli* 188). Eve's reaction reveals the anger she feels at her grandmother's intentions: "She planned to send me to the American Culinary Federation's annual convention just to get me out of the way so she could *tart up our precious restaurant until you couldn't tell it from any other Italian restaurant from fifty years ago. It was diabolical. It would be disastrous*" (188, emphasis added). Eve's strong response suggests a desire to distance herself and the restaurant from being just like any other generic Italian eatery serving generic Italian food, not the haute cuisine of Miracolo. This brief scene, unrelated to the murder that has occurred in the restaurant or the investigation that is well under way at this point, highlights the ways the small town setting complicates the representations of those aspects of character and social expectations that are presumed to be obvious.

Sherry Harris' Garage Sale Mystery series featuring Sarah Winston are set in the fictional community of Ellington, MA, a town with a history stretching back to colonial times and home to Fitch Air Force Base, also fictional. The military base becomes the location of the murder that instigates the investigation in *Tagged for Death*, the first novel in the series; the town's past is an integral component in the second novel, *The Longest Yard Sale*, because the death that occurs is connected to the forgery of an historic painting depicting an important battle that took place in the town during the Revolutionary War. The use of the town's history is limited, however, to the story surrounding the painting's history. Ellington is not presented as pristine a setting as Quaker Hills. Harris describes a place where readers see the trendy shops, but also the ordinary stores and the people who work there. The inhabitants include children, a group noticeably absent in Quaker Hills. Other crimes are referred to, particularly illegal drugs on the base; this becomes a possible motive when CJ has been accused of Tiffany's murder in *Tagged for Death* since he was involved in arresting those who were involved. Political and social tensions in *The Longest Yard Sale* are alluded to that undercut the idea of Ellington's perfection.

It is Sarah's involvement with the crimes at the center of both novels that focuses the reader's attention to how these places work through the plot to shape Sarah's sense of belonging; she is the ex-wife of CJ, the commander of the air force base's security detail and who, after retiring from the Air Force, is now the chief of police of Ellington. Sarah's best friend Carol, also the wife of a Air Force officer, is an artist who owns a shop for people to throw painting parties. Carol has become involved in the murder at the center of the second novel because she has been working on a copy of the historic painting. Sarah Winston's revelation that she is an outsider, not only to Ellington in terms of geographical place, but also in her integration into the routines of the town will become an important factor as she undertakes to solve both cases.

Sarah was born in Pacific Gove, CA, and, as the wife of a military man, has moved many times, eventually ending up at Fitch Air Force Base. In *Tagged for Death* Sarah must deal with the consequences of her husband's affair with Tiffany, a young servicewoman from the base; the divorce means that Sarah has lost her place on the base—her home and the supportive community of officers' wives where she played a major role in the social life of the base. The early chapters of this novel describe Sarah's reduced income and her search for a place to live and a source of income. She must also deal with the constant harassment—tickets for speeding one mile over the limit, not using her turn signal, and other minor infractions that typically would be waived. The members of Ellington's police force, Sarah feels, "had [CJ's] back" because they see her as a detriment to the chief's happiness (2). Over the course of the narrative, Sarah pursues two goals, investigating the murder of Tiffany and learning that she feels connected to Ellington:

> Anyone who either made the military a career or married someone in the military knew what it was like to start over: new towns, friends, doctors, dentists, and, the worst, trying to find a new hairstylist. It was always a huge adjustment. What would moving on be like this time, now that I was alone? I wouldn't live on a base or have an instant support group. Would I move away from Ellington. Even with all that had happened, I didn't want to go. *I liked it here* [220, emphasis added].

What Sarah has come to appreciate is Ellington's past and the attitudes of the people. On her travels looking for garage and yard sales, Sarah often comments on the depth of the area's history. Readers learn what the Massachusetts' Patriot Day celebrates (114), as well as Sarah's appreciation of regional food (160). Most importantly, Sarah begins to understand what Stella, her landlady, means when Stella says, "A New Englander's roots run to the middle of the Earth" (72). By the end of the first novel, Sarah has begun to establish a feeling of belonging to the community of Ellington, even as her links to the base have begun to loosen.

Kate London, the main character in Susan Goodwill's *Brigadoom* and *Little Shop of Murders*, has returned to Mudd Lake, MI, to live with her grandmother, who had raised Kate after the car accident that killed both parents. As its name suggests, Mudd Lake has little in common with Quaker Hills or Ellington. The town center is described as the "town's seedy underbelly" with the crumbling Egyptian theater—the location of vandalism and murder in *Brigadoom*—and the Acadia building, home to Fast Eddie's Pawn Shop, Lickity-Split Paycheck Advances, and Benny's Bail Bonds—not exactly the idealized version of a small town (42). Mudd Lake also has strip malls with tattoo parlors and discount pharmacies, outlet malls, and untrendy places to eat. Throughout the first novel the town is also dealing with the periodic appearances of the Naked Bandit, which only emphasizes the eccentricity of the town: "Word had it he snatched women's purses wearing only a ski mask and Adidas" (4). Kate lives in an upstairs apartment in the Egyptian not only as a way to save money, but to help her eccentric grandmother, Kitty, fulfill her dream of putting on musicals. At the beginning of *Brigadoom*, Kate has lost her job after an accident on a golf course involving a cheating fiancé (who is also her employer), a portable toilet, and a golf cart. In spite of the trouble Kate faces, she feels at home in Mudd Lake; this was the place that took her in as a traumatized child, the place where she found her best friend, Charlene, and developed her first romantic relationship with Ben, now Mudd Lake's police chief. Over the two novels, Kate's connection to Mudd Lake deepens, especially with the possibility of reconnecting her romance with Ben.

Playing to Type

The absence of any distinctive architectural feature or other indicator of a particular historical period in Quaker Hills bleaches out any suggestion of a strong, distinct ethnicity in its inhabitants. Eve's surname, Angelotta, clearly identifies her Italian heritage, but her first name is actually Evelyn, not a name typically given to Italian women. This distancing from close ties to one's heritage is replicated in the first names of Eve's cousins, Kayla and Landon. These choices may simply reflect a generational shift, especially since most of the older characters in the novels have much stronger ethnic names—Maria Pia, Gian Carlo Crespi [Miracolo's bartender]. But Giuseppe (Choo Choo) Baciagalupo, another cousin, is Eve's contemporary. Names may seem an innocuous indicator of one's ethnicity, given the ease with which they can be changed, and while it is true that people's reactions to them may be based on clichéd ideas more than specific experience, surnames, specifically, help establish frames of reference for further interactions. The surnames of other characters in the novels—Dana Cahill, Joe Beck, Courtney Harrington, for example—reflect the English origins of Quaker Hills. The Angelottas and their relatives become the sole carriers of a clear ethnic identity; they seem to be the only Italians in the immediate environs of the town. In *Basil Instinct* the number of Italian names increases; interestingly, though, the reader learns that the majority of these characters are related to Eve and her family in some way. Such discoveries underscore the long-standing stereotype of the large Italian family with its complicated degrees of familial connections. In Costa's novels these family connections become important to the solution to the murder, as the motives are traced back to the past where families have been broken (*Basil Instinct*) or where personal relationships have ruined lives (*You Cannoli Die Once*). The Angelottas also seem to be the only family in the town that is made up of more than husband and wife; Dana Cahill, for example, is married but is childless and does not appear to regret this situation. Quaker Hills refuses to adhere to the stereotypical expectation of mothers pushing strollers and making play dates. This omission further isolates and emphasizes the separateness of Eve and her relations. Rather oddly, too, no other extended families of any particular racial or ethnic identity appear in either novel.

This is not to suggest that the population of Quaker Hills is only made up of white inhabitants. Li Wei, a young Chinese man, works in the Miracolo kitchen. This is the only information about the character presented in the novels. The other non-white character is Akahana Takei, who is seen moving through Market Square rummaging through trash cans and dumpsters. The obvious conclusion readers make is of an anomaly; Quaker Hills does not seem a community to tolerate a homeless person, especially one so visible. Several issues arise with Takei's presence in the novels; the first is her race. While homelessness can affect anyone, the percentage of Japanese-Americans who are homeless seems small.[2] Why then does Costa make the character Japanese, except perhaps to play against stereotypes or to imply that being Japanese and homeless is permissible in Quaker Hills, where African Americans or Latinx-Americans would not be accepted? However, towards the end of *You Cannoli Die Once* Akahana Takei is revealed to be a PhD in Cognitive Anthology who is writing a book on the origins of consciousness (199–200). Eve learns this when Akahana, who has contacted her to provide information on the identity of the killer, hands Eve a business card with "[t]hree different phone numbers, two different email addresses, a website, and an address on West Fourth Street in Quaker Hills" (200).

This information problematizes Takei's presence; does this information indicate that homelessness can't exist in Quaker Hills because the only representative of the condition really isn't homeless; she may just be eccentric. However, she may also be suffering from some mental disorder. This belief is given credence in *Basil Instinct* when Eve goes looking for her to find out if she has seen anything suspicious during her scrounging: "Her presence in Market Square at all hours had led to a petition drive to persuade town council to enact an obnoxious curfew law, but it was met with enough resistance from the rest of us that it failed. The fact that Akahana herself had signed the petition made the council wonder whether anyone quite that innocent was a threat to public safety" (336). The use of the word innocent allows any potential threat that Akahana might represent to be contained and can be seen as a reinforcement of a racial stereotype of the Japanese as docile. Making this character a white woman would have altered nothing regarding her use to the plot; in fact, until the race is revealed, readers assume she is white. Akahana Takei, then, creates a fissure in the situation of both novels. Her role as witness is needed to move the plot to its conclusion since her testimony confirms Eve's suspicions, but as Maureen Reddy in *Traces, Codes, and Clues: Reading Race in Crime Fiction* points out:

> Whiteness is taken for granted in most crime fiction authored by whites and that implicitness is one of the ways in which whiteness is reproduced and maintains its cultural hegemony.... Other varieties of crime fiction are less centrally concerned with upholding a white ideology, yet they usually do so reflexively, and thus participate in the cultural circularity of racial construction. That circular pattern goes like this: whiteness is the norm (and the ideal); the norm requires no comment; whiteness therefore is not commented on; ... readers of that fiction are not asked to consider whiteness consciously; the normativity of whiteness thus is validated and reproduced; the norm requires no comment; and so on [115–116].

If Akahana's function is determined by the conventions of the detective story, why mention her race, by implication of the name, at all. Calling attention to her race serves only to emphasis the lack of diversity in Quaker Hills.

Costa makes deliberate use of Italian cultural stereotypes throughout both texts, usually for comic effect. When the body is discovered in *You Can Only Die Once*, Eve wonders who would dump a body in a restaurant kitchen in what is a clear reference to Mafia activity: "I mean it's not like we're a construction site or anything" (14). Other such ethnic clichés appear in both Eve's and Kayla's quick temper and Maria Pia's wearing the black clothes standard for an Italian widow, even though her husband has been dead for many years. Generally, it is Eve, the stories' narrator, who references such ethnic clichés. Interestingly, the majority of her comments are directed only to family, where she uses them to play against type or to reinforce it. She describes her cousin Choo Choo as having a "taste for wise-guy movies and moves," but who is also "afraid of spiders and allergic to most laundry detergents" (*Basil Instinct* 145–46). In Chapter 10 of *Basil Instinct*, Eve creates an elaborate ploy to extract information from two of her students who reside at the Callowhill Residential Institute for Behavioral Success by presenting Choo Choo as Don Lolo Dinardo, a made member of the Mafia, in order to scare them into revealing what they witnessed when they attempted to break into Miracolo. Since their knowledge of the mob appears limited to movie clichés, the two young men are easily persuaded, even though Choo Choo's and Eve's mannerisms are clearly exaggerated. Costa is relying on the popular images of a certain type of Italian male and, by undercutting it, hopes the reader will appreciate the joke.

This constant use of humor seems to be both an affirmation of and yet a deflection of her Italian heritage. Shame may, perhaps, be too strong a criticism of Eve's attitude; she also expresses a deep-seated love for her family and, as the narratives of both novels show, will do anything, even bending the law, to save her family from false accusations. What must be questioned, though, is why, outside the walls of Miracolo, Eve drops these expressions of her ethnicity. In her interactions with Dana Cahill, her best friend in Quaker Hills; Joe Beck, a lawyer who becomes her love interest; or any of the other business owners in the town, Eve appears to have assumed the mannerisms and attitudes of the rest of the town; her unique ethnicity seems to have been washed out. Beyond the boundaries of "Miracolo world," Eve's behavior is no different than is typical for the main female character of the cozy (*Basil Instinct* 206). Most importantly, this reframing of her Italian-ness is not because of any biases directed towards Eve or her family; it seems to be automatic, as though her public and private selves must be kept distinct. There is also a self-deprecating tone throughout both novels in Eve's apparent instinctive references to exaggerated conceptions of Italians; it is as though she relies on them to let her balance familiarity and distance from her own background. Eve can be Italian in the restaurant, where she imbues her ethnicity into dishes that are well-received by the larger community; outside of Miracolo, however, her Italian background is non-existent, suggesting that Quaker Hills appreciates the culinary efforts but prefers that that remain the only permissible expression. Costa plays on the way certain ideas about Italians have become part of the popular landscape in order to distract from the real horrors attached to the murders—false accusations, family secrets revealed, one's sense of control and order shaken. Yet such behavior also reinforces those same negative stereotypes about Italians, and by placing the Angelotta family against the background of Quaker Hills the stereotype becomes the reality.

Ellington's colonial roots mean that the dominant racial and ethnic character of the town is white and primarily English. The only other major ethnic group in the town are Italians; however, no other ethnic group is mentioned, which seems at odds with the town's geographic location. As in Costa's novels, the Italian characters embody the same popular conceptions: they are involved in the food industry; they have large extended families; they could possibly have mob ties. A reader would reasonably assume that some inhabitants would have Portuguese or Canadian French heritage, as well as a small, but noticeable African American population. This lack of diversity is surprising especially with Fitch Air Force Base being a major component of the setting, although Sarah, on a visit to the base, passes the base chapel and comments on how it holds services for "many different faiths, including Protestant, Catholic, Jewish , and Islam" (*The Longest Yard Sale* 61). Yet, it is religion, not race, that Sarah's comment highlights. Only one character is specifically identified as racially different, Laura, the manager of the base's thrift shop: "a slightly taller version of Halle Berry" (*The Longest Yard Sale 62*). The silence regarding the race of other characters in the novels becomes a focal point for interrogating the reason behind the omission. Maureen Reddy points out that

> Given popular fiction's dual role of simultaneously responding to the fantasies of readers and shaping those fantasies, the absence of people of color from most crime fiction is a comment on the profound unknowingness about race that is clung to by many whites, to offer the least sinister interpretation. White readers who want their crime fiction all white, even if they are not consciously aware of that desire, have a plethora of choices [117].

There seems to be no purpose to identifying Laura as African American, except to point out that she is African American. As with Costa's explicit marking of the homeless woman as Japanese in the Eve Angelotta mysteries, Harris' underscoring Laura's race calls attention to the absence of other people of color.

The absence of racial and ethnic diversity in Mudd Lake can be explained due to its geographic location, which seems to be far from any major city but close to Lake Michigan. This relative isolation offers some rationale for this lack of racial diversity among the town's inhabitants. What Goodwill does in the novels is exaggerate the stereotyped characteristics of the dominant ethnic groups of the area—Scandinavian and German—for their comic effect. Chapter Seven of *Little Shop of Murders* is set at Mudd Lake's Sausage Festival, a fund raiser for the town. The scene is replete with a polka band, men wearing lederhosen, kielbasa, and beer; also highlighted is the loud and obnoxious behavior of many of the Festival goers when a free-for-all food fight erupts as Kate pursues the thief who has stolen a cash box. A second set of characters also receive this same overblown description—older men and women. They are generally portrayed as eccentric, opinionated, and forgetful. Even Kitty, Sarah's grandmother, is not spared. She appears in the first chapter of *Brigadoom* wearing high-top sneakers, a feathered headdress, and a kilt. Kitty's outfits become more outrageous during this and the subsequent novel. Kitty's memory is fluid; sometimes these lapses may be age-related, but often they appear deliberate. For example, she remembers her seven ex-husbands by the cars they drove rather than by name. Vera, Kitty's friend and contemporary, also falls into a standardized picture of the reticent, housecoat wearing old lady. Many of the older male characters display similar odd behavior like the Naked Bandit in *Brigadoom* and the bank robber in *Little Shop of Murders*. The main purpose of these characters, whatever role they may have in the narrative, is to provide another source of humor as the investigation works towards its conclusion. Both of Goodwill's novels present exaggerated portraits of their characters and their behaviors perhaps because of the strong humorous tone that dominates them. Everything that happens throughout the texts is played for comic effect, so much so, that the murders in the novels almost disappear from the narratives.

Everyone Is Middle-Class

Many small-town settings in the cozy not only present a homogeneous racial and ethnic context in the narrative, but they often project a sense that everyone shares the same class position. Quaker Hills appears to have no inhabitant who is not comfortably middle or upper-middle class. The majority of the people who live there enjoy the privileges of a comfortable life, as most of the adults own successful businesses; even those who don't seem to work at jobs that would provide a living wage have little trouble surviving. Landon, Eve's cousin, works at Miracolo, but wishes to pursue a career on Broadway; however, his salary as a sous-chef could not realistically support his classes in Philadelphia, the necessary transportation, or his own home (Landon lives alone). Eve describes him as a "trust fund baby whose six-room condo is in the upscale Innerlight Estates" (*You Cannoli Die Once* 50). Readers discover in *Basil Instinct* that Landon has inherited a large fortune from his father which removes the dilemma of making ends meet typical of others in his position. Akahana Takei's class status is unclear, given that she may be delusional, but when Eve reads the address on her business card—West Fourth Street—it suggests a residential area that, if it adheres to the standards of Quaker Hills, is most likely made up of comfortable homes suited to a scholar of cognitive anthropology. However, neither novel provides an extended description of the town or the people who live there outside of the shops on Market Square. Only in *Basil Instinct* does the reader see the home of Fina Parisi, Eve's former school mate, who is one of the complications of the novel's plot. Fina's home is quite large; Eve notes that in the "'foyer' you could park half a dozen of my little Tumbleweeds" (256). Eve is referring to her trendy tiny home, which is an actual brand available for purchase.[3]

Descriptions of Eve's little house appear occasionally in both novels, her home serving as a momentary resting place during the investigation. As noted, the majority of the novel's narrative is centered on what happens at the restaurant and in Market Square. What is notable about these moments in the novels is the constant refrain that the house is tiny, that the amount of living space has been pared down to the minimum. The size of her home is a point of pride for Eve, perhaps indicating a reverse snobbishness since many of the homes in Quaker Hills seem quite large. At the time of the novel's publication, the tiny house was becoming a popular choice of housing; the typical home had to be ordered, and the buyer had a number of design options. The cost of the home depended on the design chosen by the buyer, but the broad price range means that the potential owner needed sufficient income to purchase such a house (rd.com). In addition to the house itself, one would have to purchase the land on which to build it. Readers have no sense of how much Eve makes in salary, but Miracolo has been in business since the 1930s, which suggests it is a thriving, successful operation. However, Eve does not own the restaurant; her grandmother does, making Eve an employee. Being family, though, suggests that should Eve need financial assistance, it would be offered. Eve's home requires enough money for its construction, but she drives a ten-year-old Volvo; this reinforces her reverse class-consciousness. Volvos are expensive cars known for their longevity, and the impression given in the novel is that Eve is the original owner.

The only time class differences explicitly appear in the novels occurs when Eve agrees to teach a ten-week course in basic culinary skills at the community college. Two of the class—Mitchell Terranova and Slash Kipperman—are residents at the Callowhill Residential Institute for Behavioral Success. Their last names let the reader assume the young men are white, although Mitchell is described by Eve as a "dreadlocked smirker" (*Basil Instinct* 53). His hairstyle, though, more likely reflects a stylistic choice than a reference to race. None of the female students seem to be residents of Callowhill. The class status of Eve's students may be inferred: most likely, they come from Quaker Hills and the surrounding area, but may not be part of the upper echelon as most Quaker Hills residents are. Community college tuition is markedly lower than the typical four-year college. The course Eve is teaching suggests that, except for Kipperman and Terranova, the students might be planning a career in the service industry, which suggests a need for employment. Again, based on the characters' names, only one of the girls is most likely African American, L'Shondra Washington, but this is all readers ever know of the character. Eve's teaching is one of the subplots of the novel that becomes linked to the main plot when Slash and Mitchell break into Miracolo and steal the purse of the murder victim. It is this theft that instigates Eve and Choo Choo's exaggerated impersonation of mobsters referenced earlier.

One notable point to be made regarding Eve's interactions with her students centers on how mean and condescending she is towards them. Eve's views are never spoken out loud, but her comments on their appearances and behaviors are demeaning. One illustration of Eve's attitude can be seen in her thoughts on meeting Corabeth:

> ...the fourth girl, a six-foot tall, 225-pound monument to late adolescence, what with her short dyed red hair separated into about a dozen ponytails sporting rubber bands with little grinning skulls got to her size-12 feet.

> This was Corabeth Potts, and she was wearing a silver tube top that could gift-wrap a Michelin man, and short plaid shorts. As she turned to head over to the fallen toaster, it became clear the shorts were not doing the job, assuming the job was to cover the flesh. With high-cut legs, a good deal of Cora was open to inspection [53].

Corabeth is the only student who receives such a detailed description. Eve highlights features that call attention to Corabeth's physical appearance in what can only be seen as cruel, emphasizing her size and weight. The implication in Eve's thoughts can be read as a rejection of someone who does not take care of herself or her appearance, a position Eve would never put herself in. Nothing in the novel suggests any reason for Eve's hostility to these characters, other than her resentment at being talked into teaching the course. Eve's reaction, however, might be attributed to an unconscious sense of her own class position. Like race, class in Costa's novels is left implied rather than openly referenced. No one comments on class differences because none overtly exist.

Harris' Ellington presents a more realistic sense of class differences. Surprisingly, Fitch Air Force base offers the better picture of a class structure than the town itself. One's status on base is linked to one's rank; enlisted soldiers' housing, for example, is smaller than the commanders' residences. Rules of conduct determine social relationships, and any infringement of them can lead to severe consequences. CJ's brief affair with Tiffany not only ruins his and Sarah's marriage but also violates the military code of conduct. CJ is a commander; Tiffany is an enlisted airman. Compounding this situation is the fact that CJ is also Tiffany's commanding officer in the security unit. When Tiffany is found missing, and presumed dead, her relationship with CJ is offered as the motive for his involvement in her disappearance. Off base the class differences in Ellington are less obvious. Most of the inhabitants appear to be middle-class, although some residents do enjoy a higher social position. Stella's Aunt Gennie, for example, over her wrestling career has amassed a great deal of capital, which she has used to furnish each room of her large house with period pieces of a particular decade. Most of the town's inhabitants, though, pay little attention to status.

The only person in Ellington who presents a vulnerability about her class position in Ellington is Sarah herself. Her divorce has severed all of her connections to social and financial status and safety. Where she was once a respected member of the circle of commanders' wives on base, she has become an unwelcome reminder of what could happened to others. Where once she had the ability to come and go as she pleased on the base, now she must ask others to sign her in. Throughout *Tagged for Death* Sarah frequently expresses this sense of her loss of status; after taking Carol on a garage sale trip, Sarah returns to her apartment and examines her life as the wife of a military commander and her current precarious situation: "None of those skills lent themselves to a career now that I needed one. The frequent military moves killed any chance of a long-term career. My responsibilities as the commander's wife at Fitch hadn't left a lot of extra time for a job, anyway" (12). Finding a job becomes a repeated concern throughout the novel, one that is solved when several other characters ask Sarah to help them organize their own garage sales. By the novel's end Sarah has suggested organizing a town-wide yard sale as a fund raiser to Nancy, the town manager, who accepts. In *The Longest Yard Sale* readers also learn that Sarah has worked in an accountant's office during one deployment, which become helpful in her determining the motives behind the murders that take place. At the conclusion of this novel, it is implied that Sarah has carved out a career as a planner and organizer of yard and garage sales for members of Ellington and the surrounding area that will provide her with a steady income and a secure social position in the community.

In Goodwill's *Brigadoom*, however, economic status becomes the instigator for the crimes committed in the narrative. The motive that drives Estelle Douglass to commit her crimes hinges on her desire for money and all that having money signifies. Estelle has become used to a lavish lifestyle and all of her actions are aimed at maintaining it. Achieving this goal means becoming part of a real estate deal that will require the destruction of the Egyptian Theatre and other buildings in the center of town as the first step in a transformation of Mudd Lake. Estelle's personal motives become entwined with a distorted sense of public duty:

> "I did it for the town. Once Medication Nation [a national drugstore chain] moves in, you'll never know this place. No more tacky theatre.... Medication Nation mores in, and the others will follow." *Her eyes glassed over with the vision.* "The clothing store chains, home goods stores, they'll all come here. Soon, we'll even be able to get a decent latte.... I'll be a rich woman. Correction. Richer woman" [225, emphasis added].

For Estelle, turning Mudd Lake into a duplicate of any other suburban community illustrates not only the importance of her self-image as a person of sophistication and her desire for the class status that accompanies it, but her sense that Mudd Lake's public image is as important as her own. Estelle cannot envision living in a place that does not reflect what she sees herself as. The ideal image of Mudd Lake that Estelle envision lacks anything distinctive; it is merely a repetition of the popular image of a prosperous small town. However, Estelle's arrest puts an end to her dreams, and Mudd Lake retains its slightly dingy atmosphere.

In *Little Shop of Murders* any reference to the possibility of the town's physical character never appears. The only similarity between the two novels is the constant threat of the demolition of the Egyptian Theatre. Estelle's plans for demolishing the theater include vandalism and arson, but the building is always close to collapsing on its own. The roof leaks, the wiring is not up to code, and the façade needs paint. One of the subplots in *Little Shop of Murders* centers on the production of the musical *Little Shop of Horrors* which Kitty and the Mudd Lake Players intend to stage. The budget for this production, however, is extremely tight. Kate, in fact, is maxing out her credit cards to acquire needed supplies for the show. The chance to win a grant to ensure the maintenance for the theater is lost due the fiasco on stage during the opening night performance. Although always teetering on the verge of ruin, Kitty and the theater manage to squeak through at the last minute. The theater is declared an historic edifice in the first novel, and in the second, Kitty earns a bounty offered by the niece of one of the suspects in the murder. Most importantly, Kate's determination to save the theater drives her efforts to help her grandmother's ambitions. Kitty, as has been noted, raised Kate in the Egyptian after the death of her parents. For Kate, the theater is home, the place where she feels safe. Therefore, Kate is willing to make every sacrifice to preserve the building. Kate's efforts are not only for herself. Her grandmother at one time was a well-known character movie actor, and Kate will do anything to help protect her grandmother's connections to her past. The Egyptian Theatre becomes the repository of both women's memories and keeping the building standing represents the continuation of its public value after is recognition as an historic building.

There's No Place

The small town in the cozy mystery serves not only as the physical setting for the novels, but also as a site for the paradoxical meanings involving race, class, and ethnicity hidden in plain sight that are embedded within the plot. Quaker Hills, Ellington, and Mudd Lake convey a clear sense of place as described by the authors: each place has its own distinct physical characteristics connected to its geographic location that contributes to its particular ethos. Sarah Winston, for example, as a native Californian, frequently comments on Ellington's sense of history, its charm, and its generous people. In spite of its discount malls and rundown sections, Mudd Lake has managed to create a sense of community among its inhabitants. Such portraits, however, merely present a superficial picture of these places: the vision of a unique space that encourages a sense of community is a deliberate construction reflecting the desire for a recognizable space that ensures a sense of an individual's security and identity. While the idea of the small town as a refuge from the city, as a place of shared values and support for individual efforts have become a given in popular culture, the reality of such environments is more complex. It is this complexity that the cozy mystery bleaches out.

The erasure of racial, class, or ethnic differences maintains the illusion of social harmony at the expense of the complex realities of human relationships. The assumption in much popular cultural representations that the world is white and middle class penetrates the way narratives are constructed and developed. Interrogating racial and class politics is not the primary focus of cozy mysteries, but the omission of such references in the novels underscores the power of this assumption of white economic privilege and reinforces, as Maureen Reddy suggests throughout *Traces, Codes, and Clues*, the damage that such erasures can perpetuate. The few times people of color or lower class status are deliberately mentioned calls attention to the dearth of such characters; the notion that everyone, even characters whose status is vague, enjoys the privileges of wealth implies that no one lacks sufficient economic security. The restrained environment of the cozy, perhaps, allows the problematic representations of class, race, and ethnicity to be kept safely contained. To allow these complexities to enter the narrative would open the cozy beyond the genre's capabilities, ruining the reading experience. The cozy mystery, after all, assures its readers that whatever intrudes into the community will be identified, controlled, and dispersed, leaving the small town unchanged by events.

Notes

1. Not all early colonists were English; immigrants from Germany, Sweden, and the Netherlands also established themselves in Pennsylvania.
2. A Google search on the percentage of homelessness among Japanese Americans resulted in no statistics. The search was redirected to homelessness in Japan.
3. One can view the range of Tumbleweed houses on the company's website tumbleweedhouses.com.

Works Cited

Costa, Shelley. *Basil Instinct*. NY: Pocket Books, 2014. Print.
_____. *You Cannoli Die Once*. NY: Pocket Books, 2013. Print.
Geherin, David. *Small Towns in Recent American Crime Fiction*. McFarland, 2015. Print.
Goodwill, Susan. *Brigadoom*. Woodbury, MN: Midnight Ink, 2007. Print.
_____. *Little Shop of Murders*. Woodbury, MN: Midnight Ink, 2008. Print.
Harris, Sherry. *The Longest Yard Sale*. NY: Kensington Publishing Corp., 2015. Print.
_____. *Tagged for Death*. NY: Kensington Publishing Corp., 2014. Print.
Hausladen, Gary J. *Places for Dead Bodies*. University of Texas Press, 2000. Print.
Poll, Ryan. "The Rising Tide of Neoliberalism: Attica Locke's *Black Water Rising* and "The New Jim Crow". In *Class and Culture in Crime Fiction: Essays on Works in English Since the 1970s*. Julie H. Kim, ed. McFarland, 2014. Print.
Reddy, Maureen T. *Traces, Codes, and Clues: Reading Race in Crime Fiction*. Rutgers, 2003. Print.

This Cozy England

England and Englishness in Cozy Mystery Series

SUSAN K. MARTIN and KYLIE MIRMOHAMADI

In Ellery Adams' "Book Retreat" series there is a country house, called "Storyton" which has been transferred, "brick by brick and shipped across the Atlantic," from England (13), along with its surrounding buildings. In its reconstructed form it creates an "English estate hidden away in the wilds of the Virginia mountains" (13), with rooms named primarily for British writers of classics and Golden Age crime: "Jane Austen Parlor, the Ian Fleming Lounge, the Isak Dinesen Safari Room, the Daphne du Maurier Morning Room," and "the Agatha Christie Tearoom" (7,8). Even the landscape markers and garden features of the English countryside form part of the vision. Jane Steward, heir to and guardian of the property's secret library and its treasures, plans to follow the dreams of her eccentric uncle and "restore the folly and the hedge maze and the orchards" (13). The natural environment—the "wilds of the Virginia mountains" (13)—will be thus domesticated, and enfolded into the vision of "an oasis ... [a] reader's paradise amid the pines" (13). This fantasy is represented as an act of displacement in time as well as place. All contemporary technology such as "computers, cell phones, handheld games, or e-reading devices" is banned from the public areas of Storyton Hall (43–44).[1]

The notion that England is at least partly reproducible, in deed and word, underlies the representation of England and Englishness in a range of contemporary American-set cozy mysteries, of which the Book Retreat series is characteristic. "England" is transferred, invoked, and invented in these novels, through specific patterns of behavior, attire, architecture, consumption, and address. In the Book Retreat series, while Storyton House is (literally) a displaced piece of England, the "Englishness" of the character of the resort's Head Librarian, Sinclair, is more performative in nature; located in his dress, habits, and speech patterns.[2] He wears bow-ties and "distinguished himself [from other staff members] by dressing in tweed suits every day of the year" (2). He writes with a fountain pen, keeps a carriage clock on his desk (5,6), and expresses himself in formal English. Unsurprisingly, given the signifying power of Agatha Christie, in this novel and its genre in general, Sinclair is, Jane reports, "very fond of Jane Marple," to whom he refers as "one of the 'shrewdest gentlewoman detectives of all time'" (47). The fact that Sinclair is formally polite in his address adds to his manufactured Englishness, by conforming to a widespread conception that, in the words of Jane, "[t]he British have such impeccable manners" (136). In the second volume [of the series], Jane's twins, Fitzgerald and Hemingway, play at Englishness in a similar manner, when they affect British accents and invite their mother "to tea" (Adams 2015, 186).

The imagined England towards which characterizations such as that of Sinclair gesture is cozy, white, and unchanging; often located out of time (as "timeless," or from the past), and in place (bucolic village settings and the country house). Storyton Village combines both these fantasies by "look[ing] like it belonged to another era" (17). While such representations of displaced England and Englishness play important narrative and referential functions in cozy series, they can be usefully read alongside depictions of England in the long-running English-set Agatha Raisin series. M.C. Beaton's novels reveal an England in flux, racially and culturally heterogeneous, and riven with class, gender, and racial distinctions, issues which have been recently brought to the fore in the political upheavals associated with Brexit.

The Book Retreat series opens with *Murder in the Mystery Suite* (2014), and this novel sets the scene. The novel, and the series are located in and around this physical reconstruction ("brick by brick") of British country house murder mystery scenarios in the same way that so many U.S.-located cozies adopt (and play with) the framework, the flavor, the language, and the references to English Golden Age crime fiction and England. Adams' house is redolent of the pleasures of reading such British mysteries. The house is full of material books, their look, feel, and scent, but at the heart of the house, and the series, is a hidden library of precious literary treasures, imbuing the building with a material core of English value(s). Cozy fictions' embeddedness in the Golden Age of British crime fiction and classic crime comes via the writing, and decades of dramatization, televization, and other representations of that fiction. *Murder in the Mystery Suite* stresses, as so many cozy novels do, the overarching influence of Agatha Christie, the "Queen of Crime" and the writer who is most persistently positioned as the direct literary foremother of the cozy genre in general, as well as the bearer of a distinct kind of literary Englishness.[3] The plot of the novel rests on the heroine's "random" selection of Christie's *Death on the*

Nile as the theme for a murder mystery costume weekend at the country house; the Agatha Christie Tea room literally ensures that visitors drink in and consume the Christie atmosphere.

Most (American) cozies employ some English tropes, or references to Classic crime novels. Like the house of books at Storyton, many cozy novels pun on Classic novel titles, and authors. As well as Ellery Adams' own *nom de plume* (potentially a play on Ellery Queen, in the way that Agatha Raisin references Agatha Christie), these include Victoria Abbott's Book Collector Series, which commences with *The Christie Curse*. The subsequent adventures in this series have titles like *The Sayers Swindle*, and *The Marsh Madness*. There is also Carolyn Hart's *The Christie Caper*, which is replete with references to Christie and a range of other crime authors and fiction. Christie's fiction and its particular features—rural village life, country houses, enclosed and stratified communities, stand for Englishness (McCaw 2010), and these elements have been picked up and elaborated in subsequent authors and adaptations, as our discussion of the *Agatha Raisin* books will show.

The cover of the first novel in the Book Retreat series locates the book in the visual conventions of the cozy mystery genre. Like many other cozies published in this format, this cover features a pet, Muffet Cat, and depicts the scene of a small business, in this case, the "Storyton Resort," with its sign above the door, and its transported old English windows. The valorization of book cultures and the codex which carries across all the novels in the series, and indeed across many cozy series,[4] is also signaled by the presence of stacks of books. These are valued, hardcover editions, not the paperback or Kindle version, even though these are the formats in which this novel is most likely to be read, and stacks or shelves of physical books appear on every cover of the series. Across the novels in this series, whose plots are predicated on the notion of the preciousness of the codex and its attendant artefacts, the materiality of books is held up as central to the reading experience. The opening lines of the first novel in the series focus on the object of the book and its sensual reception—the sight, scent, and feel of the "[h]undreds of books. Thousands of books" (1). The fourth novel in the series fetishizes the remains of a buried book, its "lost" text, and the attempt to retrieve the physical written words from the page.

The serial nature of the novels is further emphasized by the uniformity of the cover design, with variations for each particular installment, and the repeated banner declaring the novel to be "A Book Retreat Mystery," with an open-book logo. These repeating features reassure the reader that they will encounter the same type of story and writing in each installment, in the same way as the inclusion of excerpts from other novels by the same author suggests that similar generic fare is also available in the author's other series.

Murder in the Mystery Suite sets the tone and scene for the series, but it is not until the second installment, the Jane Austen-themed *Murder in the Paperback Parlor*, that the volumes begin to include a map of Storyton village. Maps, as paratext, threshold "productions" which "surround" and "extend" a text, "to *make present*, to ensure the text's presence in the world, its 'reception' and consumption in the form ... of a book" (Genette 1997, 1) allow readers to locate themselves in the fictional landscapes that they are, imaginatively, about to traverse. Just like maps of real places, the cartography of fictional places involves processes of knowledge, control, and dominion, but the maps that precede the novels in the Book Retreat series also lay out the landscape in distinct ways. The depiction of buildings, whose architecture is a combination of American colonial, contemporary, Alpine and English country house, allows for a sense of the community and commerce that supports the bookish activities of the (undepicted) Storyton Hall. The map also, by its miniaturization effect, visually emphasizes the small-town environment, which is a pervasive element of cozy mysteries. Bounded by a bridge, river and mountains, this place is depicted as contained, isolated, and out of time. It maps the perfect setting for a mystery and promises a discursive journey through a (now) familiar place, which reflects the genre-dictated movement of the narrative through problem, detection, and resolution.

This representation relies on the idea of the enclosed, contained and containable community, common to cozies. Susan Rowland suggests that the entire village of St Mary Mead in the original Miss Marple stories stands in as "a kind of expanded country house" (cited in McCaw 2010, 44). In such feats of miniaturization, whole English landscapes can be re-imagined as walled places; unassailable and immutable. This vision of England stands in contrast to the depiction of England in the Agatha Raisin series which, while acknowledging, appealing to, and playing with these tropes, is also layered with destabilizing details. As the series progresses over almost thirty years of installments, Beaton's novels reveal an English countryside of changing demographics and declining economic fortunes, in an England rife with social, cultural, and racial divisions, and porous borders with Europe.

Agatha Raisin and the Case of the English Village

M.C. Beaton's long-running Agatha Raisin series (1992–), set in the Cotswolds region of south central England, is often characterized as the definitive cozy mystery representation of English village life.[5] Beaton, who for some time was the most borrowed adult British author in British libraries (e.g., "MC Beaton"), is hailed on the covers of the Constable editions of the later novels as "Queen of the Village Mystery." This description, like the name of the protagonist, and like the metareferencing carried out by the American novels, invokes Agatha Christie. This version of Englishness is focused on the village and evokes the rhythms and rituals of largely racially homogenous small rural communities.

Beaton's village narratives are further identified as occurring in the "natural" English landscape, by the logo's depiction of green hills beneath the assertion of Beaton's monarchical status. The covers of the British editions of the early novels in the series also visually reinforced this association of village space and rural place, through their depiction of village scenes nestled in distance-distorted rural scenery of fields and mountains, featuring sheep and winging birds of prey. These suggest that the English countryside extends over distance, disrupted only by roads and villages, and untroubled by the cities which lie out of frame.[6]

The intense identification of the Agatha Raisin series with ideas about English countryside and village life both shapes, and is shaped by, reader response to the novels. Book reviewers in print media often comment upon the English village settings of Beaton's novels. Connie Fletcher made an oft-quoted characterization in a *Booklist* review of *Agatha Raisin and the Day the Floods Came*, in which she asserted that the series "just about defines the British cozy: she gives us an individualistic sleuth working out of a thatched cottage in an achingly picturesque Cotswolds village" (Fletcher 2002). The *Independent* also noted the "picture-postcard village" setting of the 24th novel in the series, *Something Borrowed, Someone Dead*, characterizing it as "like a satire on the 'Mayhem Parva' school of English detective fiction" (Robshaw 2014).

The idea of English place also pervades the online review sites and book blogs which form a key component of the publishing circuit of genre fiction. These often provide more personal accounts of responses to place and space in the series, describing the village settings as emotional or psychic places of pleasure and retreat. Darcia Helle recounted in a review of *The Witches' Tree* on her blog that, despite her stated reservations, "[s]pending time in the village while the mystery unravels was enjoyable" (Helle 2017). A reviewer on Amazon's Goodreads reader review website underscored the emotional dimension of this textual travel, and its connection with the idea of home, when she asserted that "[i]t's always comforting to see Agatha again and the village of Carsley [sic], almost like coming home" (MacDonald 2017). In another typical comment from this site, "Kate" claimed that "I really like this series and spending time with Agatha in the English Cotswolds" (Kate 2013). In a review of *Agatha Raisin and A Spoonful of Poison*, "Robin" matched a textual journeying through the series with the idea of geographical travel through narrative in the joint observations that the novel "reminded me of the first Agatha Raisin book" and that it "[t]ook us all along the countryside to various locales" (Robin 2012).

Readers of the Agatha Raisin novels often reveal a desire for a literary encounter that will purportedly give them access to some kind of essentially English village experience. Beaton's long-time editor, Hope Dellon, nurtured this image of authenticity in an origin story of the series which appeared in a profile of the author in *Publisher's Weekly*. After Beaton had relocated to the Cotswolds, Dellon said, they met together and she "told me such terrific stories about her village, and the people who lived there, that we somehow started talking about the Cotswolds as a possible setting for a series about an amateur sleuth" (Picker 2014).

So closely is the Agatha Raisin series associated with England and Englishness, and the English village, that readers assign an anthropological role to the novels. The blogger Patricia Garry attributed an educative role about Britishness to the 13th novel in the series, *Agatha Raisin and the Case of the Curious Curate*. She describes this book as giving "several tours of several parts of London, [and] introduces us to duck races, English style." The novel, she concludes, is "[g]ood for the brain, good for the funny bone," because, amongst other features, it offered "lots of chances to figure out how British villages work" (Garry 2016). This reading is echoed in a Goodreads review of *Agatha Raisin and the Potted Gardener*, which observed that "[t]he everyday life of the village was dissected in detail" (Kavita 2014).

For transatlantic readers, especially, the "England" that is constructed in Beaton's series is, uncannily, both familiar and unfamiliar space. One such reviewer, for example, wrote that "[r]eading an Agatha Raisin cozy" as "like going home to very a familiar, friendly neighborhood. … I read these cozies to meet the inhabitants of this little village in the English countryside, and to see what my old friend Agatha is up to nowadays" (Katz 2003). It is "*like* going home" [our italics], but it is not going home, not only because the archetypal English village is a product of the imagination, but also due to the fact that Beaton's England is geographically remote from the place of reading.

Unsurprisingly, the prospect of travelling to and dwelling in the actual English place of the Cotswolds, and the act of reading an Agatha Raisin novel, are often conflated in online commentary on the series, such as Annie's comment in a Goodreads review of *Agatha Raisin and the Potted Gardener* that "you really want you would be able [sic] to purchase her cottage" (Annie 2016). The possibility of physical engagement with places in the novels is given cartographic shape on the Booktrail website, which features eight of the Agatha Raisin novels, by mapping out itineraries for Raisin-related travel in the Cotswolds region. The online map of the Cotswolds for *Agatha Raisin and the Quiche of Death* on this website features four pinpoints: for the village of Charlbury, accompanied by the text "This is a nice little village. Could it be Carsely?" and one for the Cotswold Hills, with the explanation that "Fictional Carsely is located here somewhere." The remaining two locate Moreton in Marsh as the place of Market Day and where "she gets off the train," and Bourton on the Hill as the place "[t]he car passes through ... [mine] on the way to carsely [sic]," with the added suggestion of visiting the Bourton House Garden. In this way, the maps on this site encourage and commend tourist travel to and within the region, even though the accompanying "Travel Guide" comments that, in the book, Agatha Raisin is "pleased" that her village of Carsely is "relatively free from the usual tourist trap of craft and tea shops and daily buses trundling around the leafy lanes" (Booktrail n.d.). The impact of the "inevitable groups of tourists" (Beaton 1992, 148), and the limitations of the experience offered within the commodity culture of tourism, are also longstanding themes in the series (e.g., Beaton 1993, 184–185; Beaton 1996, 101; Beaton 2001, 55; Beaton 2002, 174; Beaton 2003, 124; Beaton 2010, 161; Beaton 2012, 14; Beaton 2014, 52; Beaton 2017, Kindle Locations 525–528).

Writing against these themes of visiting and touring the Cotswolds, because of and through the books, some online reviewers claim a local, specialized, knowledge in their readings of Beaton's novels. Toria Forsyth-Moser's review of *Agatha Raisin Dishing the Dirt* on The Crime Warp blog, for example, claimed that "[a]nyone who has ever lived in an English village will recognize the ensemble of characters" (Forsyth-Moser 2016), when she could just as accurately have claimed that anyone who has ever read a village mystery could recognize these types. The blogger Hugh Ashton's scathing critique of the latest novel in the series, *Dead Ringer*, draws upon details of ecclesiastical architecture, the Church of England hierarchical structures, and periodization of English history, to suggest that Beaton's book (unlike his review) is not based on a specialist local, or national, knowledge base. To give one example, he writes that the cover of the edition he found at the Lichfield Library, in Staffordshire, "shows a church which hardly corresponds to the Norman church of Thirk Magna in the book, and the bells look like a stock illustration cut from a wedding programme clipart set," while "the American edition ... shows an even more ludicrously inappropriate church on the cover" (Ashton 2018).[7] This shows an interesting understanding of the essentially phatic, rather than mimetic work that covers like this, and those of Ellery Adams' series are performing.

Agatha Raisin and the Rural Idyll

The valorization of rural landscapes that inflects many of the accounts of the series' appeal, in literary journalism and online community reviews, participates in discourses of the rural idyll—the representation of rural space as preserving a cultural, natural and national integrity by virtue of its remoteness from the degradation of the city and the challenges of modernity, and its connectedness to nature, landscape, and agriculture. In this fantasy, rural places like the Cotswolds are produced as culturally and racially homogenous, in much the same way as, prior to a major re-calibration in 2016, the cast of *Midsomer Murders* was white.[8] This was explicitly tied to a version of Englishness in the (job-ending) pronouncement of its co-creator and producer, Brian True-May, that "the television series was the last bastion of Englishness because it did not have actors from ethnic minorities" (Hutchison 2011). True-May's comments, which prefigured the anxieties about a purportedly beleaguered Englishness mobilized in the Brexit debate, provide evidentiary support of David Bell's characterization of the rural idyll as "first and foremost a symbolic landscape into which is condensed and onto which are projected a whole host of things: identifications, imaginings, ideologies," including acting as "a receptacle for national identity" (Bell 2012, 151). The idea of the rural idyll is also heavily invested with the fantasy of a simpler, unified past, untroubled by the complexities of urbanization, globalization, and financial upheavals. This "mythical, pastoral England," sold by the heritage, tourist and creative industries, and captured in the enduring calendar image of "picturesquely thatched cottages clustered around village greens ... thrives on presentations of England as a country idyll unspoilt by 'modernity'" (Berberich 2015, 159).

The specific setting of the Cotswolds reinforces the claim to archetype that informs and inflects the promotion and reception of the series. This area is famous for its pretty villages with whimsical names, and a preponderance of thatched roofs and cottage gardens. These places, with their flower-hung buildings and historic pubs, operate in a signifying circuit by appearing to reproduce the idealized visual images from the lids of biscuit tins and chocolate boxes. This semiotic reflexivity is playfully referenced in some of the novels in the series. In *Agatha Raisin and the Vicious Vet*, for example, the "frost-covered landscape ... reminded Agatha of the Christmas calendars of her youth where the winter scenes were decorated with glitter" (Beaton 1993, 13), and in *Agatha Raisin and the Murderous Marriage*, Agatha tells James that the clouds they are watching "are like those neat and regular water-colour ones painted by the Cotswolds amateurs" (Beaton 1996, 90). In another, Agatha's cottage is considered by Toni

Gilmour to be "the kind she had seen on chocolate boxes and calendars with its deep thatched roof" (Beaton 2007, 38).

The region of the Cotswolds, often itself imagined as a garden (see Brace 1999), plays a heavy symbolic role in the construction of certain fantasies of being English and living in the landscapes of England, as "a semi-mythical South Country" which is the "defining landscape of Englishness" (Brace 366). The pervasiveness of this representation is evident in the manner in which the region functions as shorthand for a quintessentially English atmosphere in Laura Childs' Cackleberry Club Mysteries, in which the Cackleberry Club Café is repeatedly described as seeming like it belonged in the Cotswolds, rather than in Kindred, Ohio (e.g., Childs 2010, 140; Childs 2012, Kindle location 138; Childs 2014, Kindle location 139; Childs 2014a, 57). The Cotswolds are the subject of many descriptive passages over the Agatha Raisin series, many of which point out the constructedness of the region, as well as its natural beauty, and highlight the role that this area, as imagined as well as geographical space, plays in the generation, and perpetuation, of ideas of essential Englishness. Beaton presents her readers with a complicated account of the role of the Cotswolds region in cultural imagining, at the same time as she draws upon its recognizable landscapes and symbolic status. The area is introduced in the first novel as the subject of Agatha Raisin's fantasy. Her lifelong "dream," the reader is told, was a Cotswold cottage, after a childhood visit to this region, "one of the few man-made beauties in the world: quaint villages of golden stone houses, pretty gardens, winding green lanes and ancient churches." To maintain the fantasy, she had "never gone back to the Cotswolds, preferring to keep the dream intact" (Beaton 1992, 7,8). In the latest installment, *Beating About the Bush*, Agatha is still in thrall of this English childhood fantasy. Out on a case, she insists on seeing a donkey because those animals "belonged in a traditionally British picture-postcard world of seaside holiday rides on the sands and family fun in the sunshine at resorts" (Beaton 2019, Kindle Location 641).

Beaton's Agatha Raisin series consistently works against stereotypical images of the village, and its valorized place in abstractions of Englishness, while at the same time drawing upon, promoting, and benefiting from, these same tropes. Instances of this cultural double dealing can be found in the representations of the cottage garden in *Agatha Raisin and the Potted Gardener* (Beaton 1994) and disputes over freehold agricultural land in *Agatha Raisin and the Walkers of Dembley* (Beaton 1994a).

Gardens, and especially rural cottage gardens, carry heavy symbolic weight in constructions and assertions of Englishness. The potency of the nationalizing cultural narratives that are built around horticulture is evident in an account of the Chelsea Flower Show in *The Sunday Times* in 2015 when, just after the election of a Conservative government, the Show is described as part of "a skein of Englishness" and "a shrine to the values that lay behind the election victory—a metaphor for an innately conservative, fiercely aspirational nation that fetishises the home and garden as a measure of a successful life." In this celebratory account, the exhibitors are displaying national qualities as well as flowers. They "combine patience with our other characteristics—pragmatism and a degree of ruthlessness—... and they play up that other staple: eccentricity." Here, gardening is, according to "the social commentator and analyst" Peter York, "a fantastically British thing" (Driscoll 2015).[9]

The third novel in the series, *Agatha Raisin and the Potted Gardener* (Beaton 1994), centers upon the politics of the traditional English cottage garden scene, a recurring theme throughout the series, and suggests that the supposedly innocent garden space of traditional flowers is as illusory as Agatha's instant garden and charade of horticultural knowledge. This installment achieves much of its drama and comedy from pointing out the dysfunctional nature of the relationships in the village's gardening community, for all its horticultural display. This revelation of the sinister spaces within the English domestic garden, represented almost literally in the "planting" of the corpse of a murder victim—"Someone had hung her upside down by her ankles and buried her head in earth in a large earthenware pot" (Beaton 1994, 76)—is made against the idealized image of the country cottage garden. This horticultural space is "a figment of the mind ... a normative ideal rather than a reality, a garden that has become almost too idealized to actually exist except in representations: paintings, picture postcards, and greetings cards" (Tilley 2008, 225).

The Cotswolds may be at the epicenter of cultural imaginings around the English rural idyll, but the fourth novel, *Agatha Raisin and the Walkers of Dembley* (Beaton 1994a), works to contradict received notions of the harmony, and neutrality, of the natural landscape. The image of rural space as "an apolitical space of tranquillity where the conflict of urban areas was inexistent" (Prendiville 2017, 35) is disturbed, not only by the genre of the village crime narrative itself, in which some level of conflict and violence is inherent, but more specifically by a plot involving ramblers and political agitation around public accessibility of private land. The longstanding status of political protest in rural landscape is underscored by an early reference to Greenham Common, where the murder victim, the activist Jessica Tartinick had been an anti-nuclear campaigner.[10] Histories of more local skirmishes, over rambler access to land, are also referenced, and there are repeated images of people consulting ordinance maps, and marking out sometimes disputed rights of way over cultivated landscapes. One of the few incidents of physical violence in the novel occurs when a belligerent landowner punches Jeffrey Benson, one of the Dembley Walkers, after he had "brandished" a map, and asserted that the group were traversing "a legitimate right of way" (Beaton 1994a, 148). This contested, disputed map is in distinct contrast to the imaginary enclosed, "settled" map which appears in cozies like Ellery Adams' Book Retreat series.

Beaton's representation of the English, and the more specific Cotswold, village is thus layered with imagery and commentary that complicate stereotypical understandings of harmonious agricultural space and rural communities. While this intensifies over the series, which charts the changes wrought to English villages by gentrification, property development and government policy, it was also at work in the early novels, part of whose project is to point to the fissures within communities which, on the surface, seem to enjoy an idyllic calm. There were, as Agatha muses in the first novel in the series, *Agatha Raisin and the Quiche of Death* (Beaton 1992), "worms in this charming polished apple," and the "serpent in this Garden of Eden" (Beaton 2015, 231–2) is not just murder, but division.

Beaton introduces these themes by mentioning cultural clashes between villagers and newcomers, commenting how villagers blame "newcomers" for the closing down of village shops when it is as much to do with the motorcar and supermarket chains, while, for their part, the new arrivals, self-styled as upper class, are condescending and "rude." This conflict, overt and covert, between the local and the outsider, the long-term dweller and the newcomer, the worker who can no longer afford a village worker's cottage and the Londoners who have inflated the property prices, and the resident and the tourist, plays out across all 29 novels in the series.

Additional fissures in these communities around the presence of migrant workers in England become visible in later novels. In *Agatha Raisin, Dishing the Dirt*, for example, published the year before the 2016 Referendum on England's exit from the EU, Agatha Raisin noted the "strong European accent" of a worker at Computing Plus, and thought he was "[p]robably Polish.... Evesham was rapidly becoming Little Poland." The presence of Polish workers in the region is further underscored when another character says that "[t]here's a good restaurant round the corner from where I live called Warsaw Home'" (Beaton 2015, 83, 87). The same presence was noted by Charles Fraith in an earlier novel, when he identifies a receptionist, described as "a tall rangy female in tight jeans, high boots and a peasant-type blouse … [with] masses of frizzy blonde hair, a narrow face and pale-blue eyes," as Polish. "These Poles get everywhere these days," he says to Phil Marshall, "But what a looker!" (Beaton 2007, 175–6). In the 2011 novel, *Agatha Raisin as the Pig Turns*, Toni Gilmour makes a more overtly racist reference when she (incorrectly, as it turns out) sums up the case for Simon Black: "It sounds like a gang.... Look at all the criminal gangs Britain let in after the European Union opened the borders: Bulgarians, Romanians and so on" (Beaton 2011, 114). This counter narrative of change and devolution places the English village at the center of ruptures and movements that are national and international in origin.

The 27th installment, *Agatha Raisin Pushing Up Daisies*, makes a significant contribution to the series' aggregated portrait of contested and divided Englishness. Published in 2016, the year of Britain's Referendum on leaving the European Union, the novel is based around the identifiably English cultural practice of allotment gardening (see King 2007), but also works to reveal the social, racial, class, and ethnic fissures on Britain's national ground that fuelled the debates around Brexit. While there are the perennial divisions around class and gender, for example one character's "public school accent" that led Agatha to sum him up as a "posh rugger bugger" (Beaton 2016, Kindle Locations 375–380), prevalence is also given to the ideas around Englishness that were being mobilized at the time in contemporary British political discourse. Charles's supposition that "Indian Summer" might now have to be referred to as "Native American Summer" (Beaton 2016, Kindle Locations 152–153) is an oblique reference to the Leave Campaign's constant bugbear of so-called "political correctness." Alex Cameron, the crime reporter, also expresses an anxiety (quickly refuted by Agatha Raisin) that a "new puritanism" (Beaton 2016, Kindle Locations 1393–1395) is taking hold in relation to sexual harassment allegations.

Throughout *Pushing Up Daisies* there are references to a sense of besieged Britishness, due to changing economies, cultural values, and laws. The characters go to a restaurant which "prided itself on traditional British cooking," and order steak and kidney pie (Beaton 2016, Kindle Locations 1120–1121), and Alex Cameron complains about the changing media landscape, dominated by "agencies and freelancers" (Beaton 2016, Kindle Locations 1385–1386), while the cityscape of empty apartments at Chelsea Harbour is explained as the result of "very rich foreigners buy[ing] them as investments" (Beaton 2016, Kindle Location 1399). These references to the cultural, social and economic anxieties that drove the Brexit movement are more explicitly tied to the campaign when Agatha wonders "Whatever happened to women's lib? One of those grand ideas, like the European Union, that kept unravelling" (Beaton 2016, Kindle Location 2141). One of the most strident voices of the Leave campaign, that of Nigel Farage, is obliquely invoked in the name of the character of Nigel Farraday. This character is a Member of Parliament who is described by Jenny Coulter as a former Conservative who "feared he might lose his seat, so he decided to leave the party and stand as an Independent, promising all things to all people with nostalgia thrown in." She continues "You know, Britain for the

British, throw all the immigrants out, bring back smoking, and double the pension money for the elderly. And as he is never likely to have any real power, he can promise what he likes" (Beaton 2016, Kindle Locations 526–529).

In her Agatha Raisin series, then, Beaton consistently references and draws upon the cultural mythologies that are built around the English village and its role in the generation and promotion of ideas of Englishness. She also complicates this picture by pointing to the conflicts and divisions that are glossed over in the villagescape images made familiar by calendars and chocolate boxes, and which comprise an important and lucrative aspect of her own publishing appeal. In this counter narrative, which is exemplified in the political language mobilized in the Brexit debate, cozy pictures of the cottage, garden, village and farm obscure much harsher and more complex realities.

England as an idea, a dream, a fantasy which threads through many cozy mystery novels. In volume after volume, series after series, the idea of Englishness, as well as the English origins of Golden Age detective fiction, is referred to, played with, and written against. A reading of Ellery Adams's Book Retreat series, centering on reassembled English houses and places in rural western Virginia, alongside MC Beaton's Agatha Raisin series set in the small villages of the Cotswolds, highlights the malleability, and in the end, longevity, of notions of England and Englishness in the cozy mystery genre.

Notes

1. The rules against technology exist, we are told, because Storyton Hall "aims to be a place … conducive to reading" (43), and vision-impaired readers will be supplied with large-print books from the library in preference to e-readers. This sets up 'reading' in opposition to technology, despite the fact that this novel, like all cozies, is likely to be consumed in digital form.

2. Theodore Kowalksi, from Eva Gates's Lighthouse Library Mysteries, more explicitly affects Englishness. The reader is told that he employs a "fake English accent" because "he thought [it] made him appear scholarly" (Gates 2015, 33), and that "[f]or reasons known only to himself, he wanted people to think that he was English, and dressed like a country squire heading off to the Highlands for a spot of grouse shooting" (Gates 2016, 6). The character of Everett Hathaway, in Carolyn Hart's long-running Death on Demand series similarly affects what is perceived as an "upper class" British manner and ways of dress and speaking (eg. Hart 2012, 2, 24).

3. See Light 1991. Other writers in this genealogy include Ngaio Marsh (despite her New Zealand origins) and Dorothy L. Sayers. Amongst many other instances across the cozy genre, Christie's emblematic Englishness is noted in Abbott 2013, 24–25; Burns 2017, Kindle location 249; Childs 2010, 142–3).

4. The valorization of the codex form of the book pervades many cozy bibliomystery novels, including, as a very select sample, Abbott 2013, 2103a, 2013b, 2014, 2016; Gates 2015, 2015a, 2016; and in a bookshop setting, Brandon 2012, 2013, 2013a, 2014, 2015, 2016; Burns 2017, 2018, 2018a, 2019).

5. M.C. Beaton was one of the pen names of the writer Marion Chesney.

6. The website of the painter of these images identifies them as "prospect" pictures and notes the long tradition, since the seventeenth century, of "bending and stretching" the landscape by depicting it from above (Farmar).

7. This commentary points to the fact that the subject of this novel, campanology, also signifies Englishness. Bell-ringing, also the subject of an episode of *Midsomer Murders* (2002) and a novel, *The Nine Tailors*, by Dorothy L. Sayers, is characterized by Jill Paton Walsh in her Introduction to this novel as having "an essentially English nature" (Sayers 2016). Studies of campanology also emphasize its Englishness (see Johnston 2006, 22; Harrison 2016, Kindle Locations 13–14).

8. This re-calibration coincided with the Brexit Referendum and there was a referential cross-pollination between the political debates and the changes to the series. In the first episode in Series 19, for example, there is a Union-Jack adorned banner proclaiming "Great Auburn Celebrates the Liberation of Little Auburn" (*Midsomer Murders* 2016). This visual gesture recognized the cultural currency of the rhetoric employed by the Leave campaign, while providing a counter image in the form of a mixed-race couple on the street. An article in the *Daily Mail*, which noted the introduction of "[a]t least 24 ethnic minority characters," most of them "in mixed-race relationships," predictably attributed the transition to 'political correctness' (Buckley 2016), a key concept in anti-European Union rhetoric.

9. This plays directly into fantasies about English rurality. The article also sees in Chelsea "strands of that vision" of John Major, who declared, when he was Prime Minister, that Britain was "a country of long shadows on country cricket grounds, warm beer, invincible green suburbs, dog lovers and old maids bicycling to communion through the morning mist." This vision is reproduced repeatedly in the opening images of shows like *Midsomer Murders*, and (though slightly more mischievously) the television adaptations of the Agatha Raisin series (2016; 2018).

10. In this inherently conservative account Jessica's activism was "fuelled by bitterness and envy' and 'by a desire for power over people" (Beaton 1994a, 14).

Works Cited

Abbott, Victoria. 2013. *The Christie Curse*. New York: Berkley.
Abbott, Victoria. 2013a. *The Sayers Swindle*. New York: Berkley.
Abbott, Victoria. 2013b. *The Marsh Madness*. New York: Berkley.
Abbott, Victoria. 2014. *The Wolfe Widow*. New York: Berkley.
Abbott, Victoria. 2016. *The Hammett Hex*. New York: Berkley.
Adams, Ellery. 2014. *Murder in the Mystery Suite*. New York: Berkley.
Adams, Ellery. 2015. *Murder in the Paperback Parlor*. New York: Berkley.
Adams, Ellery. 2016. *Murder in the Secret Garden*. New York: Berkley. Kindle edition
Adams, Ellery. 2018. *Murder in the Locked Library*. New York: Kensington Books. Kindle edition
Adams, Ellery. 2019. *Murder in the Reading Room*. New York: Kensington Books. Kindle edition
Agatha Raisin Television Series. 2016. Sky 1.
Agatha Raisin Television Series. 2018. Acorn TV.
Annie. 2016. Review of *Agatha Raisin and the Potted Gardener*, Goodreads, 8 August 2016. https://www.goodreads.com/book/show/40604452-agatha-raisin-and-the-potted-gardener?from_search=true. Accessed 4 March 2019.
Ashton, Hugh. 2018. Dead Ringer (M.C. Beaton)—Review. Books by Hugh Ashton blog, 9 November 2018. https://hughashtonbooks.com/2018/11/09/dead-ringer/. Accessed 4 March 2019.
Beaton, M.C. 1992 [2002]. *Agatha Raisin and the Quiche of Death*. London: Constable and Robinson.
Beaton, M.C. 1993 [2002]. *Agatha Raisin and the Vicious Vet*. London: Constable and Robinson.
Beaton, M.C. 1994. *Agatha Raisin and the Potted Gardener*. New York: Ivy Books.

Beaton, M.C. 1994a [2002]. *Agatha Raisin and the Walkers of Dembley*. London: Constable and Robinson.
Beaton, M.C. 1996. *Agatha Raisin and the Murderous Marriage*. New York: Minataur.
Beaton, M.C. 2001. *Agatha Raisin and the Love from Hell*. New York: Minataur.
Beaton, M.C. 2002. *Agatha Raisin and the Day the Floods Came*. New York: Minataur.
Beaton, M.C. 2003. *Agatha Raisin and the Case of the Curious Curate*. New York: Minataur.
Beaton, M.C. 2007. *Agatha Raisin and Kissing Christmas Goodbye*. London: Constable. Kindle edition.
Beaton, M.C. 2010. *Agatha Raisin and the Busy Body*. London: Constable and Robinson. Kindle edition.
Beaton, M.C. 2011. *Agatha Raisin As the Pig Turns*. London: Constable. Kindle edition.
Beaton, M.C. 2012. *Agatha Raisin Something Borrowed, Someone Dead*. London: Constable. Kindle edition.
Beaton, M.C. 2014. *Agatha Raisin and the Blood of an Englishman*. London: Constable. Kindle edition.
Beaton, M.C. 2015. *Agatha Raisin Dishing the Dirt*. London: Constable. Kindle edition.
Beaton, M.C. 2016. *Agatha Raisin Pushing Up Daisies*. London: Constable. Kindle edition.
Beaton, M.C. 2017. *Agatha Raisin and the Witches' Tree*. London: Constable. Kindle edition.
Beaton, M.C. 2018. *Agatha Raisin and the Dead Ringer*. London: Constable. Kindle edition.
Beaton, M.C. 2019. *Agatha Raisin: Beating About the Bush*. London: Constable. Kindle edition.
Beaton, M.C. n.d. *M.C. Beaton* website. https://www.mcbeaton.com/us/reviews/. Accessed 26 February 2019.
Bell, David. 2006. "Variations on the rural idyll." In *Handbook of Rural Studies*. Edited by Paul J. Cloke, Terry Marsden and Patrick Mooney. London: SAGE. 149–160.
Berberich, Christine. 2015. "Bursting the bubble: Mythical Englishness, then and now." *Journal of Postcolonial Writing* 51.2: 158–169.
Booktrail, The. "Agatha Raisin and the Quiche of Death," 7 April 2012. https://www.thebooktrail.com/book-trails/agatha-raisin-and-the-quiche-of-death/. Accessed 4 March 2019.
Brace, Catherine. 1999. "Gardenesque imagery in the representation of regional and national identity: the Cotswold garden of stone." *Journal of Rural Studies* 15: 365–376.
Brandon, Ali. 2012. *A Novel Way to Die*. New York: Berkley.
Brandon, Ali. 2013. *Words with Fiends*. New York: Berkley.
Brandon, Ali. 2013a. *Double Booked for Death*. New York: Berkley.
Brandon, Ali. 2014. *Literally Murder*. New York: Berkley.
Brandon, Ali. 2015. *Plot Boiler*. New York: Berkley.
Brandon, Ali. 2016. *Twice Told Tail*. New York: Berkley.
Brewer, Mary F. "Exporting Englishness." In *Contemporary British Television Crime Drama: Cops on the Box*. Edited by Ruth McElroy. London and New York: Routledge, 2016.
Buckley, Jemma. "After Midsomer race row." *Daily Mail*, 18 February 2016. https://www.dailymail.co.uk/tvshowbiz/article-3451971/After-Midsomer-race-row-latest-20-episodes-feature-24-minority-characters-Villages-set-political-correct-former-producer-s-departure.html. Accessed 18 February 2019.
Burns, V.M. *The Plot is Murder*. 2017. New York: Kensington. Kindle edition.
Burns, V.M. *The Novel Art of Murder*. 2018. New York: Kensington. Kindle edition.
Burns, V.M. *Read Herring Hunt*. 2018a. New York: Kensington. Kindle edition.
Burns, V.M. *Wed, Read and Dead*, 2019. New York: Kensington. Kindle edition.
Childs, Laura. 2010. *Bedeviled Eggs*. New York: Berkley.
Childs, Laura. 2012. *Stake & Eggs*. New York: Berkley. Kindle edition.
Childs, Laura. 2014. *Eggs in a Casket*. New York: Berkley. Kindle edition.
Childs, Laura, 2014a. *Scorched Eggs*. New York: Berkley. Kindle edition.
Driscoll, Margarette. 2015. "Everything's Coming Up Roses." *The Sunday Times*, 17 May 2015, 18.
Farmar, Francis. n.d. http://www.francisfarmar.com. Accessed 25 February 2019.
Fletcher, Connie. 2002. Review of *Agatha Raisin and the Days the Floods Came. The Booklist*, 98.21: 1824.
Forsyth-Moser, Toria. 2016. 'Dishing the Dirt by M.C Beaton Book Review,' The Crime Warp,

2 June 2016. http://thecrimewarp.blogspot.com/2016/06/dishing-dirt-by-mc-beaton-book-review.html. Accessed 4 March 2019.

Garry, Patricia. 2016. "Book Review: Agatha Raisin and the Case of the Curious Curate." 2 June 2016. http://www.patriciagarry.com/2016/06/02/book-review-agatha-raisin-and-the-case-of-the-curious-curate/. Accessed 26 February 2019.

Gates, Eva. 2015. *Booked for Trouble*. New York: Obsidian.

Gates, Eva. 2015a. *By Book or By Crook*. New York: Obsidian.

Gates, Eva. 2016. *Reading Up a Storm*. New York: Obsidian. Kindle edition.

Genette, Gérard. 1997. *Paratext: Thresholds of Interpretation*. Cambridge: Cambridge University Press.

Harrison, John. 2016. *Bells and Bellringing*. Shire Library. Kindle edition.

Hart, Carolyn. 2012. *Death Comes Silently*. New York: Berkley.

Helle, Darcia. "Book Review—The Witches' Tree: An Agatha Raisin Mystery by M.C. Beaton." Quiet Fury Books, 25 October 2017. http://quietfurybooks.com/bookreview-witches-tree-agatha-raisin-mystery-m-c-beaton/. Accessed 26 February 2019.

Hutchison, Peter. 2011. 'Midsomer Murders producer steps down over race row.' *Telegraph*, 23 March 2011. https://www.telegraph.co.uk/culture/tvandradio/8400208/Midsomer-Murders-producer-steps-down-over-race-row.html. Accessed 18 February 2019.

Johnston, Ron. 2006. "A most public of musical performances: the English art of change-ringing." *GeoJournal* 65: 17–31.

Kate. 2013. Review of *Agatha Raisin and the Walkers of Dembley*, 26 February 2013. https://www.goodreads.com/book/show/139177.Agatha_Raisin_and_the_Walkers_of_Dembley?from_search=true. Accessed 4 March 2019.

Katz, Sharon. 2003. Review of *Agatha Raisin and the Haunted House*, Reviewing the Evidence blog, October 2003. http://www.reviewingtheevidence.com/review.html?id=3451. Accessed 4 March 2019.

Kavita. 2014. Review of *Agatha Raisin and Potted Gardener*, Goodreads, 6 January 2014. https://www.goodreads.com/book/show/40604452-agatha-raisin-and-the-potted-gardener?from_search=true. Accessed 4 March 2019.

King, Heather. 2007. "Allotments as Cultural Artefacts." *Material Culture Review* 65. https://journals.lib.unb.ca/index.php/MCR/article/view/18086/19410 accessed 12 March 2019.

Light, Alison. 1991. *Forever England: Femininity, Literature and Conservatism Between the Wars*. London and New York: Routledge.

"M C Beaton: The most borrowed adult British author in UK libraries." *Midas Public Relations*. https://www.midaspr.co.uk/news-stories/m-c-beaton-borrowed-adult-british-author-uk-libraries. Accessed 26 February 2019.

MacDonald, Fiona. 2017. Review of *Agatha Raisin and Potted Gardener*, Goodreads, 17 April 2017. https://www.goodreads.com/book/show/40604452-agatha-raisin-and-the-potted-gardener?from_search=true. Accessed 4 March 2019.

Mccaw, Neil. 2010. Adapting Detective Fiction: Crime, Englishness and the TV Detectives. London: Bloomsbury Publishing PLC, Continuum Literary Studies.

Midsomer Murders. 2002. "Ring Out Your Dead." Series 5, Episode 2: aired 15 September 2002. ITV.

Midsomer Murders, 2016. "The Village that Rose from the Dead." Series 19, Episode 1: aired 18 December 2016. ITV.

Picker, Leonard. 2014. "An Interview with M.C. Beaton: Mysteries and Thrillers 2014." *Publishers Weekly* 261:46, 17 November 2014.

Prendiville, Brendan. 2017. "Rural Protest in England." In *The English Countryside: Representations, Identities, Mutations*. Edited by David Haigron. New York: Palgrave Macmillan.

Robin. 2012. Review of *Agatha Raisin and A Spoonful of Poison*, 1 January 2012. https://www.goodreads.com/book/show/2866846-a-spoonful-of-poison?from_search=true. Accessed 4 March 2012.

Robshaw, Brandon. 2014. "Agatha Raisin: Something Borrowed, Someone Dead." *The Independent*, 27 April 2014, 20.

Sayers, Dorothy L. 2016 [1934]. *The Nine Tailors*. Hodder and Stoughton. Kindle Edition.

"Tea Time with Truffles: Blood of an Englishman by M.C. Beaton Review and

Giveway." *Melissa's Mochas, Mysteries and Meows*, 18 September 2014. https://www.mochasmysteriesmeows.com/2014/09/tea-time-with-truffles-blood-of.html. Accessed 26 February 2019.

Tilley, Christopher. 2008. "From the English Cottage Garden to the Swedish Allotment: Banal Nationalism and the Concept of the Garden." *Home Cultures* 5.2: 219–249.

Extending Cozy Boundaries

Kathryn Heltne Swanson

There seems to be general agreement among authors and readers alike about definitions of the cozy mystery. Traditionally, cozies have featured a Miss Marple-esque character who is not a professional detective, who is often discounted as a nosy busy body by police persons around her, and who lives her life in a relatively small, quiet, and restricted setting. While most often this setting is a small village, certainly other bounded environments can serve as well. Requisite is that the sleuth is a member of a specific, rather insular community where she is thought to be somewhat innocuous; a place where the protagonist is comfortable and where those with whom she interacts know and trust her is essential. She is generally likeable, moves easily in her world, may own a small business or have a hobby that endears her to those around her, and is able to intuit characteristics of those around her The cozy sleuth is often privy to local gossip, history, and protocols of her world, understands motives and secrets of her neighbors and coworkers, and is thus able to unmask the guilty with relative grace and ease, putting pieces of a puzzle together as no one else seems able to do. Because others in her world trust her, she can investigate surreptitiously and is able to garner information that is often inaccessible to the local police force. Members of the local police department and community detectives are often somewhat inept although there can be a romantic connection between the sleuth and one of the local investigators. Important, also, is the novels' audience: Readers of the cozy mystery often inhabit worlds similar to those of the sleuth (for example, academic and medical environments). Thus, they can identify with the protagonist and her world and understand the often-unstated rules of behavior that are operative within particular boundaries. Violence is minimal in the cozy, and when it occurs, it is off stage, either having taken place before the beginning of the novel or reported early in the novel. Cozy mysteries end well as the sleuth eventually solves crimes that baffle officials around her, and the perpetrator is caught and punished at novel's end.

While these insular communities are frequently small towns in which most inhabitants are known by the sleuth, there are other insular environments and specifications that also qualify as suitable ground for a cozy sleuth. For example, the protagonist in a traditional cozy may be a cat lover such as the sleuth in novels by Rita Mae Brown's Mrs. Murphy series written with her Tiger Cat Sneaky Pie and Lilian Jackson Braun's *The Cat Who...* series, or she may be a dog trainer in the show dog competition world presented by Laurien Berensen. The cozy sleuth's world may also be centered by her work as a needlecrafter as in the novels of Monica Ferris; the proprietor of a tea shop as in the cozies by Laura Childs; a cook such as Hannah Swenson in Joanne Fluke's work; a caterer such as Goldy in Diane Mott Davidson's novels; a librarian such as Helma Zukas in novels by Jo Dereske; a bookstore owner and mystery fiction aficionada such as Carolyn Hart's Annie Lawrence; an antiques dealer as is Abigail Timberlake in the series by Tamar Myers; a creator of crossword puzzles as is Parnell Hall's Cora Felton; or even a golfer as in novels by Roberta Isleib, an intrepid traveler such as Dorothy Gilman's Mrs. Pollifax, or an archaeologist such as Amelia Peabody in the work of Elizabeth Peters. The protagonists in these novels are successful because of their particular skills and their immersion into specific communities. Interestingly, there is an extremely high number of crimes committed in these particular communities, and someone who is a knowledgeable and trusted member is always able to solve the mystery without using violence but by using her wits, empathy, and intuition.

Notably, academe has long also provided such a cozy setting. From Dorothy Sayers' *Gaudy Night* to Carolyn Heilbrun/Amanda Cross's *Death in a Tenured Position* (and more) novels featuring professor Kate Fansler, the academic has used her membership in a particular community to gain access, trust, and information that others, certainly members of the local police forces, are denied by members of the community. The sleuth who lives in academe knows all too well its rules, pretensions, and expectations. She is entrenched in her academic community and understands it as no non-academic can. She navigates the many academic land mines, whether the setting is an Ivy League university, an urban community college, a community education site, or a public high school, staying in tune with her colleagues and, most importantly, most often with her students. These are the teachers who feel responsible when a student in their class is inexplicably distracted, falls apart during an office hour conference, goes missing or is arrested, and who must figure out the cause and find a solution for this aberrant academic behavior. These are also the professors who face fierce competition for tenure, promotions, and grant funding. This desperation is at the base of the plot in the academic work presented in *Give Me Your Hand* by Megan Abbott, for example.

Indeed, there are many elementary, middle, and high school teachers who inhabit the academic cozy. For example, Gillian Roberts' Amanda Pepper is a high school English teacher and Diane Mott Davidson's Goldy, in addition to her catering business, is a prep school teacher. Many cozy sleuths who move in academe are college English Professors. A few examples of these cozy academics appear in Ann Waldron's Princeton Murders Series; Leigh Perry's (Toni L.P. Kelner) Family Skeleton Mystery Series; Cynthia Kuhn's Lila Maclean's novels; Alice Boatwright's Ellie Kent series; J.S. Borthwick's work and the Murder 101 series by Maggie Barbieri featuring English professor/amateur sleuth Alison Bergeron.

More specifically, note examples provided by Jincy Willett's protagonist, Amy Gallup, an experienced albeit jaded, writing instructor who facilitates a creative writing group in Willett's novel *The Writing Class* (2008). Teaching her weekly evening class offered as a university extension course for non-traditional students is Amy's only reason to leave her house and her Bassett hound. Among her students are the usual players: the enthusiastic repeater, the joker, the unrealistic egotist, the silent talent—all categories of students well known to teachers. But in classic closed room fashion, when one of the students is murdered, Amy has to sift through threatening messages, nasty peer editing comments, and bizarre events in the classroom to determine which of her students is the murderer. She uses her knowledge of the academic system to ferret out the perpetrator and to create an insular academic world for her readers. For example:

> On the first night of class, Amy made a little show of studying her pre-registration list, which she would turn before the night's end, into her own mnemonic cheat sheet.... She needed the money; she couldn't afford to alienate potential students (*customers*, the university extension people called them).... But she hated first nights, hated not knowing if she'd have enough people to run the class ... hated most of all having to work a cold room. In a few weeks' time she'd feel comfortable with these people, and most of them would like her. Right now, she wanted them all to buzz off [*Writing Class* (6–7)].

The class goes on, the intrigue mounts, a student is murdered, and at the end of one of the writing class meetings, Amy is left alone with the student who turns out, surprisingly, to be the murderer about whom Amy says, "And now she came right out with it, the same dumb question they all asked, like a college junior waving round a notebook crammed with loopy violet paragraphs" (*Writing Class* 313). The student rages, "Why don't they publish me? ... You know it. I've got something to say. I have a mind" (313). Always the creative writing teacher, Amy bravely and honestly replies, "Yes, but you don't know how to tell a story.... If you want to send a message, use Western Union" (313).

Despite the honest critique, Amy escapes being murdered and, at the end of the novel, realizes that the experience has brought her out of seclusion and has enabled her to start thinking about her own life and the shape of the novel she might write which "Might get finished, and might get published, and might make money, and might even be worth reading" (*Writing Class* 326).

In Jane Isenberg's *Hot Wired* (2005), community college instructor Bel Barrett enters the world of rap in order to understand one of her troubled students, a talented rapper who received a D in her class because he turned in only four of twelve required journal entries. He eventually retaliated with vicious comments on pickurprofs.com and filed a grievance with the dean. Bel does some investigating and finds enough paper generated by committee meetings, hearings, reports, interviews, proposals, and counterproposals regarding her case to "cause the destruction of entire forests" (*Hot Wired* 47). After all the protocol and academic hoops have played themselves out, the student is found responsible, drops out of school, and leaves Bel feeling guilty, often asking herself (as many of her readers in academe would do), "But what if I had given him an incomplete or even a C...." (*Hot Wired* 59). She feels even more responsible—and vulnerable—when the student, returned from fighting in Iraq, dies from being hit on the head and thrown in front of a subway car. Bel becomes a suspect in his murder and has a difficult meeting with the college president who seeks her retirement as a way to placate his Board; she enlists the faculty union's support and, disguised, ingratiates herself with the rapper community and solves the mystery—but only after agonizing over her role as professor, evaluator, and upholder of academic standards at her urban New Jersey community college.

As is the case in the closed world of *The Writing Class*, the academic environment presented by Isenberg is one of students' competition for grades and professors' immersion in departmental politics and struggles for positions, promotions, tenure, and favor from their students, administrators, and Regents. Academe is, indeed, an insular world known very well by its inhabitants, but not easily accessible to outsiders.

A writer who knows the world of academe through and through is the 2015 winner of the Thurber Prize for Humor for her novel *Dear Committee Members* (2014). Julie Schumacher is a professor of English at the University of Minnesota where she has also served as the Chair of the University Judiciary Committee. Although she is the first woman to win the Thurber Prize, her novel also fits criteria for a cozy mystery. It is bounded by the day-to-day rigors and frustrations of a long-time tenured professor who, as an influential member of his English Department, deals with matters generally unfamiliar to those outside a university setting. *Dear Committee Members* centers around a professor, the protagonist Jason Fitger, who teaches creative writing at a Midwestern (and mid-prestige) University. Indeed, the author has stated in interviews that the protagonist's office bears an odd resemblance to the building in which she works. Fitger's life is glimpsed through the seemingly endless number of recommendation letters he is asked to write for colleagues, students, and even strangers. Schumacher's experience teaching creative writing and inhabiting the same insular community as Professor Fitger makes her satire very authentic and believable to readers who are also members of academe, an insular world, indeed. In this epistolary novel, the restrictive academic community inhabited by author and main character alike, the shared familiarity with rigors and frustrations of mundane academic tasks, and the departmental squabbling and political maneuvering all provide parameters around a discrete community. The protagonist's full immersion into this specific community and his intimate knowledge of its particularities qualify the novel as a cozy. And, yes, there is a death.

The peculiarities and particularities of academe are captured in letters Fitger writes during one academic year. The satire is biting as Fitger's frustrations with academe build and he uses his letters to vent. For example, in a letter to his department chair in which Fitger is recommending a colleague for a position as a teaching assistant mentor, he writes:

> You understand, of course, that Ms. McCoy is a stranger to me. I may have glimpsed her in the hall, poor burdened wight, as she trudged from one lecture to another in her yard-sale clothes, thick piles of yet-to-be-graded undergraduate essays under a raw-boned arm; but, mainly, as required, I have skimmed her CV and her letter of interest, both of which express the requisite theater-of-the-absurd language about pedagogy and the euphoria of learning. Suffering creature! By all means, yes, yes! I endorse her bid for the mentorship: May the bump in salary allow her to avoid scurvy by adding fruit to her diet once a week [*Dear Committee Members* 26].

Easily recognizable to anyone living in an academic environment is Fitger's letter to the chair of another department on behalf of an associate administrator in the English Department who has applied to move to a similar job in a different department: "We can only interpret a desire to exit the Department of English as a mark of sound judgment...." Continuing, Fitger notes the English Department has "long vied for recognition as the most dysfunctional of departments" and that the reason for the candidate's seeking reassignment and leaving English might be due to:

> the fisticuffs in the lounge over the issue of undergraduate curriculum, or the faculty meeting (where she was faithfully taking minutes) during which a senior colleague, out of his mind over the issue of punctuation in the department's mission statement, threated to "take a dump" (there was a pun on the word "colon" which I won't belabor here) at a junior faculty member's door [*Dear Committee Members* 132–33].

And, more seriously, perhaps, Fitger writes this letter to the dean of the College of Arts and Sciences:

> In the context of the hiring freeze—we can't afford to sacrifice even one teaching colleague to the funeral pyre of administration. You want undergraduates who can write, think, and read? Stop pretending that writing can be taught across the curriculum by geologists and physicists who wouldn't recognize a dependent clause if it bit them on the ass [*Dear Committee Members* 52].

Often Fitger's recommendations are intended to support students' applications for literary residencies, again, a request understood by those in academe. The most heartfelt of these is in support of Darren, a student who reminds Fitger of himself when he was an eager, promising young writer. Darren is working on a novel that retells Melville's "Bartelby the Scrivener," and he needs to obtain a residency in order to have the funding he needs to concentrate and to finish his novel. Fitger's pleas on behalf of Darren are repeatedly refused, even by Fitger's own literary agent to whom he writes on Darren's behalf:

> I feel a moment of reckoning approaching.... On a day-to-day basis I often find myself overwhelmed by the needs of my students—who seem to trust in an influence I no longer have and in a knowledge of which, increasingly, I am uncertain.... If there is anything you can do for Darren Browles, any assistance similar to that which, twenty-two years ago, you extended to me, I would so appreciate the favor.... Thank you.... Still gazing up at you on that pedestal [*Dear Committee Members* 136].

Despite that serious and poignant appeal, Darren does not receive the funding and, in fact, Fitger later realizes that his former mentor has, in fact, passed off some of Darren's work on the adaptation of Bartleby as his own, again a grievous sin understood by anyone in the academic world.

Fitger continues writing letters in vain attempts to help Darren. One of last is sent to Carole, his former lover and the Associate Director of Student Services and the Fellowship Office. Noting the spurning of Darren and the treachery of his former mentor, Fitger pleads for at least some summer funding for Darren whom he describes as "living on borrowed cigarettes and the castoffs from business school catered lunches" (*Dear Committee Members* 162). Finally, he receives a letter from Carole in which she informs him of Darren's suicide. Fitger responds with his intent to establish a scholarship in Darren's honor and states:

> I suppose this is the last letter of recommendation anyone will write for poor Darren Browles.... He was patient and industrious and quietly determined. Buffeted by setbacks and rejection and his own limitations, he persevered. Furthermore, he was kind—an admirable person. I wish I had told him these things directly, rather than saving my praise of him for letters and e-mails sent to other people: a correspondence Browles would never benefit from or see [*Dear Committee Members* 171].

In Schumacher's novel, the closed world of academe persists. Despite his increased isolation from his department and the administration, Fitger is elected English Department chair (again) and in the final letter of the novel, written to a former colleague, Fitger writes:

> Enjoy the summer.... Fall will arrive soon enough, with requests from students trickling in via e-mail and the trees that shade Willard Hall flushing red at the hem. There is nothing more promising or hopeful than the start of the academic cycle: another chance for self-improvement, for putting into practice what one learned—or failed to learn—during the previous year [*Dear Committee Members* 179–80].

Another insider to the world of academe is Joanne Dobson's Karen Pelletier, an English professor at Enfield College, a liberal arts institution modeled after Dobson's own Amherst where she received her Ph.D. Dobson's sixth mystery novel featuring protagonist Dr. Pelletier is *Death Without Tenure* (2009). In the tradition of a cozy, the protagonist moves easily in an insular world, known best by its insiders. She deals with students, academic pressures, and rivalries among colleges and departments, e.g., an English Department chair who seeks to maintain political correctness and a Visiting Professor of Whiteness Studies. In this novel, there are quotes embedded from the work of Emily Dickinson as well as many literary allusions. In addition to the bounded world the protagonist inhabits in this novel, as in many cozies, she has an ongoing relationship with a police detective, here Lt. Charlie Piotrowski. Even though in this novel, he is serving in Iraq in the National Guard, he is a constant presence in Pelletier's life as he supports her from afar with almost daily communications.

As the title suggests, the novel also vividly captures the struggle and accompanying anxiety those in academe experience when they seek tenure. The stakes are certainly high as academics in their sixth year of review understand too well. The files they present to the tenure review committee and with which they make the case of their strong community involvement/service, excellent teaching with glowing student evaluations, and a substantive record of published scholarship can determine whether or not they remain employed. The world represented by Enfield College is, indeed, an insular one and one which Karen Pelletier (and her creator Joanne Dobson) fully understand and navigate regularly. As Pelletier states:

> ...race and culture have always been in flux. That's academic speak [and] what it means for English professors is that career advancement depends on whatever literary fiefdom the individual scholar has carved out for him or herself, and therefore, lines are drawn in the theoretical sand as if they were etched into concrete [*Death Without Tenure* 140].

The English Department at Enfield College is given only one tenure position yearly, and Pelletier learns that despite her thorough preparation, she has a rival in Professor Joseph Lone Wolf, a Native American. Pelletier is warned that the Department may favor him because of his ethnicity and the push for diversity (even though Lone Wolf has not finished his dissertation and has no publications). A friendly colleague tells her that Lone Wolf may be granted tenure because:

> Joe is Native American. According to (the Department Chair), because Joe Wolf is a member of a native tradition where, from prehistory, knowledge has been transmitted orally, he should not be judged on his writings, but on his "speakings." Evidently it would perpetuate hegemonic oppression to expect him to complete a written dissertation. In his case we must practice radical equalitarianism [*Death Without Tenure* 5].

Political correctness and identity politics swirl around the Department and the College; Pelletier's tenure materials disappear; and then Lone Wolf is found dead from an overdose of Peyote buttons. Two of Pelletier's students, a Muslim woman and a coal-miner's son on full scholarship, seem to be involved, and Dr. Pelletier becomes almost as concerned about their well-being as about her quest for tenure. With little progress being made in solving the murder (and because she has become a primary suspect), Pelletier realizes—as do many cozy protagonists—that "...if I'm ever going to get my life back, I'm going to have to get serious and investigate this murder myself" *(Death* 129).

In the midst of the political furor, Karen Pelletier remains steadfastly an English professor enmeshed in her cozy world. For example, she looks for clues in the murdered professor's gradebook; she often corrects her own (and others') grammar; she worries about plagiarism; and she comes up a very significant clue when she realizes that Lone Wolf has listed his mother's residence as Erewhon, Montana which, when spelled backward, as in *Erewhon*, a nineteenth century novel by Samuel Butler, is Nowhere but for the transposition of two letters. She persists, navigates her world of academe, and by novel's end has solved the murder.

And so, from Dorothy Sayers and Carolyn Heilbrun and many others, to the facilitator of a creative writing group in *The Writing Class* by Jincy Willett, to the English professor in Jane Isenberg's *Hot Wired*, to the university professor who writes recommendation letters in *Dear Committee Members* by Julie Schumacher, and to the angst-ridden, tenure-seeking English professor in Dobson's *Death Without Tenure*, the academic world is a viable setting for the cozy mystery. Bounded by the rules and often-unstated protocols known best by insiders in academe, especially those inhabiting the world of English professors, their departments, and their administrators, academic mysteries do extend the boundaries of the traditional cozy mystery.

Maintaining the traditional criteria for a cozy, one can extend boundaries to include other environments in which the cozy sleuth operates and which her readers often inhabit. If, indeed, a primary criterion of the cozy mystery is its insular setting and a sleuth who intimately knows her world, has gained the trust of those who inhabit this world, and thus can move easily within it, the insular setting can extend the traditional boundaries of the cozy to a Thai hospital and to David Casarett's protagonist Ladarat Patalung, a nurse ethicist who works (and sleuths on the side) at a prestigious hospital in Chiang Mai, Northern Thailand, a very old city nestled in the mountains. Near the infamous golden triangle of Thailand, Laos, and Myanmar (Burma)—the epicenter of the opium trade—this city is the ancient capital of the Lanna kingdom, and today is home to Hmong hill tribes.

The author of the two Patalung books in this series is David Casarett, a physician, researcher, and Professor of Medicine at Duke University School of Medicine and Chief of Palliative Care at Duke Health. He is widely published in medical journals and is well known for his research on the use of cannabis in treatment programs for cancer patients. Dr. Casarett is also a frequent and knowledgeable visitor to Thailand, has taught in Chiang Mai, and knows a great deal about Thai expressions, food, and concepts of farangs (foreigners). These observations and details are woven into his two cozies: *Murder at the House of Rooster Happiness* (2016) and *The Missing Guests of the Magic Grove Hotel* (2017).

Like other cozy protagonists, Nurse Ladarat is an insider to a particular community and is intimately familiar with members of that environment. Curious to a fault, Ladarat is an astute observer of those around her, and she cares that order, justice, and—most of all—ethics be maintained within her community. She easily blends into the world of her hospital and enjoys trust from patients, nurses, and physicians alike, as well as full access to hospital records and procedures. In fact, Ladarat seems almost invisible in her world and is described as knowing that "she lacked a presence that was either appealing or commanding. But for the work of an ethicist—and, occasionally, as a detective—an unassuming appearance proved to be quite useful" (*The Missing Guests of the Magic Grove Hotel* 5). She can move surreptitiously among victims and suspects and use her inside awareness to solve crimes much more quickly than local male detectives and police officers are able to do. Indeed, particularly in the first novel, *Murder at the House of Rooster Happiness* (*Rooster*), there is a degree of tension between Ladarat and Detective Wiriya Mookjai of the Chiang Mai Royal Police Force. He enters, very nervously, on the first page of the novel to ask for Ladarat's help to investigate a mysterious woman who has dropped off her dead husband at the hospital. Ladarat knows Wirija is nervous because he is wearing a green tie on Monday, the day on which the king was born and the day when all proper Thais wear yellow in honor of their beloved (and now, late) king, the longest reigning monarch in the world. Ladarat, always patient, agrees to work with Wiriya and gains his respect and friendship; in the cozy tradition, their relationship develops further although he remains condescending and patronizing at times, much to Ladarat's annoyance.

In Casarett's novels, all violence—and there is little—occurs off stage (as with the case presented to Ladarat above) and involves relationships among individuals or people within small intimate groups rather than disputes involving people vs. cartels, terrorists, spies, or the mafia which would come complete with the requisite assassinations and gun battles. Rather, the plots present puzzles to be solved, and the happy endings reveal all pieces neatly in place as life goes on.

There are four puzzles, really two main plot lines, presented to Nurse Ladarat in *The House of Rooster Happiness*. The first is the one presented by police detective Wiriya and involves the woman who has dropped off her dead husband at Ladarat's hospital, but is found to have done the same thing several times in the past with other husbands, all bearing the same name. To solve this puzzle, Ladarat seeks the help of her cousin Siriwan, the proprietress of a very proper Thai brothel (Thais have quite an enlightened view of the function of properly managed brothels). The two women and Wiriya manage to lure the suspect to the brothel when Wiriya poses as a potential fresh new husband in a match-making scheme. Eventually, all pieces come together, and justice prevails when this case is tied to a second puzzle in the hospital: a strange and elusive man who is lurking around waiting areas and hiding in stairwells. He is connected to the mysterious woman who has been poisoning her husbands and finally admits that Siriwan, the brothel owner, knows how dangerous the murderer is and has asked him to look out for the safety of her cousin Ladarat. So, the protector has been guarding Ladarat in the hospital and trying to dissuade her from continuing her sleuthing in the best Thai manner: by leaving a ripe durian, an incredibly foul-smelling fruit, in her beloved VW beetle (again, note the absence of blood and violence).

The second main plot line also has two moving parts. The main one centers around an American couple who has been injured, the new husband seriously so, by an elephant which became startled when they were riding him. The newlyweds are joined in the hospital by the husband's parents, and Ladarat is summoned to make sure they understand the severity of the husband's condition. Again, it is her position and status in her hospital world that enables her to gain information and access to patients' charts, information, and conversations. Nurse Ladarat calls upon the year she spent studying medical ethics at the University of Chicago and her accompanying immersion in the ways of Americans in order to understand the injured couple and the husband's parents. When asked by the hospital administrator to run interference with the family so the hospital doesn't lose face, she thinks:

> Of course she would help. There was no question of that. Wasn't this why she'd been sent to receive ethics training at the University of Chicago? Wasn't this why she had

braved a year of extreme cold and rude people, and bland salty food? Food, in fact, that was so tasteless that eating a meal was no more satisfying than reading a menu. She suffered all of that for a year so she could bring the principles of ethics back to the best hospital in northern Thailand [*Rooster* 27].

Regarding her awareness of Americans, when Ladarat is asked to serve as interpreter for the injured couple and parents, she reflects: "No wonder Thailand had never been in a serious war. We are allergic to conflict whereas Americans seemed hardwired to seek it out" (*Rooster* 41) and later explains to a colleague, "Americans will often rearrange the world to suit themselves" (74). Near the end of the novel, as all seems to be going well, Ladarat again reflects, "But if there was one thing she had learned from her year in America, it was that Americans always surprised you. You never could tell" (*Rooster* 26).

In addition to using her study abroad experience, when she needs guidance, Ladarat also calls upon the wisdom of her mentor, Julia Dalrymple, a nurse PhD and professor of nursing at Yale. Dalrymple's book, *The Fundamentals of Ethics*, is always present for Ladarat; she seeks its wisdom, and often quotes from it. For example, "In order to care for the patient … you must care about the patient" (23) and "One must never tell a patient that there is no hope. There is always hope. It's just a matter of helping our patients hope for what is reasonable" (28) and "You must always treat a patient's family as an extension of your patient"(33).

This second plot line also involves a hospital-lurker, a poor hill tribesman who seems to be living in the waiting room and who spends his days staring at Doi Suthep, a mountain in Chiang Mai populated by Hmong families. Eventually, Ladarat gains his trust and learns why he is staying close to the American family. He is a mahout, the keeper of the elephant which caused the near fatal injury; he feels responsible and is waiting to see if everything is going to be all right (It is). Ladarat arranges for him to apologize on behalf of his beloved elephant (which was killed as is the Thai custom when an elephant hurts a person). He comes dressed up, prostrates himself before the family, and with Ladarat's translation, asks for forgiveness. Again, the pieces of the congruent story lines fall into place.

Casarett's second novel is *The Missing Guests of the Magic Grove Hotel (Missing Guests)*. Nurse Ladarat and Police Detective Wiriya return with a new puzzle. Again, there are actually several overlapping plot lines in this cozy novel that depends much more on relationships among characters and ethical questions about palliative hospital care than on complex mysteries rife with violence and murder. There are, however, mysterious events and deaths. *Missing Guests* opens with Ladarat noting that "a frail woman sitting alone below in the courtyard was sad … and brushing away a tear as casually as she could" *(Missing Guests* 3). Soon after this observation,

Detective Wiriya asks for her help in determining why so many foreigners have entered Bangkok, flown to Chiang Mai, and then disappeared, leaving no trace. It seems that some of them have spent time in the palliative care unit of Ladarat's hospital, a unit which has an amazingly low number of recorded deaths relative to the seriousness of the patients' diagnoses. Ladarat and the hospital's intrepid and beloved therapy dog Chi befriend one such patient, the woman observed crying as the novel begins, and are surprised to learn after a few days that she has checked out of the hospital and has gone to the Magic Grove Hotel. Ladarat manages to get a friend hired by the hotel owner/manager, and he monitors those guests entering and leaving the hotel. Meanwhile two young nurses ask for Ladarat's help in determining what is causing a doctor's strange behavior and frequent mistakes; Ladarat's assistant is convinced she has witnessed the actions of a smuggling ring; and foreigners and Thais alike are seemingly being drugged and then robbed as they travel by bus between Bangkok and Chiang Mai. As in *The House of Rooster Happiness,* there is a convergence of these story lines, and at the end, all the pieces of the larger puzzle come together.

Again, the plot/mystery is not really the draw for Casarett's novels. Rather, readers become enticed by (and very fond of) Nurse Ladarat and by Casarett's knowledge of Thai culture and his presentation of Thais' observations about Americans ("farang")—done with subtlety, grace, even humor. For example, he notes that when studying in Chicago, Ladarat suffered "what was easily the worst, most tasteless food ever imagined" (*Missing Guests* 64) and presents Ladarat wondering:

> Everyone had their theories about why farang did what they did. It was a national Thai pastime, trying to explain the strange behaviors of Germans and Australians and Americans. Like pancakes. Why did backpacker hostels all serve pancakes? Banana pancakes usually. What was the appeal of a big, tasteless slab of fried dough? [*Missing Guests* 205].

Casarett (and Nurse Ladarat) also understand that Thailand, often called the "Land of Smiles," has, indeed, many kinds of smiles and they don't all signify happiness. Using phonetic Thai phrases, he presents varieties of smiles that mean, "Of course, I respect your opinion even though it's completely wrong" and "Oh, it could be worse" (*Missing Guests* 22, 83). There are also smiles by people who don't really mean to smile; the teasing smile by someone who knows something another person doesn't; a tolerant smile for someone who is talking nonsense but has to be humored; and a smile that is intended to mask wicked thoughts, but which doesn't quite succeed. Such detail solidifies the insular world of a Thai hospital, known by inhabitants of that world.

But, indeed, these cozies with their insular settings, lack of violence, endearing characters, and final restoration of order also raise ethical questions relevant to end of life care by Casarett's very likeable and believable characters, primarily nurse ethicist Ladarat. For example, there is a point early in the novel when Ladarat is determined to read the charts of every patient who has died at her hospital in order to see if these patients were dying well. She asks herself: "Didn't she have an obligation to ensure that their patients' deaths were good deaths? If they couldn't keep someone alive—and often, too often, they couldn't—then they had an obligation to make sure that the person's death was as peaceful and comfortable as possible" (*Missing Guests* 26). To this end, she labels all files as "Good," "Bad," or "Mixed." Channeling her mentor, Dr. Dalrymple, Ladarat questions the admonition to physicians, "Do No Harm" and concludes that it makes no sense: "In medicine, doctors always do harm. They give medications with side effects and give treatments that make patients feel bad. We just need to try to ensure that those harms we cause are outweighed by benefits" (*Missing Guests* 183). At the novel's end, when Ladarat and Wiriya realize what has happened at the Magic Grove Hotel, they take different positions on a patient's right to die. Wiriya argues that because the bodies in the hotel's teak grove are not registered deaths, a crime has been committed. He states, "They're not buried in a cemetery or cremated. That's a crime, you see?" Latarat replies, as a nurse ethicist must, "A crime against whom?" (*Missing Guests* 337). Thus, in creating Ladarat and the "Ethical Chiangmai Detective Novels," David Casarett has provided authentic glimpses into Thai culture and values and has extended cozy boundaries.

From early definitions of the cozy, with the requisite unobtrusive sleuth who is a trusted member of a specific group, lives and works in a particular environment, and who, therefore, has access and intimate knowledge of participants in her world, the protagonist in cozy mysteries—while retaining these requisite criteria—has also inhabited insular worlds beyond, for example, small country villages or manor houses. Specifically, settings for cozy mysteries can (and do) include academe, especially the world of teachers and, even more specifically, of English professors, and even the medical world of, for example, a nurse ethicist in northern Thailand. Writers of cozy mysteries have definitely extended the boundaries of their sleuths' environs and, perhaps, of their readers' as well.

Works Cited

Casarett, David. *The Missing Guests of the Magic Grove Hotel*. New York: Redhook Books/Orbit (Hachette Book Group), 2017. Print.

Casarett, David. *Murder at the House of Rooster Happiness*. New York: Redhook Books/Orbit (Hachette Book Group), 2016. Print.

Dobson, Joanne. *Death Without Tenure*. Scottsdale, Arizona: Poisoned Pen Press, 2009. Print.
Isenberg, Jane. *Hot Wired*. New York: HarperCollins (Avon Books), 2005. Print.
Schumacher, Julie. *Dear Committee Members*. New York: Penguin Random House (Anchor Books), 2014. Print.
Willett, Jincy. *The Writing Class*. New York: St. Martin's Press (Thomas Dunne Books), 2008. Print.

The Body in the Library
The Library in the Cozy Mystery
Mary P. Freier

The body in the library has been a part of the mystery genre since Anna Katherine Green wrote *The Leavenworth Case* (1878), the first mystery to feature a body in a library. Charles A. Goodrum pointed out in 1979 that the early bodies in libraries in mystery fiction were found primarily in private libraries in the homes of nobility or wealthy landowners, but that, since the publication of Agatha Christie's *The Body in the Library* (1942), public libraries are as likely to feature bodies as private ones (Goodrum "Overdue" 269–70). Since Goodrum's writing, however, bodies are more likely found in public libraries, usually small, rural, nonacademic libraries funded by the community and open to the public. These public libraries are government-funded entities that serve the entire community and are considered by many to be a feature of democracy. Like the public library, the cozy mystery is more democratic than its predecessor the traditional, Golden Age mystery. Cozy mysteries set in libraries focus on the community and an employee of that community, as opposed to Golden Age novels, which focused on the elite and a gifted individual detective. Although the community supports and funds these libraries, they are often at risk. Since the 1970s, library novels focus on threats to libraries and their communities. The body discovered in the library brings attention to these threats, and, when the murder is solved, the threat to the library is also removed, and the community celebrates its library. The library may have to make some changes to deal with the threat or prevent future threats, but resilience is a sign of a healthy library. The body, therefore, serves to emphasize the health of the library. As S.R Ranganathan, in his fifth Law of Library Science, declared, the library "is a growing organism" (Ranganathan 382). Thus, the body in the library serves to show that the library is alive and well.

The body in the library was already a cliché when Agatha Christie wrote a novel of that name; she admitted as much in the Author's Foreword. Christie also thought that the body should be dissonant with the setting of the library (Cook 43). Despite the continued use of the cliché, murder set in a library is still shocking; as Aurora Teagarden thinks in *Real Murders*, the threat of violence is particularly distressing "in this quiet and civilized building where people came to pick out nice quiet civilized books" (Harris *Real* 230). The presence of a murdered body in a library is still an effective device because the library is still culturally significant. What libraries signify, however, is a matter of discussion.

Libraries inspire fear, for various reasons. This fear might be inspired by libraries' traditional architecture, which can be reminiscent of a Gothic cathedral. However, the fear of libraries is rooted in more than surface architectural qualities. Matthew Battles suggests that the fear of libraries is really the fear of the weight of accumulated knowledge (Battles 14–15), while Gary P. and Marie L. Radford look to Michel Foucault to suggest that the idea of a complete collection of materials in perfect order makes the library patron feels like a transgressor and creates fear as well as guilt (Radford and Radford 308, 310–11). Patrons fear violating the rules, but their fear is made greater because they are not certain that they know the rules or even how the library is organized. In Jorge Luis Borges' "The Library of Babel," the organizing principles of the library are unknown, even to the librarians: although the narrator can tell us how many letters are in the alphabet that the books are composed in, and how many pages in each volume, he must admit that although he has perhaps searched for "the catalogue of catalogues," the idea that the Library contains "all books" and is therefore complete has not lead to lasting "extravagant happiness" for any of the librarians (Borges 52, 54–55). The magnificent fictional library in Umberto Eco's *The Name of the Rose* has organizing principles known only to the librarian, who has been using his knowledge to hide materials (Garrett 374). Eco admitted that his actual experiences in European research libraries that treat all patrons like thieves inspired his fictional library (Eco 10).

The perfectly-ordered, complete library where the patron is made to feel at least unwelcome and at most like a thief is essentially static. Library policies, procedures, and personalities may make the patron feel like a transgressor simply for using materials; removing an item from the collection, even through a legitimate transaction, destroys the perfection of the collection, but preserving the collection's completeness and perfection also renders it static. Library paraprofessional turned historical romance novelist Kate Ivory recognizes this stasis and connects it with death when she thinks of the Bodleian Library in *Oxford Exit* as a dead space holding the works of dead male authors, since the materials are not used because they are of little interest to the university community. At the conclusion of the novel, she is pleased when stolen materials that have been sold to a special collection in the United States cannot be recovered; the materials will actually be used in their new home (Stallwood 37, 180–81).

But not everyone connects the library with perfection, order, stasis, and death. John Buschman uses the work of Jürgen Habermas on democratic principles as well as that of Ray Oldenburg's theory of the "third space" to describe the cultural significance of the library. Buschman believes that libraries might, like coffeehouses, be a third space: a place outside of work or home where people gather to exchange ideas in a democracy. Having information freely available in a space that is open to all promotes democracy, and libraries welcome patrons to use this space for meetings as well as for access to information. Buschman's image of the library, needless to say, is certainly one that librarians seek to promote (Buschman "Integrity" 290–92; Buschman "Transgression" 37–40; Buschman and Leckie 21).

Mystery fiction, even cozy mystery fiction, portrays both the fear-inspiring and welcoming elements. At first glance, the library in these novels seems like a place that inspires fear. After all, these libraries are settings for murder. The fact that the body in the library could even become a cliché seems to validate the negative, threatening interpretation of the library. But libraries are often presented as dangerous simply because they are libraries. Bookstacks in large research libraries obscure sightlines. The trademark quiet of the library magnifies any noise. Placing a character in one of these spaces after closing and with the lights off creates instant suspense, and, if a killer joins that character in the stacks, the situation immediately becomes threatening. For example, a serial killer chases librarian Katie Townsend through the stacks of the New York Public Library in *Katie's Terror* (Fisher 251–57), and a murderer tracks down Crighton Jones in the closed and dark Werner Bok library in *Dewey Decimated* (Goodrum *Dewey* 172–82). Even small public libraries are threatening after closing: A murderer chases librarian Lucy Richardson through the Lighthouse Library in the Lighthouse Library series (Gates *Book* 296–305), and a murderer ambushes library director Lindsey Norris in her small public library after closing in the Library Lover's series (McKinlay *Books* 290–93). On another occasion in this series, a man shoots at Lindsey and chases her through the stacks even before the library closes (McKinlay *Borrowed* Kindle Locations 2643–2669). In *Library, No Murder Allowed*, two men injure the children's librarian while they fight with a pair of scissors, someone terrifies a library page in a tunnel between parts of the building, and the murderer takes the library director to the roof of the library with intent to kill (Steiner 16, 50–51, 54, 240–44). In *Real Murders*, Aurora Teagarden becomes convinced that one of her co-workers is the murderer while working at night in the library (Harris *Real* 227–33). In *Last Scene Alive*, while Aurora works the evening shift, a terrorist on the run interrupts her, and then the murderer disrupts that encounter. The terrorist rescues Aurora from the murderer and then escapes (Harris *Last* 244–54).

Kathleen Paulsen has a number of "accidents" in the library where she has just started work in the Magical Cats Mysteries. In *Curiosity Thrilled the Cat*, a shutoff valve burns her when the radiators are removed, she slips on some water in the library entryway, and a large, heavy roll of plastic falls from some scaffolding and injures her (Kelly *Curiosity* 105, 227). While Kathleen cannot imagine why the contractor is sabotaging the renovation and attacking her, it is clear from his refusal to take her calls and his constant slowdowns on the work that he is doing so. In another novel in the series, a murderer threatens Kathleen in the library (Kelly *Copycat* 307).

Many fictional people also die in fictional libraries, and most of these deaths are murders. In Terry Curran's *All Booked Up*, enough people are murdered in the library that the police tell a librarian that "I don't presume to know what you folks do in this library that generates dead bodies, but this place is straining its per capita limit and frankly gives me the creeps" (Curran 100). But murder in the library is hardly unusual in the mystery genre. Bodies are found in storage closets (Abbott 24; Adams 18), in public areas of the library (Borthwick 251; Cannell 12, 266; Davidson 25; Davis 209–10; Dean 31; Grant 94; McKinlay *Borrowed* Kindle Location 273–78; Steiner 52–3; Wingate 45; Wolzien 1), in librarian offices (Davis 30; Gates *Read* Kindle location 774; Mills 56), crushed in the compact shelving (James *No* 112, 144), in the bookstacks (Goodrum *Dewey* 48; Madison 14, 17, 23, 25; Miller 18–19), in the basement (Belle 29–32; Meier 10; Sprinkle 27; Van Gieson 5), bricked up in walls (Buehler 45; Thomas 1), during library occupations to protest budget cuts (Coward 8), in the rare book stacks (Dobson 94; Gates *Book* 35; Gates *Spook* Kindle Location 927; Paton Walsh 7), and the ladies room (Ludwig and Mowery 20–21; Skom 3–4).

Library-related deaths occur in every entry in Eva Gates' Lighthouse Library series. So ubiquitous are the murdered bodies in or near the Lighthouse Library that when Lucy Richardson reports the latest discovery to her library director, she responds, "Not again!" (Gates *Reading* 69). Multiple library murders occur in the Miss Zukas novels, although the murders take place in different institutions: the Bellehaven Public Library, a Native American cultural institution, and the site for the new public library building (Dereske *Catalogue* 46; Dereske *Library* 30–31; Dereske *Raven's* 9–10).

Another library that attracts murder is the bookmobile belonging to the Chilson District Library in the Bookmobile Cat Mysteries. Minnie

Hamilton and her cat, Eddie, find bodies on two separate occasions while out on the bookmobile (Cass *Lending* 42; Cass *Wrong* 12), and Minnie's volunteer assistant is murdered during a lunch break (Cass *Borrowed* 59). Minnie also discovers a corpse in the Chilson District Library building (Cass *Cat* 12–13). Even cozy mystery fiction portrays libraries as dangerous for both patrons and employees.

However, in mystery fiction and in reality, libraries are more under threat than threatening. Libraries in mystery fiction are endangered by a multitude of forces, from finances to people who want to challenge library holdings to library boards to wealthy and influential citizens. These fictional threats mirror many of the real threats that libraries face: Wayne Wiegand tells of a council meeting in Tacoma, Washington, where a suggestion to close all of the library buildings was welcomed as "thinking outside the box" (Wiegand 378–79). Similar thinking threatens libraries in mystery fiction.

The Bellehaven Public Library, setting for the murder in *Miss Zukas and the Library Murders*, is very successful, but it is "overcrowded and overused" (Dereske *Library* 7). Miss Zukas is a bit disgusted when the police ask her if she had noticed anything unusual about a patron who might be involved in the murder, as she doesn't really have time (or space) to notice such things (Dereske *Library* 42). The Bellehaven Public Library is also threatened by budget cuts, since, as one city councilman claims, all information is now available on the internet (Dereske *Bookmarked* 16). When planning begins for a new library building, the staff's hopes are dashed when their major donor is murdered (Dereske *Catalogue* 53).

Mark Salinger, the director of the Santa Linda Library in *Library, No Murder Aloud*, perceives his library as being "under siege" by a man named Perry Webb, head of an organization called Citizens Against Higher Taxes, This group is campaigning in support of a public referendum that would replace the public library with a private rental service. Mark is no stranger to defending his library's funding, but this referendum could cost the library all of its municipal funding (Steiner 18, 21).

Minnie Hamilton in the Bookmobile Cat Mysteries proposed a bookmobile when her library district closed a number of its smaller branches (Cass *Lending* 13–14). While the library budget provides funding for the vehicle itself, it cannot provide funding for staff. Minnie must rely on volunteers since she needs the help to deal with bookmobile patrons and it isn't safe to be out in rural areas alone. Throughout the series, Minnie worries that the board will cancel bookmobile programming altogether and is concerned about making her case to the library board for continued funding. When the primary donor for a foundation declares bankruptcy, possible grant funding disappears (Cass *Borrowed* 27). When one of Minnie's volunteers is killed, his sister files suit against the library for negligence. Minnie must prove he was murdered in order to preserve the bookmobile and even her own job (Cass *Borrowed* 76). Later, the bookmobile's budget is jeopardized when the board hires a director who is more interested in electronic products than in face-to-face service (Cass *Wrong* 24).

Smaller academic libraries, like that of Athena College, where librarian-sleuth Charlie Harris works as archivist in The Cat in the Stacks series, also face financial threats. Charlie explains that college budget money goes to sports teams, not "A piddly little thing like an archive with rare or irreplaceable documents" (James *Arsenic* 110–11). In another entry in the series, a murder takes place in the basement of the library, and the lack of security cameras prompts Charlie to again bemoan the lack of funding available to libraries (James *No* 125).

But even large, supposedly well-funded research libraries like *Dewey Decimated*'s Werner Bok are not financially secure. The director of the Werner Bok explains to Edward George, retired library director of Yale University, that someone has been writing letters to the library board suggesting that recently-purchased rare books are not particularly valuable. While that possibility alone is disturbing, the real threat is that "the foundations are cancelling grant programs right and left and we've been running on grants for the past twenty years.... We've had a rich game going on our vast dignity and tradition, but if the word gets out that we don't know what we're doing, they could wipe us out in a week. We couldn't even cover salaries" (Goodrum *Dewey* 38). This novel was written in 1977, and fictional libraries have been threatened by loss of funding well into the twenty-first century.

United States libraries are not unique in being under financial threat. Early in the twenty-first century, Great Britain's library councils closed so many public libraries for financial reasons that a group of authors published a collection of essays about the importance of libraries (The Reading Agency). A number of mysteries published during this period portray the effect of these budget cuts and closures.

In *Open and Closed*, a murder takes place in a London library during an all-night sit-in protesting the local Council's decision to close it, despite its success by every kind of library measure—headcount, circulation, gatecount, and customer satisfaction (Coward 21). When Israel Armstrong takes a job in Tumdrum, a small village in Northern Ireland, he discovers to his horror that the library building has been closed due to a "resource allocation" and, worse, that he will be driving the "mobile learning centre" or bookmobile (Sansom 4–5, 14, 17). The bookmobile isn't even in good condition: "the remains of a bus in a faded, rusting cream and red livery: there were rust patches as big as your fist, and what looked like mushrooms growing around the windscreen." It also has no shelving. Israel also learns that all of the books are missing, and he is expected to find them (Sansom 39, 46, 92).

The Blessed Oliver Plunkett library, a small library in a rural area of Ireland, is old, the furnace doesn't work, and most of its patrons are impoverished and elderly. Things are so dire that when her supervisor, Miss Tuohy, wants librarian Ellie to add up the user statistics for a report to the Library Committee, Ellie suspects that the statistics are more likely to hasten their closure than to demonstrate the need for the library (Mills 36). When the Library Committee announces that the library is being closed, the regular patrons respond by occupying it (Mills 167–68).

The Blessed Oliver Plunkett's staff also finds the existence of another library in a nearby town to be threatening. This library is the antithesis of the Blessed Oliver: "a superstructure housing community information services and the latest technology ... staffed by bright young things on first-name terms with their public. The chief librarian, William R. Pender, wore aftershave. He was energetic and ambitious. The only person in the municipal system to have achieved this rank below the age of forty, he was known as Billy the Kid" (Mills 15). The staff of the Blessed Oliver perceive Billy the Kid and his library as enemies, enemies who will eliminate them.

Libraries, however, are threatened even when well-funded. The local public library in *A Firm Foundation* is closed because a city board member believes that there is a vein of gold beneath it (Rodgers 238). The Lighthouse Library is under constant threat from some of its own board members, who hire an efficiency expert to evaluate the library, certain that the expert will recommend that the library be closed (Gates *Booked* 263; Gates *Reading* 97). At the same time, a local mayoral candidate runs on an explicitly anti-library platform; he wants the library closed so that the lighthouse can become "an income-generating tourist attraction" (Gates *Booked* 169–70).

In *Died in the Wool*, a small-town public library must compete for funding in a public town meeting. Monah Trenary, the librarian, worries about the ethics of listening to gossip about another town office's strategy, but realizes that "the battle for the funds donated to the city kept getting more and more intense .... The library, woefully behind the times, needed new computers, and she needed to learn something—anything—to keep the playing field level" (Ludwig and Mowery 8).

Censorship campaigns can also threaten libraries. Censorship became a threat in both real and fictional public libraries in the 1990s, when a group called Family Friendly Libraries (FFL) formed to battle the American Library Association's (ALA) supposed "stranglehold" on library collections. FFL maintained that ALA encouraged librarians to treat parental concerns as "censorship cases," and, when the internet became a part of public libraries, FFL demanded internet filters on library computers because of concerns for children (Gaffney 187–90).

A similar group attacks the Bellehaven Public Library in the Miss Zukas mysteries by submitting a list of books they want removed: "Two of the books, including Madonna's *Sex*, weren't even owned by the library, although twenty-three patrons had requested them since the article appeared in the Bellehaven *Daily News*" (Dereske *Island* 1). In another entry in the series, a new member of the library board claims that the library makes "smut" available to the public (Dereske *Death's* 23–24). At the Mirabeau Public Library in the Jordan Abbott series, a woman attempting to ban materials seems to follow the FFL model by claiming that materials are "anti-family" (Abbott 5–6). In *Library, No Murder Aloud*, a local woman loudly announces that the library "is making dirty books available to children!" (Steiner 18–19).

Of course, the murders that take place in these libraries also threaten their existence. The director of the Lighthouse Library starts warning her staff about referring to the location of the most recent murder near or in the Lighthouse Library; when a body is found near the library wall, she wants them to "to imply she was found in the marsh, rather than in the shadow of the lighthouse wall" (Gates *Booked* 133). When a third body is discovered near the library, she wants it made clear that the most recent body was not found in the library or on the library grounds, but in an area near the library (Gates *Reading* 96–97). Minnie Hamilton's friend, restaurateur Kristen Jurek, asks if having a body found in the library would be as bad for library business as it would be for her if a body were found in her restaurant, and the idea gives Minnie pause (Cass *Cat* 21). Kayley Burke, new curator of the Fowling First Editions Society Collection (of Golden Age mysteries) must also contend with negative publicity when a body is discovered in the Society's library, although some wonder if it isn't an appropriate occurrence, given Christie's novel (Wingate 55).

Bodies in libraries underscore the threats to libraries, and even create new ones; having a murderer on the loose is even more worrisome than bad publicity. But as the crime is solved, the community recognizes the library's value. When the library is threatened, its supporters rally around it. Indeed, the library's position as a "third space" or heart of a community is strongly reinforced. The warmth and community that the library provides is contrasted with the violent death that has taken place in it. Since cozy mysteries celebrate small communities, the library is thus portrayed as the center of such a community. As the crime is solved, the threat to the library is removed. Many of these mysteries end with a celebration of the library.

After the murder in the library is solved, when Minnie Hamilton presents her case for the bookmobile to the library board, they give her strong support (Cass *Wrong* 329). The efficiency expert tasked with evaluating the Lighthouse Library concludes that "you have a highly unorthodox library.... But extremely efficient and wildly popular with both local residents and visitors" (Gates *Booked* 263). The Lighthouse Library holds a celebration of voting during the mayoral campaign to underscore the library's value to democracy. The celebration is so successful that the anti-library candidate's wife comes out in favor of the library, telling Lucy that her husband will have to change his campaign: "I've missed this.... I love this library, but [the campaign manager] told me Doug wants to close it down so it would be better if I stopped coming.... I think I'll tell him that Doug needs to get rid of that idea instead" (Gates *Reading* 298).

Other libraries find themselves celebrating at the end of the trials that have beset them in these novels. Kathleen Paulsen manages to complete the renovations at her library, to local acclaim: "You turned the library back into an important part of this town" (Kelly *Cat* 241). Despite being accused of murder in her first months in Sweet Briar, librarian Tori Sinclair ends *Sew Deadly* by celebrating the opening of her library's new children's room (Casey 269). The destruction of the library in *A Firm Foundation* is halted when a child begins a sit-in to protect a nest of endangered squirrels, a tactic that stops the wrecking ball just long enough for the whole town to join him, and for minister's wife Kate to arrive with the paperwork proving that the council member has no claim to the land (Rodgers 270–74). When Monah Trenary, in *Died in the Wool*, makes her presentation requesting grant money from the town council, she tells them about the Digital Divide and how libraries close it. Monah manages to make her case effectively by emphasizing the library's contribution to an informed citizenry, and her request is granted (Ludwig and Mowery 108–09).

When "Billy the Kid" tours the Blessed Oliver Plunkett, Ellie tries to see the library through his eyes. Unfortunately, she sees only how the library has fallen into rather irregular habits in the service of their patrons: for example, they serve soup in the afternoon to help keep their elderly patrons warm. But Billy sees something entirely different. He not only recommends that the Blessed Oliver Plunkett remain open with a larger budget, he threatens to quit if the committee doesn't meet his demands (Mills 268–70).

These novels also illustrate how much libraries have changed. As librarian Lindsey Norris explains: "Libraries aren't really known for being that quiet anymore.... And while higher learning is awesome, we're also the place where you can learn how to actually do stuff ... whatever you can think of, we can find the directions" (McKinlay *Likely* Kindle

Location 2529). Librarian Cassandra Mitchell, in the Karl Alberg mysteries, shares Lindsey's confidence in the library mission. She looks around her small-town public library: "at the senior citizens sharing newspapers and comfortable chairs with the unemployed; at Paula, checking out books for a young mother whose infant slept in a stroller at her feet; at the shelves of books, hundreds of books—my work, my comfort, and my joy, she thought, feeling slightly dizzy; Cassandra looked around the library, a place of learning, of diversion, of refuge" (Wright 111). Cozy mysteries show how libraries change to serve their communities.

In *The Case of the Missing Books*, Israel Armstrong discovers that the books weren't missing. Community members, who distrusted the council that regulated the library and bookmobile, appropriated the entire collection and maintained and even circulated it. When Israel decides to leave Tumdrum, the community has a farewell party for him, and he surprises himself by having no farewell speech: "He thought ... that he would say something about how libraries were important to communities, how they brought people together, and represented all that was good about mankind's striving for knowledge and self-understanding. But ... There was no point in him telling people what they already knew" (Sansom 317). He leaves the party in order to say goodbye to the bookmobile and finds his feelings about the bookmobile have changed: "Israel went up to the van, to the rusty creamy red flanks of the van, and patted her, as though patting the rear of a cow—something he must have seen Ted do dozens of times, but not something that he himself had ever before had either the urge or intention to do, but which suddenly seemed to come naturally...." (Sansom 318). He enters the bookmobile to take one last look at the shelving that has finally been installed, and discovers that "on every one of those beautiful grainy shelves there were books—hardbacks, paperbacks, sitting like old friends gazing down at him in silent amusement. They were back" (Sansom 319). He then learns about the villagers' deception, that they were determined not to lose their library. They returned the books because they decided that Israel could be trusted. Israel responds to that trust by deciding to stay in Tumdrum (Sansom 321–23).

The body in the library, while a durable cliché, does not represent the death of libraries. While libraries can be perceived as dead, unused spaces bound by order and regulations, they are also used a places to explore ideas and learn. The library represents learning and democracy to its small community. Libraries in cozy mysteries are important community centers, where people can even sometimes get the information to solve a murder. A body in the library serves to emphasize how much a living organism a library truly is.

Works Cited

Abbott, Jeff. *Do Unto Others*. Ballantine Books, 1994. *Jordan Poteet Mysteries*.
Adams, Deborah. *All the Crazy Winters*. Ballantine Books, 1992.
Battles, Matthew. *Library: An Unquiet History*. Large Print ed., Thorndike, 2003.
Belle, Josie. *50% Off Murder*. Berkley Pub. Group, 2012. *Good Buy Girls*.
Borges, Jorge Luis. "The Library of Babel." *Labyrinths: Selected Stories and Other Writings*, edited by Yates, Donald A. and James E. Irby, New Directions, 1964, pp. 51–58.
Borthwick, J.S. *The Student Body*. St. Martin's, 1986.
Buehler, Luisa. *The Rosary Bride*. Echelon Press, 2003.
Buschman, John. "The Integrity and Obstinacy of Intellectual Creations: Jürgen Habermas and Librarianship's Theoretical Literature." *The Library Quarterly*, vol. 76, no. 3, 2006, pp. 270–299.
———. "Transgression or Stasis? Challenging Foucault in LIS Theory." *The Library Quarterly*, vol. 77, no. 1, 2007, pp. 21–44.
Buschman, John, and Gloria J. Leckie, editor. *The Library as Place: History, Community, and Culture*. Libraries Unlimited, 2007.
Cannell, Dorothy. *How to Murder the Man of Your Dreams*. Bantam Books, 1995. *Ellie Haskell*.
Casey, Elizabeth Lynn. *Sew Deadly*. Berkley Pub. Group, 2009. *Southern Sewing Circle*.
Cass, Laurie. *Borrowed Crime*. Obsidian, 2015. *Bookmobile Cat Mysteries*.
———. *Cat with a Clue*. Obsidian, 2016. *Bookmobile Cat Mysteries*.
———. *Lending a Paw: A Bookmobile Cat Mystery*. Obsidian, 2013.
———. *Wrong Side of the Paw*. Berkley Prime Crime, 2017. *Bookmobile Cat Mysteries*.
Cook, Michael. *Narratives of Enclosure in Detective Fiction: The Locked Room Mystery*. Palgrave Macmillan, 2011. *Crime Files Series*, general editor Bloom, Clive.
Coward, Mat. *Open and Closed*. Five Star, 2005. *Don Packham and Frank Mitchell*.
Curran, Terrie. *All Booked Up*. Dodd, Mead, 1987.
Davidson, Diane Mott. *Sweet Revenge*. William Morrow, 2007.
Davis, Lindsey. *Alexandria*. St. Martin's Minotaur, 2009. *Falco Series*.
Dean, S.F.X. *By Frequent Anguish*. Walker and Co., 1982.
Dereske, Jo. *Bookmarked to Die*. Center Point Large Print ed., Center Point, 2006. *Miss Zukas*.
———. *Catalogue of Death*. Avon, 2007. *Miss Zukas*.
———. *Miss Zukas and the Island Murders*. Avon, 1995. *Miss Zukas*.
———. *Miss Zukas and the Library Murders*. Avon, 1994. *Miss Zukas*.
———. *Miss Zukas and the Raven's Dance*. Avon, 1996. *Miss Zukas*.
———. *Miss Zukas in Death's Shadow*. Avon, 1999. *Miss Zukas*.
Dobson, Joanne. *The Maltese Manuscript*. Poisoned Pen Press, 2003.
Eco, Umberto. "What Is the Name of the Rose: Umberto Eco and Libraries." *FOCUS*, vol. 14, no. 1, 1989, pp. 11–15.
Fisher, David E. *Katie's Terror*. Morrow, 1982.
Gaffney, Loretta M. "'Is Your Public Library Family Friendly?' Libraries as a Site of Converavtive Activism, 1992–2002." *Libraries and the Reading Public in Twentieth-Century America*, edited by Pawley, Christine and Louise S. Robbins, University of Wisconsin, 2013, pp. 185–99. *Print Culture History in Modern America*, general editor, Danky, James P. et al.
Garrett, Jeffrey. "Missing Eco: On Reading The Name of the Rose as Library Criticism." *Library Quarterly*, vol. 61, no. 4, 1991, pp. 373–388.
Gates, Eva. *Booked for Trouble*. Obsidian, 2015. *Lighthouse Library Mysteries*.
———. *By Book or by Crook*. Obsidian, 2015. *Lighthouse Library Mystery*.
———. *Read and Buried*. Crooked Lane, 2019. *Lighthouse Library Mysteries*.
———. *Reading Up a Storm*. Obsidian, 2016. *Lighthouse Library Mysteries*.
———. *The Spook in the Stacks*. Crooked Lane, 2018. *Lighthouse Library Mysteries*.
Goodrum, Charles A. *Dewey Decimated*. Crown Publishers, 1977.
———. "An (Overdue) Tribute to the Librarian." *Murderess Ink: The Better Half of the Mystery*, edited by Winn, Dilys, Workman Publishing, 1979, pp. 269–71.
Grant, Charles L. *The Hour of the Oxrun Dead*. Doubleday, 1977.
Harris, Charlaine. *Last Scene Alive*. St. Martin's, 2002. *Aurora Teagarden*.
———. *Real Murders*. Berkley Pub. Group, 1990. *Aurora Teagarden*, 2010.

James, Miranda. *Arsenic and Old Books.* Penguin, 2015. *Cat in the Stacks.*
_____. *No Cats Allowed.* Berkley Prime Crime, 2016. *Cat in the Stacks.*
Kelly, Sofie. *Cat Trick.* Obsidian, 2013. *Magical Cats.*
_____. *Copycat Killing.* Obsidian, 2012. *Magical Cats.*
_____. *Curiosity Thrilled the Cat.* Wheeler Publishing Large Print Cozy Mystery ed., Gale, 2011. *Magical Cats.*
Ludwig, Elizabeth and Janelle Mowery. *Died in the Wool.* Barbour Pub., 2011. *Massachusetts Mayhem.*
Madison, Ada. *The Probability of Murder.* Berkley Prime Crime, 2012. *Professor Sophie Knowles.*
McKinlay, Jenn. *Books Can Be Deceiving.* Center Point Large Print, 2011. *Library Lover's.*
_____. *A Likely Story.* Berkley Pub. Group, 2015. *Library Lover's.*
_____. *On Borrowed Time.* Penguin Publishing Group, 2014. *Library Lover's.*
Meier, Leslie. *Valentine Murder.* Kensington Books, 1999. *Lucy Stone.*
Miller, Jeffrey. *Murder at Osgoode Hall.* ECW Press, 2004. *Amicus Curiae.*
Mills, Jackie. *Ellie.* Brandon, 2000.
Paton Walsh, Jill. *The Wyndham Case.* St. Martin's, 1993. *Imogen Quy.*
Radford, G. P., and M. L. Radford. "Libraries, Librarians, and the Discourse of Fear." *Library Quarterly*, vol. 71, no. 3, 2001, pp. 299–329.
Ranganathan, S. R. *The Five Laws of Library Science.* The Madras Library Association, 1931.
The Reading Agency. *The Library Book.* Profile Books, 2012.
Rodgers, Anne Marie. *A Firm Foundation.* Guideposts, 2009. *Mystery and the Minister's Wife.*
Sansom, Ian. *The Case of the Missing Books.* Harper, 2006. *Mobile Library.*
Skom, Edith. *The Mark Twain Murders.* Council Oak, 1990.
Sprinkle, Patricia Houck. *Murder at Markham.* St. Martin's Press, 1988.
Stallwood, Veronica. *Oxford Exit.* Scribner's, 1995. *Kate Ivory.*
Steiner, Susan. *Library: No Murder Aloud.* Fawcett Gold Medal, 1993.
Thomas, Emily. *If Walls Could Talk.* Guideposts, 2014. *Secrets of the Blue Hill Library.*
Van Gieson, Judith. *The Shadow of Venus.* New American Library, 2004. *Claire Reynier Mysteries.*
Wiegand, Wayne A. "To Reposition a Research Agenda: What American Studies Can Teach the LIS Community about the Library in the Life of the User." *The Library Quarterly*, vol. 73, no. 4, 2003, pp. 369–382.
Wingate, Marty. *The Bodies in the Library.* Berkley Prime Crime, 2019. *A First Edition Library Mystery*, vol. 1.
Wolzien, Valerie. *All Hallows' Evil.* Fawcett Gold Medal, 1992. *Susan Henshaw Mysteries.*
Wright, Laurali R. *Strangers among us.* Scribner's, 1996.

Aurora Teagarden, the Cozy and the Southern Gothic

Jessica Gildersleeve

Perhaps surprisingly for those familiar with her immensely popular *The Southern Vampire Mysteries* (2001–2013) and its television adaptation *True Blood* (2008–2014), Charlaine Harris's earliest publication and longest-running collection is her *Aurora Teagarden* series (1990–present), a series of cozy mysteries featuring a librarian amateur sleuth. The popularity of the cozy as a genre fundamentally depends upon its capacity for comfort and order, or as Richard B. Schwartz has pointed out, "[t]he belief that crimes actually can be solved and criminals brought to justice provides emotional reassurance as well as the lineaments of a larger worldview, a middle-class reading of life that will not be an interim one, but rather an eternal one, as stable as the societies it is designed to preserve" (7). This essay will consider the extent to which the *Aurora Teagarden* novels and their Hallmark adaptations (2015–present) commit to such reassurance and stability through two main arguments. First, I suggest that rather than upholding the genre, the *Aurora Teagarden* book series seeks to destabilize the veracity of the cozy: that is, the very possibility of the genre as in any way associated with something like "real life" by increasingly permitting the intrusion of the violence and darkness of the Gothic as the series progresses. Despite its efforts, the cozy cannot keep these invasions out: the Gothic asserts its primacy over the tamer genre. By associating violent crime with the leisure activity of the "Real Murders Club," as well as with librarian Aurora's love of crime fiction, the novels show how we attempt to put those disruptions at a distance, making them safe by their association with story. In addition, the sequence of romantic subplots in which the narratives engage, and the ultimate establishment of Aurora in the shelter of marriage and motherhood, are explicitly positioned as the desire for an escape or a balm for such invasions.

In contrast, however, I posit that the *Aurora Teagarden* television series attempts to undo this relationship between the cozy and the Gothic, and thereby remove any real sense of threat or danger. Indeed, the adaptations, produced by Hallmark, a studio noted for its conservative values, star Candace Cameron Bure, an actor whose wholesome public image is most prominently identified with the family television shows *Full House* (1987– 1995) and *Fuller House* (2016–present).[1] The innocence and resolution foregrounded in the television adaptation firmly reestablish the narrative as "a cozy" in a number of ways, primarily the characterization of Aurora by Cameron Bure, and the relocation of Aurora's hometown of Lawrenceton from Georgia, in the historically fraught location of the American South, to the northern state of Pennsylvania, a site associated with civilization and order. More than this, the television series constructs for Aurora a static identity which keeps her in a position of virgin girlhood, more akin to Nancy Drew or Miss Marple than her sexualized novel counterpart. Importantly, then, the *Aurora Teagarden* television adaptation depends upon the containment and negation of the Gothic threat of Harris's more disturbing and supernatural narratives, as well as the threat associated with the Southern Gothic as a genre. In its conservative reconstruction, however, the series ironically highlights the extent to which Harris's novels can be read as engaged with the Southern Gothic as a construction of American historical identity. This essay will suggest, therefore, that the conservatism of the *Aurora Teagarden* television series is dependent on the active management and containment of the Gothic disruptions of the contemporary nation which repeatedly invade the small town of the novels. Together, these arguments make clear the sense in which Harris's work ironically mobilizes the cozy as a socio-political commentary inextricable from its Gothic roots.

Like its literary predecessors in detective fiction of the Golden Age, the cozy mystery is a genre characterized by its revulsion of disorder and chaos and the return to Edenic innocence. Crucially, the cozy

> ...assumes the existence of a once-happy society under challenge by evil (or at least, reactionary) forces that, we are assured, will not finally prevail.... The course of the narrative is to chart the actions of the perpetrators who have overturned or are at least threatening the status quo, block or blunt them, and, ultimately, exile them, so that the society they are undermining or obstructing can be returned to its previous, happy condition [Schwartz 5].

Such narratives are often accused of being formulaic, dominated by tropes: the female, middle-aged amateur sleuth owns a bakery or bookshop in a quaint village populated by unusual figures, lives alone with her cat, and has romantic links to a detective or police officer. She is heavily involved with her orderly and hierarchical community, as well as her friends and family (Vester 31). Her identity is thus bound to her small-town location:

as Aurora observes, the "idea of moving out of my normal orbit scared the heck out of me. I was okay, right here in Lawrenceton. I knew who I was, here" (Harris, *Last Scene Alive* 113). The amateur female sleuth of the cozy works alone to solve the crimes occurring close to home and, as in Golden Age detective fiction, any bloodshed associated with these murders is kept firmly out of the picture (31). The emphasis, for the (typically female) fan of the cozy, is on following the clues and solving the mystery, so that order is restored by the novel's end, "thus experiencing the satisfaction of a world that is unambiguous and in which chaos ... can be overcome" (31, 33). It is a "predictable" world, one "not unlike that of the children's book," Schwartz notes (6). The comparison identifies the sense in which the cozy might be said to be prey to a naiveté of both plot and genre, refusing complication, preferring not simply rationality but formula and expectation, from "once upon a time" to "happily ever after."

However, cozy mysteries are often far more engaged with their social and economic contexts than such a view might express. In their emphasis on the disruptions to a small community explored from the perspective of an observant female sleuth, cozies can be seen to "articulate, explore and offer a response to contemporary anxieties, specifically: the role of the individual in an increasingly fragmented and alienating society; the impact of global and national economics and finance on the individual and the community; and the particular effect of these anxieties on women" (Waters and Worthington 199–200). Importantly, such disruptions come from outside of that close-knit community, so that rather than suggesting a rotten core at work to undermine the social idyll, any disturbance is shown to be a product of the invasion of modern pressures (201). In the novels Aurora and her neighbors frequently complain about the expansion of Lawrenceton's nearest urban center, Atlanta, so that her own small town is becoming simply a suburb of the larger urban sprawl. More than this, however, this urban growth is associated with an increase in crime, as the dangers of the city reach out to its satellite towns. "Lawrenceton used to be such a quiet town," the Lawrenceton Chief of Police notes, "but the city is reaching out to us here, and I guess in a few years we'll have a crime rate like Atlanta's" (Harris, *Three Bedrooms, One Corpse* 18), while a woman who makes her living repairing windows broken by burglars tells Aurora that the crimes should be attributed to "[t]hose people coming out from the city.... They come out here to get away from the city, but they bring their city habits with 'em'" (Harris, *A Bone to Pick* 43–44).

It is in this engagement with the problems and anxieties of the modern world, rather than the exclusion and containment so often assumed of the genre that these particular iterations of the cozy find resonance not only with detective fiction of the Golden Age, but the literary predecessor of both forms: the Gothic. American Gothic literature often demonstrates the nation's struggle with understanding and integrating its violent history into an understanding of modern identity. In particular, the American South is subject to a Gothic stereotyping (Lloyd 79) which means that it "functions as an 'Other' place to cast off the rest of the nation's difficult past and social problems, so that the ghosts haunting contemporary society become a regional matter that finds the South bearing all Gothic burdens" (82). Positioning the South as the nation's Other in this way is a form of Gothic repression, Teresa Goddu asserts:

> Identified with Gothic doom and gloom, the American South serves as the nation's "other," becoming the repository for everything from which the nation wants to dissociate itself. The benighted South is able to support the irrational impulses of the Gothic that the nation as a whole, born of Enlightenment ideals, cannot ... the imaginary South functions as the nation's "dark" other [and] neutralizes the Gothic's threat to national identity [4].

Harris's *Southern Vampire Mysteries* and their television adaptation, *True Blood*, typify the Southern Gothic, emphasizing the geographical isolation of the small town of Bon Temps, Louisiana, and the way in which the extreme heat of the region leads to similar states of emotional and psychological extremes in its characters, particularly a kind of languid passion for sex and violence. In these narratives, "the 'deviance' of the regional setting, seen in relation to the supposedly heteronormative and cohesive larger American nation," is exposed through the lurking presence of the supernatural (Leavenworth 39). But it is not only the "construction of peoples or individuals as monstrous or 'other' which mark out the contemporary American Gothic, Catherine Spooner notes, but 'the legacies of the past and its burdens on the present'" (qtd. in Troy 59).

Indeed, Southern Gothic literature "has as much to do with location, and the nature of life as determined by geography, as it does with the supernatural and the monstrous," Caroline Ruddell and Brigid Cherry point out (41). The American South is "haunted by slavery" (Amador 164), tainted by America's fraught history of "repression" and "racism," such that it is, Sabrina Boyer says, "an emotionally loaded geographic idea" (27). Harris's Sookie Stackhouse narratives are thus "a loose but obvious allegory," explicitly engaged with these discourses of America's violent past and its legacies of civil rights in the present, as well as other modern debates about marginalization and tolerance, such as those to do with gender and sexuality (Tyree 32). It is in this respect that Southern Gothic literature might be seen to disturb the expectations of regional narratives, since these works are persistently preoccupied with such larger questions about the contemporary nation. Considering the cozy in terms of its intersections with the Southern Gothic in Harris's narratives, therefore, complicates the sense in which the cozy upholds the "belief that crimes actually can be solved and criminals brought to justice[,] provid[ing] emotional reassurance as well as the lineaments of a larger worldview, a middle-class reading of life that will not be an interim one, but rather an eternal one, as stable as the societies it is designed to preserve" (Schwartz 7). Rather, the *Aurora Teagarden* novels expose such a conviction as a fiction readily destabilized by forces of social change.

The series' first novel, *Real Murders* (1990), establishes the *Aurora Teagarden* narrative as one interested in the failures of the fictional constructs preferred by the cozy. A meeting of the "Real Murders Club" is interrupted when Aurora discovers a club member brutally killed in the same manner as one of the famous cases the club has discussed. Aurora's investigation uncovers a copycat killer hoping for widespread notoriety by mimicking the details of "real murders." The crimes the club discusses are thus underscored as, precisely, "real," reminding the club members and the reader that these violent crimes are not simply a hobby, a story rendered safe by their club meetings, but a function of violence and horror in the real world. In this brutal interaction between the real and the imitation the story points up the impossibility of the cozy's naïve protection of the moral boundaries of the community through its fictive idyll. Diane Waters and Heather Worthington observe that "cozy characters frequently remind readers that they are in a fictional world, which enhances the sense of safety the texts confer. Where used, punning titles also implicitly inform the reader that the content is light and that graphic violence, explicit sex, or bad language will be absent" (205). However, this is not the case in the *Aurora Teagarden* series. Harris does make frequent use of punning titles—for instance, *A Bone to Pick* (1992), *Dead Over Heels* (1996), *Last Scene Alive* (2002). The novels also make regular reference to the stories' fictionality: not only is Aurora a librarian, employed in the business of books and an expert in mysteries and detective fiction (a subject in which she holds a Master's degree), but the authenticity of her name is regularly called into question, as is her ability to survive repeated attempts on her life despite her comically small frame. In addition, her sometime boyfriend and eventual husband, Robin Crusoe, is a mystery writer in possession of a similarly unlikely name. *Last Scene Alive* makes this particularly explicit in a series of self-referential moves: the novel Robin published based on the murders committed in *Real Murders* has been adapted to film and is to be shot on location in Lawrenceton. That the fictional world of the film, based on the real world of Aurora's life, is then disrupted by real violence and murder, confirms the impossibility of the cozy's belief in justice and order.

Each of the novels also works to refuse any kind of happy resolution: even when Aurora marries her first husband, Martin Bartell, he is quickly established as a "frightening" character rather than a figure of safety and security (Harris, *The Julius House* 40), that is, as any kind of conclusion to a marriage plot for Aurora. He is nothing like the husbands of her friends: "a hardware store owner, an insurance salesman, a farmer, a lawyer" (105). Indeed, even her relationship with Detective Arthur Smith, a staple of the cozy, had been thought "exotic" by her peers: "Police officers were too close to the wormy side of life, the side we didn't see because we didn't turn rocks over" (105). The distinction between Aurora and her friends suggests, however, her ironic distance from the tropes of the cozy: here, a police officer is not a reassuring moral center, but a symbol of proximity to danger. But it is Martin who figures the greatest threat, entirely disrupting the resolution of the marriage plot. Just like the house he purchases for Aurora to renovate and restore, but which is revealed to harbor the horrific remnants of a family murder, rather than being the tall, dark, handsome stranger as whom he first appears, Martin is revealed to have a dangerous history of arms dealing and criminal connections.

> What we did was ... sell guns. Really, we were giving them away.... I thought, at least at the beginning, that I was doing something good for my country. I never made any personal profit. But it's become harder and harder to know who the good guys are.... Some of these people were okay, some were crazy. They were all very tough. A few were just—bandits (99).

As Martin admits, then, there is no stable point of morality in the *Aurora Teagarden* novels: it is "harder and harder to know who the good guys are." Martin is ultimately killed as a result of his own niece's attempts at fraud and blackmail, so that Aurora is moved from new bride to widow within the space of just a few novels. Even when Aurora eventually marries Robin and gives birth to a daughter, they are still subject to domestic invasion and criminal disruption (*Sleep Like a Baby* [2017]). There is no site of resolution or safety, the *Aurora Teagarden* novels suggest, least of all marriage and motherhood for women.

Despite this, it would be difficult to assert the *Aurora Teagarden* narrative as a feminist one, but rather a series which considers the impossibility of the cozy's insistence on a "utopian space" of empowerment and freedom from expectations and norms. Although Aurora often exhibits the traditional characteristics and behaviors of the "Southern Belle," she also self-consciously uses these as a kind of mask or a process of anonymity to protect her true intentions as part of an investigation: "Anytime you pull that fluff-headed southern eccentric routine," her ex-lover Arthur complains, "you're putting out a smoke screen" (Harris, *Poppy Done to Death* 23). Such a bland identity, Aurora suggests in her attitude to the actress playing her in *Last Scene Alive*—"Her accent was generically southern. I rolled my eyes, all to myself. Why can't Hollywood comprehend that there are regional accents in the South, besides Cajun?" (59)—is emblematic of an inattention to the nuances of a region, and thus the construction of an illusion of small-town life in the cozy. Aurora's attention to her appearance and her weight—her self-consciousness about her height, the clothes she selects, a regular exercise habit, and comparisons to her glamorous mother and friends—also suggests the way in which she is subject to, rather than "outside dominant beauty norms" (Vester 31). The extraordinary strength and beauty of her friend Angel Youngblood—whose own name also implies her fictionality or supernaturalism—provides an ironic counterpoint highlighting the unlikely possibility of a preternaturally beautiful heroine. But it is in her refusal of such ideals of the female detective that Harris mobilizes the cozy as social critique. Indeed, John Charles, Joanna Morrison, and Candace Clark argue that "[t]he appeal of the amateur sleuth to many mystery readers is that the detective is so very ordinary. Amateur sleuths lack the skills and training professional investigators have and instead must rely on their own instincts and wits" (18). The amateur female sleuth, they add, uses that anonymity, their immersion in a known community, as well as their freedom from the legal regulations which can restrict a professional detective's behavior, to gather gossip, information, and clues (19).

It is true that Aurora therefore finds her origins in the amateur sleuths of Golden Age detective fiction, but her professional research training as a librarian, as well as her extensive knowledge of old murders as part of her commitment to the Real Murders Club, signifies her adoption of popular characteristics of professional female detectives of late twentieth-century fiction. Linda Mizejewski has pointed out the transition from the "amateur female sleuth—Nancy Drew in her roadster, Miss Marple in her rocker" to the professional female detective or forensic specialist in popular mysteries of the late twentieth century (1–2). For Mizejewski, the shift indicates growing "empowerment and equalization" for women, as well as an important sense of "freedom—the detective earns her own paycheck but isn't tied down to a desk, computer, cubicle, kitchen, or nursery" (4). Jennifer Burek Pierce insists that Aurora should not be considered as anything but an amateur sleuth since "[h]er professional skills do not aid her in solving the murder" (20), and any reference to her profession "draws heavily on stereotypes," such as Aurora's dowdy clothes and large glasses (19). However, I suggest that Aurora Teagarden can be seen to represent an evolution of these two categories of female sleuth, since she is not employed as a detective (and indeed actively dislikes Detective Lynn Liggett-Smith, a frequent antagonist of the series), but uses her research training and her profession as a librarian to inform her cases. That she is made independently wealthy through an inheritance from an elderly female friend in the second book of the series (*A Bone to Pick*) gives her an even greater freedom: Aurora is from then on not beholden to either her work or the finances of a romantic partner or family member. In this respect she is a disruptive force: another ex-lover, Father Aubrey Scott, "is not the only one who found the concept of a woman of leisure unsettling" (Harris, *Three Bedrooms, One Corpse* 29).

Aurora's troublesome presence also extends to her social attitudes and their conflict with her broader community. Although Aurora solves the crimes presented in the novels, the fundamental social problems they indicate remain: not simply negative emotions which motivate crime, like revenge and jealousy, but a sense of a broader social dis-ease. Resolution, their presence indicates, is not then so simple. For example, the novels indicate a pervasive and insidious racism in Lawrenceton: "there are many, many churches in Lawrenceton," Aurora explains, parenthetically, "and I am sorry to say there is little racial mixing on Sundays" (Harris, *Last Scene Alive* 67). This persistent racism is exhibited by several members of Aurora's community, as one witness she interviews comments on the unlikelihood of the name "Duncan for a black man" (Harris, *The Julius House* 92), while another is "none too fond of having to do work for a black man.... Though having Debbie working for *her* didn't seem to be a problem" (Harris, *Three Bedrooms, One Corpse* 39), and one of her mother's employees casually notes that "younger couples don't mind having a black realtor, and the black clients love it" (Harris, *A Bone to Pick* 174). Importantly, however, such attitudes are not attributed to Aurora, and she internally if not externally critiques the prejudice. Rather, she often exhibits a greater worldliness than those around her, a kind of outsider view of the attitudes of the small town. For instance, when she witnesses a friend hide her homosexuality she asks: "Why do you do that, Eileen? ... Is that really you?" (Harris, *Three Bedrooms, One Corpse* 113). These are, of course, not issues particular to Lawrenceton, but are indicative of broader social problems at work. By introducing these into the protected world of the cozy, Harris insists on the impossibility of ignoring the association of social injustice with the presence of crime and violence.

The *Aurora Teagarden* novels are therefore preoccupied with ironically establishing and ultimately undoing the expectations of the cozy mystery as part of their social critique. They refuse "a world that makes moral, political, and cultural sense, a world whose structures and values are generally acceptable to us, a world whose coherence we seek to preserve and extend" (Schwartz 5), mobilizing a readerly dissatisfaction which might lead to social change. The series' television adaptation, however, does not invoke such a strategy. I will turn now to a discussion of the Hallmark *Aurora Teagarden Mysteries* in order to consider how their conservatism reestablishes the stereotypical conventions of the cozy but undoes the broader social engagement provided by the novels.

The Gothic—typically in the form of horror and the supernatural, like Harris's *True Blood* series—can be seen to be particularly suited to the television format, Helen Wheatley argues, because of its association with the domestic, as well as its episodic and thus suspenseful form. In this way Gothic television also reaches its ideal audience, the female viewer (qtd. in Subramanian 114). Indeed, "[i]t is television's ontological status as a domestic medium which potentially emphasizes the Gothic rendering of homes and families, drawing parallels between the domestic space on screen and those homes in which the dramas are being viewed" (Wheatley qtd. in Keetley 91). Thus, television Gothic finds its niche in the way that it reflects (literally) our own homes and families, suggesting the way in which the home becomes a site of instability and danger rather than stability and reassurance. As Ruth Griffin asks, "what happens if the home is no longer the safe haven that we imagine?" (87). However, the construct of popular mysteries, like the cozy narrative, seeks to reassure the viewer anxious about such a question. The production of cozy mystery television programs thus acts as a counter to such pervasive Gothic instability and uncertainty "invading" the domestic space via the television. In the resolution and punishment of the crime, as well as the upholding of wholesome family values, cozy television mysteries like the *Aurora Teagarden* adaptation function to reassure viewers of the order of the known world. It is for this reason, however, that the adaptation misses the opportunities for social engagement offered by its novel counterparts.

Agnieszka Stasiewicz-Bieńkowska has shown how the "dynamics between the literary and the televised versions of [the] Sookie Stackhouse story ... shed light on the ways in which *True Blood* complicates, resists and reconfigures the gendered scripts of sexual freedom and constraint produced by the novels" (231). For example, whereas Sookie is infantilized in the novel series, presented as the student to her lover Bill as teacher, the television adaptation renders her as an agent of her own sexuality to a greater extent (231). The opposite is true of *Aurora Teagarden*: whereas the novels present Aurora's character as undergoing a series of dark changes as a function of her encounters with violence and murder, such that she becomes increasingly isolated, bitter, and withdrawn as the series progresses, the television program presents her character as a static one. That is, while her refusal of Martin's marriage proposal and purchase of her own property, for example, might seem to figure her as independent, the way in which these are coupled with Aurora's insistence upon traditional feminine values restricts the growth she is offered in the novels as she grapples with conflicts between her own sense of agency and the expectations of women according to Southern values. More than this, the television adaptation of *Aurora Teagarden* may be seen to present a wholly conservative interpretation of the novels which counter their critical engagement with the cozy as a genre.

The program stars Candace Cameron Bure, an actress whose wholesome family image is a product of her early starring role on *Full House* and its later reprisal in *Fuller House*, frequent roles in other Hallmark movies, typically Christmas romances, and her position as a kind of Christian spokeswoman through the authorship of books advocating traditional Christian values in the modern world. This re-envisioning of Aurora through such a chaste perspective positions her as a kind of virginal Nancy Drew or Miss Marple figure, far more aligned with traditional cozies than the novels might present. Mizejewski suggests that such amateur female sleuths are thrilling to female readers because of "their mobility, their capacity to follow their curiosity on forbidden nondomestic and nonromantic quests. Even though the girl sleuth might flirt with her beau, she ended her adventure snaring a criminal rather than a husband" (16). However, the adaptation does not figure Aurora's status as a single woman in such independent terms: rather, her insistence on a certain number of dates before permitting Martin to be known as her boyfriend and her rejection of his marriage proposal, as well as her refusal of the possibility that he stay overnight in her home, associates those decisions with her chastity rather than her agency. Similarly, the reconfiguration of Martin as a former CIA agent rather than an arms dealer casts him as wholly good and lawful, rather than dangerous, as in the novels, as does the removal of his friends and bodyguards, the Youngbloods. That he does not die, widowing Aurora, as in the book series, but leaves Lawrenceton in order to protect a CIA colleague, reinforces this view. This Aurora would never receive a poison pen note, as does her novel counterpart, reading, "You Whore she's not even buried and your after her boyfriend" (*sic*; Harris, *Last Scene Alive* 154), nor would she confess that she "would be a terrible minister's wife, inwardly if not outwardly" (Harris, *Three Bedrooms, One Corpse* 27).

The relocation of Aurora's hometown, Lawrenceton, from Georgia in the American South to Pennsylvania in its North also points to the television adaptation's conservatism. The shift indicates a rejection of the possibility of understanding the television narrative in terms of the Southern Gothic, and thus even of any Gothic association at all. The move North would be shocking to the novels' Aurora, who harbors a xenophobic grudge against "Yankees": "Who'd want to name a street after Gettysburg?" she asks. "I'm not one of those unreconstructed southerners who refers to the War of Northern Aggression, but it seemed I'd been indoctrinated to some extent" (Harris, *A Fool and His Honey* 117; see also Harris, *The Julius House* 61). Moreover, since the Southern Gothic "imagery of relaxation, decadence and heat" is removed in favor of its contrasting "general American national identity of the moral Protestant with a strong work-ethic," the adaptation removes or represses the capacity of the narrative to "[blur] the boundaries of race, gender and sexuality" associated with that genre (Amador 163). For instance, the program removes Perry Allison's (now Perry Dell) psychological instability; the homosexuality of characters integral to crimes and their resolution; the representation of gory violence, especially that enacted by Aurora herself; Aurora's broken family; and the awareness of informal racial segregation. Instead, the narrative shifts to a Gothic tradition associated with Washington Irving's "The Legend of Sleepy Hollow" (1820): in other words, an ironic use of the genre which refuses its possibility in the modern world.

Whereas the *Aurora Teagarden* television series does its best to minimize the presence of the threat of the Gothic and the moral instability of the modern world, Harris's original narratives question the constructs of the cozy and its exclusion of such dangers. Considering the influence of the Southern Gothic on the *Aurora Teagarden* novels permits an understanding of their social critique, and thus the capacity of the cozy to disrupt its generic expectations.

Notes

1. In 2019, the channel faced criticism after it removed advertisements which featured a lesbian couple (Murphy).

Works Cited

Amador, Victoria. "The Gothic Louisiana of Charlaine Harris and Anne Rice." *The Modern Vampire and Human Identity*. Ed. Deborah Mutch. Houndmills: Palgrave Macmillan, 2013. 163–76.
Bailey, Peggy Dunn. 'Female Gothic Fiction, Grotesque Realities, and *Bastard out of Carolina*: Dorothy Allison Revises the Southern Gothic.' *Mississippi Quarterly* 63.1–2 (2010): 269–90.
_____. "Talismans of Shadows and Mantles of Light: Contemporary Forms of the Southern Female Gothic." In Street and Crow, *The Palgrave Handbook of the Southern Gothic*, 445–60.
A Bone to Pick. Dir. Martin Wood. Hallmark Movies & Mysteries, 2015.
Boyer, Sabrina. "'Thou Shalt Not Crave Thy Neighbor": *True Blood*, Abjection, and Otherness.' *Studies in Popular Culture* 33.3 (2011): 21–41.
Brown-Syed, Christopher, and Charles Barnard Sands. "Some Portrayals of Librarians in Fiction—A Discussion." *Education Libraries* 21.1/2 (1997): 17–24.
A Bundle of Trouble. Dir. Kevin Fair. Hallmark Movies & Mysteries, 2017.
Charles, John, Joanna Morrison, and Candace Clark. *The Mystery Readers' Advisory: The Librarian's Clues to Murder and Mayhem*. Chicago: American Library Association, 2002.
Dead Over Heels. Dir. Terry Ingram. Hallmark Movies & Mysteries, 2017.
The Disappearing Game. Dir. Terry Ingram. Hallmark Movies & Mysteries, 2018.
Edwards, Justin D. "Contemporary American Gothic." *The Cambridge Companion to*

American Gothic. Ed. Jeffrey Andrew Weinstock. Cambridge: Cambridge University Press, 2017. 71–83.
Ford, Jennifer. "Murder with Southern Hospitality: An Exhibition of Mississippi Mysteries." *Primary Source* 26.1 (2004): 8–15.
A Game of Cat and Mouse. Dir. Mark Jean. Hallmark Movies & Mysteries, 2019.
Goddu, Teresa. *Gothic America: Narrative, History and Nation*. New York: Columbia University Press, 1997.
Griffin, Ruth. "Dreams, Nightmares and Haunted Houses: Televisual Horror as Domestic Imaginary." *Imago* 6.4 (2015): 86–104.
Harris, Charlaine. *Real Murders*. 1990. New York: Berkley Prime Crime, 2007.
_____. *A Bone to Pick*. 1992. New York: Berkley Prime Crime, 2008.
_____. *Three Bedrooms, One Corpse*. 1994. New York: Berkley Prime Crime, 2008.
_____. *The Julius House*. 1995. New York: Berkley Prime Crime, 2008.
_____. *Dead Over Heels*. 1996. New York: Berkley Prime Crime, 2008.
_____. *A Fool and His Honey*. 1999. New York: Berkley Prime Crime, 2009.
_____. *Last Scene Alive*. 2002. New York: Berkley Prime Crime, 2009.
_____. *Poppy Done to Death*. 2003. New York: Berkley Prime Crime, 2009.
_____. *All the Little Liars*. New York: St Martin's, 2016.
_____. *Sleep Like a Baby*. New York: Minotaur, 2017.
An Inheritance to Die For. Dir. Michael Robison. Hallmark Movies & Mysteries, 2019.
The Julius House. Dir. Terry Ingram. Hallmark Movies & Mysteries, 2016.
Keetley, Dawn. 'Stillborn: The Entropic Gothic of *American Horror Story*.' *Gothic Studies* 15.2 (2013): 89–107.
Last Scene Alive. Dir. Martin Wood. Hallmark Movies & Mysteries, 2018.
Leavenworth, Maria Lindgren. '"What Are You?": Fear, Desire, and Disgust in the *Southern Vampire Mysteries* and *True Blood*.' *Nordic Journal of English Studies* 11.3 (2012): 36–54.
Lloyd, Christopher. "Southern Gothic." *American Gothic Culture: An Edinburgh Companion*. Ed. Joel Faflak and Jason Haslam. Edinburgh: Edinburgh University Press, 2016. 79–91.
Mizejewski, Linda. *Hardboiled and High Heeled: The Woman Detective in Popular Culture*. London: Routledge, 2004.
Murphy, Heather. "Hallmark Channel Pulls Zola Ads Featuring Brides Kissing." *New York Times* 13 Dec. 2019 <https://www.nytimes.com/2019/12/13/style/hallmark-channel-ads.html>.
Pierce, Jennifer Burek. "Professional Reading? Or the Case of Librarian Detectives in Mystery Fiction." *Indiana Libraries* 24.2 (2005): 19–22.
Real Murders. Dir. Martin Wood. Hallmark Movies & Mysteries, 2015.
Reap What You Sew. Dir. Terry Ingram. Hallmark Movies & Mysteries, 2018.
Ruddell, Caroline, and Brigid Cherry. "More than Cold and Heartless: The Southern Gothic Milieu of *True Blood*." *True Blood: Investigating Vampires and Southern Gothic*. Ed. Brigid Cherry. London: IB Tauris, 2013. 39–55.
Schwartz, Richard B. *Nice and Noir: Contemporary American Crime Fiction*. Columbia: University of Missouri Press, 2002.
Stasiewicz-Bieńkowska, Agnieszka. "Lustful Ladies, She-Demons and Good Little Girls: Female Agency and Desire in the Universes of Sookie Stackhouse." *Continuum* 33.2 (2019): 230–41.
Street, Susan Castillo, and Charles L. Crow. "Introduction: Down at the Crossroads." In Street and Crow, *The Palgrave Handbook of the Southern Gothic*, 1–6.
Street, Susan Castillo, and Charles L. Crow, ed. *The Palgrave Handbook of the Southern Gothic*. Ed. Street and Crow. London: Palgrave Macmillan, 2016.
Subramanian, Janani. "The Monstrous Makeover: *American Horror Story*, Femininity and Special Effects." *Critical Studies in Television* 8.3 (2013): 108–23.
Three Bedrooms, One Corpse. Dir. Lynne Stopkewich. Hallmark Movies & Mysteries, 2016.
Troy, Maria Holmgren. 'The Nineteenth Century in Jewelle Gomez's Vampire Novel *The Gilda Stories* and the TV Series *True Blood*.' *American Studies in Scandinavia* 42.2 (2010): 57–73.
Tyree, JM. "Warm-Blooded: *True Blood* and *Let the Right One In*." *Film Quarterly* 63.2 (2009): 31–37.

A Very Foul Play. Dir. Martin Wood. Hallmark Movies & Mysteries, 2019.
Vester, Katharina. 'Bodies to Die For: Negotiating the Ideal Female Body in Cozy Mystery Novels.' *Journal of Popular Culture* 48.1 (2015): 31–43.
Walsh, Christopher J. "'Dark Legacy': Gothic Ruptures in Southern Literature." *Southern Gothic Literature*. Ed. Jay Ellis. Pasadena, CA: Salem Press, 2000. 19–34.
Waters, Diane, and Heather Worthington. "Domestic Noir and the US Cozy as Responses to the Threatened Home." *Domestic Noir: The New Face of 21st Century Crime Fiction*. Ed. Laura Joyce and Henry Sutton. Houndmills: Palgrave Macmillan, 2018. 199–218.

Clara and Solange

Two Very Modern Detectives in a Very Cozy World

Jon Wilkins

Clara, Baroness of Linz, strolls along Pall Mall; ahead she sees Solange Fontaine. Solange waves discreetly, Clara nods, regally. We can see why Clara is compared to the "Mona Lisa for her smile, to Fra Filippo Lippi's Madonna for the exquisite clearness of her eyes and the transparency of her complexion, to Viola Tree for the delightfully humorous curve of her lips..." (Phillips Oppenheim 176) and as she approaches, we immediately notice that Solange is a beauty as well, with "Her mouth, small-lipped but fine of long-drawn curve, like a bow before it is bent for the arrow.... Hers was the modern beauty of line not of bloom...." (Tennyson Jesse 4).

We see before us two of the most beautiful women in all of London. But behind their beauty are minds as sharp as knives. It is always interesting to see how the female detective is viewed in literature, this perhaps before the onset of any idea of cozy crime. In the late nineteenth century, we had the pot boiler and the magazine story and they were very different from the detective stories we read in the Golden Age. Solange Fontaine does come from that background, but she is a beauty whereas Catherine Louisa Pirkis in her book *The Experiences of Loveday Brooke, Lady Detective* of 1893 introduces us to a character whose "nondescript appearance allows her to carry out her detective work without being unduly noticeable but, more than this, it also sets her up as a species of 'everywoman'" (Hendrey-Seabrook).

Indeed, two of the most popular women detectives of this time, Mrs. Gladden and Loveday Brookes, pride themselves on the ability to be unseen so that they could insinuate their way into any company. Mrs. Gladden states in *The Female Detective*: "The woman detective has far greater opportunities than a man of intimate watching and of keeping her eyes upon matters near which a man cannot conveniently play the eavesdropper" (Forrester 4). How different they are from my two beautiful detectives Clara and Solange. Mrs. Gladden and Loveday Brooke may have been transgressive in their day, but they were not going to be portrayed as anything other than ordinary so as not to disrupt the status quo.

At the time, Mrs. Gladden and Loveday Brookes were a breath of fresh air in the crime writing genre, but they still had to know their place. They had to show subservience to men and according to Joan Warthling Roberts, the female detective is "a model of submission, outdoes and out thinks her male colleagues without causing a snarl or murmur. She is deferential to every male, offers her own ideas, but does not press them, dresses and speaks unobtrusively" (3). Stephen Knight, on the other hand, writes that "the creators of the early women detectives were trying, against the tide of the male magazines as much as against social attitudes, to offer different and inherently subversive positions and values for detecting crime. The idea that they all pursued ... was that crime can both threaten and be explained by a woman as much as a man" (Knight 79).

All well and good, but what did she look like? In cozy crime how important are looks? Do we as the reader have to suspend belief to the extent that we are the creators of the heroine's beauty? For an example, Oppenheim in his earlier cozy crime novel *Miss Brown of X.Y.O* describes his lead thus: "Miss Brown was wearing a brown mackintosh which had seen better days, and a plain little felt hat, suitable for the weather. Her gloves had been mended, her shoes were tidy and her skirts not too short. She had blue eyes, a rather broad forehead and an attractive mouth. Her complexion, except for the presence of an occasional freckle, was unusually fair and delicate" (6). The non-descript woman. Nothing outstanding, unless we see the brain as a beautiful object. Dorothy Sayers' creation Harriet Vane could never be said to be classically beautiful. Indeed, Wimsey's mother describes her coolly: "...so interesting and a really remarkable face, though perhaps not strictly good-looking, and all the more interesting for that, because good-looking people are so often cows" (*Strong Poison* 26). It is her background that is all important here, not her looks. Her behavior that commands comment and negativity. She does not fit into the mode of a beautiful woman nor does her behavior follow societies norm. She is different. That is her beauty.

For Agatha Christie, Miss Marple was not a beauty. Indeed, if she ever had been, her looks would have faded anyway. Like a Tricoteuse at the guillotine, we first meet Miss Marple in "Thirteen Problems": "Miss Marple wore a black brocade dress, very much pinched in around the waist. Mechlin lace was arranged in a cascade down the front of the bodice. She had on lace mittens, and a black lace cap surmounted the piled-up masses of her snowy hair. She was knitting—something white and soft and fleecy" (1). We later have a more positive description from *Murder at the Vicarage*: "Miss Marple is a white-haired old lady with a gentle, appealing manner...." (22). And a few pages further on: "Miss Marple was an attractive old lady, tall and thin with pink cheeks and blue eyes and a gentle rather fussy manner. Her blue eyes often had a little twinkle in them" (14).

Attractive? Perhaps, but an old lady. Interesting face? But no beauty. Characteristic? Whatever that means, though it seems to be damning with faint praise. None of our lead characters are beauties, but they are the personification of cozy crime of the era, the bench-mark for detective agency. But mostly a realization of the superiority of brains over beauty. But then we have Clara and Solange.

Where does cozy crime fit in? How should we define cozy crime and how do our beautiful protagonists fit into the genre? Alan Bradley, author of the wonderful Flavia de Luce stories, told me: "I must say that I dislike intensely the phrase 'cozy crime.' I prefer to think of the genre (another despised word) as one which exercises the brain rather than the emotions, although that's not an easy concept to trot out in a catchy phrase. 'Intelligent murder?'" (Bradley). He is not alone amongst authors who dislike the phrase cozy crime. But there again, he is one of the very literary crime authors who does not understand why we must package stories into certain slots. I agree. They should be taken on merit.

Erin Martin the cozy-mystery web site founder writes, in as nearly perfect a definition as we can get, and the one which I will take as my starting point for discussion:

> Cozies very rarely focus on sex, profanity or violence. The murders take place off stage and are often relatively bloodless ... while sexual activity ... between characters is only ever gently implied and never directly addressed. The cozy mystery usually takes place in a small town or village. The small size of the setting makes it believable that all the suspects know each other. The amateur sleuth is usually a very likeable person who can get the community members to talk freely about each other. There is usually at least one very knowledgeable, nosy, yet reliable character in the book who is able to fill in all of the blanks, thus enabling the amateur sleuth to solve the case [https://www.goodreads.com].

Solange Fontaine and Carla Baroness of Linz contradict this. Solange is university educated, has written theoretical and academic books, and is an advisor to the French police as well as a renowned private investigator. Clara is a professional, and a highly paid one at that, who can pick and choose her cases from a wide range of upper-class contacts. For small town or village substitute the small enclosed world of upper-class London. She frequents the salons and tea rooms of only the very best establishments.

Do we then have to define domestic setting? Do all cozy mysteries have to be set in the drawing room or the library? If the murder does not occur inside the house what do we then have? This definition seems to exclude so much, and I don't think we can take it on board. However, in almost every cozy crime novel I have read, the crime will "take place in a small, picturesque town or village, with characters who I could envision having as neighbors or friends. On the whole, they are usually normal, everyday characters you might have known at one time in your life. Cozies don't usually involve a lot of gory details or explicit 'adult situations'..." (https://www.cozy-mystery.com).

But firstly, I will investigate Solange Fontaine, who appears in two volumes of short stories: "A pale slim young woman, half French, elegant and intelligent...." (Colenbrander 167). Solange Fontaine appeared in Fryn Tennyson Jesse's series of short stories, run in *Premier Magazine* and included "Mademoiselle Lamotte of the Mantles," "The Lovers of St. Lys," "Emma-Brother and Susie-Sister," "The Green Parrakeet," "The Mother's Heart," "What Happened at Bout-du-Monde," "The Sanatorium," and "The Railway Carriage."

"Mademoiselle Lamotte of the Mantles" was published in *The Metropolitan* (August 1918) as well. "The Lovers of St. Lys" was also published in *Metropolitan* (August 1919). Tennyson Jesse next wrote another set of Fontaine stories: "The Black Veil," "The Pedlar," "The Reprieve," "The Canary," and "Lot's Wife." "The Black Veil" and "The Pedlar" both appeared in *The London Magazine* (respectively, September 1929, and December 1929). All five later works were reprinted in *The Solange Stories* (London: Heinemann, 1931).

Fryn Tennyson Jesse was fascinated by crime and murder: "Murder, to my mind, is the most fascinating of all phenomena, because it is the one in which the game can never be worth the candle, also because it has behind it a more endless combination of motive than any other act" (www.batteredbox.com).

In the stories, Solange Fontaine is the daughter of an English mother who has died and a French father, Professor Fontaine, who has a laboratory in their house in southern France near Nice. He is a criminologist and sometimes works for the Sûreté. We are never quite sure what he is up to, though in an early story he is "...investigating the vagaries of a disease he supposed to be brought on by a venomous insect" (*http://www.batteredbox.com*). Solange has also written a book on criminology, and of what makes a murderer. This theme, of what exactly makes a murderer tick, runs through many of the Solange stories. In "The Green Parrakeet," we find that "Solange and her father, Professor Fontaine, were occupied in compiling a treatise upon the relative amount of convolutions in the brains of apes, of moral imbeciles, and in normal human brains" (http://www.batteredbox.com).

She has this intellectual bent that is constantly being reinforced for the reader, lest we forget she is all about brains as well as beauty. It is her intellect that is more important than her beauty for Fryn Tennyson Jesse, but for the reader it is her beauty. We are perhaps nowadays more enamored of the appearance of our lead detective. We rarely see a dour drab detective on screen, save perhaps for "Vera" in the eponymous series by Anne Cleeves, but that is played to excess, I feel, and takes us away from the story. No, most lead characters at this time are stunning because beauty interferes with the perception that these women are capable of intellectual endeavor. So perhaps we just accept that Solange is stunning, and in our unpleasant twenty-first century view just dismiss her as a vacuous woman because when the books were written women were still held in that Victorian view of being decorative items on the arm of a man. In this way the transgressive manner of the female detective was able to flourish. She is seen, but unappreciated. Her beauty is all that counts. Her intelligence, if she had any, is ignored as it was not the thing to be. A woman, fighting crime? Their clients have to bite the bullet and move on. What is interesting is that for all the initial misgivings their clients do accept them and are soon won over and appreciate the talents of the detective and not the woman. But then does the woman rely too much on her looks to inveigle her way into conversations and plots? If she sees this as her main oeuvre, does this demean her sex and make a caricature of her working relationship? For me, the woman is a woman, powerful and assertive. For the onlooker the narrow view of beauty has to be ignored and the skills of the detective enjoyed and treasured.

Several of the stories in the first series take place in southern France, where Tennyson Jesse's own father had been a chaplain, and some are set in the Caribbean. They still remain in the cozy environment as they are in secluded, hard to get to spots where the participants in the novel are part of a closed community. In this first series of stories, the characters are quite complex and often have unconventional romantic relationships, which can lead to murder. Solange is involved in the lives of these characters, which fits in with the cozy crime definition. The murders, though not the main crimes that Solange investigates, are not explicit, the love making unseen. In this way we see the cozy crime attitude emphasized. We have the transgressive act, highlighted in Auden's essay, but it is unseen. The sex is unseen. Nothing is shown that will take us off the scent of the crime. We know what has taken place and do not need the sensational hyperbole that can go alongside it. We have the cozy environment, the cozy players. The setting of villages in the Caribbean again fall into the correct category. Not all the characters are, of course, sympathetic, but neither are all the people we meet in real life. Solange often intrudes on the lives of these characters. Solange believes that some people are born to be murderers, or at least have a strong predisposition to commit murder. In the story "Emma-Brother and Susie-Sister," Solange seems to think that people who murder are just that, murderers, no matter what the influences are upon them.

The relationships between husband and wife or parent and child are often destructive. There is no overt sexualization in her stories. Another tick in the cozy crime box. Indeed, many of the Solange stories show a rejection of sexuality as if she is afraid of it. This does not really fit into the cozy definition, as we do not like to see overt statements about sex in our reading. Solange, as the first series ends, is deciding whether to allow herself to fall in love. Tennyson Jesse explains it in these words:

> She had always recognized that her nicely balanced instincts would not only be upset, but probably destroyed by the intrusion of "falling in love." Just as a woman who is an artist is bound to lose her artistry—for all but the art of living—as long as the madness lasts, even if her art of creation be enriched afterwards, so Solange would lose that instinct for being aware of evil, together with the science with which it was allied, as soon as she allowed herself to be swept away by the common lot of women [http://www.batteredbox.com].

The meaning is clear, that for women physical sex can ruin their intellectual abilities. Tennyson Jesse explains it in these words: Despite the discussion of "nicely balanced instincts" and "art of creation," the meaning is clearly that physical sex can ruin higher abilities, so there is no place for sex here!

Fryn Tennyson Jesse's emphasis was on female sexuality, and she is very negative about British attitude toward adulterers. This British attitude is reflected in the Solange story, "The Canary," in which we learn that a young woman has taken up with a lover, but hopes to keep her respectability. But Fryn Tennyson Jesse's attitude toward sexuality was not, however, as straightforward as this comment might indicate. In the same story, a man who can understand but not experience sex and love is effectively dead. Of course, it is once again "of its time," but the affairs of the heart or sex are quite prominent here. There is no overt discussion of this, but it seems to overlay the text, a classic case of "show not tell" by the writer allowing the readers to imagine and make up their own mind. Does Solange use her charms to inveigle the murderer Ames into his confession? Does he delay in killing her because she is so beautiful? It seems plain that he does, though there is no overt telling us of how this came about from Fryn Tennyson Jesse; we just get the feeling the writer wants to achieve, which is a wonderful talent. We see that Charles Evelyn, the man she saved from the gallows who had been accused of murder, says his heart has been taken by Solange, but she is able to deflect this by stating: "Not for me—I don't want that. I should lose my gift if I ever gave way to that supreme and beautiful selfishness" (Tennyson Jesse 97).

Charles Evelyn in "The Reprieve" is beguiled by her; he is taken by her beauty and wants to marry her. However, we can see that this theme in only the second story of the first book is one that Solange will not fall into, the trap of marrying, so any comments now about her sexuality or so-called need for a man are superfluous. She is very much her own woman and will cut her own path; she will not take on any man as her work depends upon her being single and alone.

A decade earlier, Fryn Tennyson Jesse had written a second series of stories about Solange Fontaine; the stories began in the August 1929 issue of *The London Magazine* and were collected in the 1931 book *The Solange Stories*. Solange is introduced thus: "…she looked so young that she could still afford to smile…. Her ashen-fair hair, close cropped in the courageous modern manner showed her small ears, high-set above the fine egg-like curve of her jaw. She was straight and well-knit as an athletic boy, and her olive-grey eyes looked out quietly and directly … hers was the modern beauty of line…" (4). So, we have an author aware of the sexuality of a woman and a character who is beautiful and takes on board her writer's world. Is Solange Fryn? I don't think so, but she does represent how a woman thinks in this era. Solange has a classical beauty that seems to cross over time. She is shown to the reader in the description above and the reader then must fill in any gaps. She is introduced as the modern woman of the time, but we can see beyond that. We interpret her beauty as pure and subtle. Solange is also aware of how she should look. After rushing for her train in "The Railway Carriage," she is quickly aware that "All was well, she was her usual clear, fine-set self, save for an unwonted flush on her pale cheeks" (Tennyson Jesse 270). Appearance is all. It is unladylike to be flushed!

It was a well-worn Victorian trope that

> Innocence was what he demanded from the girls of this class, and they must not only be innocent but also give the outward impression of being innocent. White muslin, typical of virginal purity, clothes many a heroine, with delicate shades of blue and pink next in popularity. The stamp of masculine approval was placed upon ignorance of the world, meekness, lack of opinions, general helplessness and weakness; in short, recognition of female inferiority to the male [Petrie 184].

What a fight the woman of that era had to break these shackles of expectation. It is no wonder that Solange was not prepared to hold up her wrists in submission.

In "The Canary," a story in the second series, a young woman has married an older man for security without understanding the physical demands that will be made upon her as a wife: "He was one of those men whose idea of love-making resembles Swedish massage; was always running his hand down her arm, or caressing her neck when a third party such as me was present. I can tell you I've seen her flesh creep with distaste" (Tennyson

Jesse 125). And "The dreams had not lasted beyond the honeymoon. To begin with, that difficult experiment had taught Marjorie, who till then had preserved an innocence in thought and deed which is rather rare, that one could pay too highly for the material comforts of four meals a day. She did not have to earn them behind a counter, but she earned them nevertheless" (Tennyson Jesse 132). In both cases we can see the distaste shown to advances made and to the duty in the bedroom that Marjorie endures. She knows her duty, but does not like to do her duty.

Solange's attitude is perhaps more manifest in "The Reprieve" when she tells us: "This farmyard world of sex, how nauseating it was!" (Tennyson Jesse 83). Tennyson Jesse's attitude toward sexuality was not, however, as straightforward as this comment might indicate. In the same story, a man who can understand but not experience sex and love is effectively dead. This is quite outspoken for its day and shows her repugnance, but also her willingness to state how she feels publicly. A very brave statement of the time, but it was a time when women in the suffragette movement were becoming more vocal in their attitudes to the patriarchy and so sex would have been included in that.

Solange does, in some cases, allow men to fall in love with her but is quick to put them out of their misery by rejecting them. She must be a free spirit, free in every sense to continue her work. She does not actively encourage this, however, and it seems that the attraction of the male in her case is a by-product of their relationship. It would be hard at any time for a young man not to become infatuated with a gifted beautiful woman who he is working with. We could either decide that this psychic trait is unsatisfactory as it requires no sleuthing or accept it as a genuine, if unusual way of solving crime. I take the latter view. There is enough investigation to allow us as the reader to accept the final denouement without griping that this is improbable or unlikely. We know that Solange has this gift. She combines this gift with her alluring beauty to enter the minds of both villains and victims and can solve the case. A practical outcome to a very impractical investigation if we view it in "modern day" terms. But one we can accept because we know it is a cozy crime read "of its time."

During the decade between the publication of the first and second series of the Solange stories, Fryn Tennyson Jesse's interest in criminology grew. In 1924 she wrote the book, *Murder & Its Motives*. She was then invited to edit new volumes in the "Notable British Trials" series, beginning with *The Trial of Madeline Smith*, a true crime book written in 1927. But she did return to her Solange mysteries. Three of the five stories take place in England, where we see Solange visiting people and places she knew in her childhood. "The Pedlar" begins with an evocative portrait of rural England, a picture of the cozy place, the home of cozy crime: "...the

England that is passing away; the divinely stupid, honest, unselfconscious because quite-sure-of-itself England" (Tennyson Jesse 2).

She is seen as an exotic by many due to her experiences of living in France. She is able to become an acute observer of British society and her stories help Fryn to investigate further. We now fit into the cozy crime genre as we are in quintessential English villages with the characters to match. But even Solange can point out to the reader: "And if they only knew what I do for a living ... thought Solange. Crime ... not very nice. Particularly for a girl..." (Tennyson Jesse 3). She knows she is subversive; she realizes her work is unusual, and as she is a professional, she does not fit into the idea of sleuth as amateur and certainly not as sleuth as a woman.

In these stories, Solange's sense of evil is presented in a more pronounced way, and we must ask ourselves whether she still is in the cozy crime genre or has moved towards the occult detective:

> It was a favourite axiom with Solange that the best clues to a crime were in the characters of the people connected with it, and were worth all the burnt matches, footprints, or even fingerprints in the world. Of course, she would add, twinkling a little, the drawback to the discovery of clues of character lay in the fact that no one ever really knew what anyone else was like. And that was where her own peculiar gift for "feeling" a moral flaw came in with such unfailing effect. For it never played her false [Tennyson Jesse 99].

Solange now senses the nature of a moral flaw. "The solution's to be found in people, in human relationships" (Tennyson Jesse 99). And she says in "The Reprieve," "...and they are the most difficult and complicated things in the world" (Tennyson Jesse 65). In "The Pedlar" "...Solange fell on silence, thinking of her own strange gift, that delicate extra sense of hers which warned her of hidden evil where blunter-natured beings did not feel it" (Tennyson Jesse 11).

There is no real explanation of her powers. They are there. She did not acquire them. She was born with them. Some critics have called Solange an Occult Detective because she uses these powers, but if she is, then so many other detectives could be described thus as well. In "The Pedlar" she has already set up the cozy crime scenario by her description of the village she is staying in. Again, it is a closed society like so many other cozy crime venues: "Here, at least, except for the grosser lapses our flesh is heir to—particularly, our novelists would have us think, in villages—there could be no ill, none of that sinister evil that had always sent its strange messages into the consciousness of Solange.... Here was peace" (Tennyson Jesse 6).

This time there is a real sinister edge to the story with threats and danger being omnipresent. How little did she expect the unexpected? Indeed, this quote with its swipe at her writing peers allows us to see that there will be disruption as Auden in his essay on crime writing expects, and it will not be pleasant. In this case it was the murder by Pasquier of his wife and children. There is no description, but the murder of children always seems more horrific. Here the story steps out of the cozy crime genre. Unusual for its day, 1919, but reflective perhaps of the horrors that had just ended with the Armistice. Her father "...treated with all respect the fact that she had experienced her 'feeling,' that sense of something intolerably evil that never warned her in vain, in the presence of the man Pasquier" (Tennyson Jesse 27). Solange here solves the problem with her senses, a problem she did not even know about until she investigated the man who had given her this feeling. But her real secret seems to be hard work. In "The Canary": "At the end of an hour's rather laborious work, Solange felt she carried a fairly complete picture..." (Tennyson Jesse 131).

What she did and how she did it we are not too sure, and, to be honest, this seems to be the pattern throughout her stories. What she does to solve crime we are never told. How she solves crimes, we can never be sure, but that she has unbridled success, that goes without saying. She tells Charles Evelyn in "The Reprieve": "Oh. clues! Clues aren't everything. People are what matter. Fingerprints are not nearly so important as faces..." (Tennyson Jesse 51) And there we get the closest to her raison d'etre, her way of working. But it isn't that helpful really is it? What we can see is that she has a sixth sense when it comes to crime. In "Lot's Wife," "She recognized the sensation for that tingling sense of evil that people gave her..." (Tennyson Jesse 198). And so, it is repeated throughout her stories. "Her 'feeling,' that warning apprehension of evil which was her great gift..." (Tennyson Jesse 77)

In terms of the cozy crime aspect it fits into the psychological solution and, of course, the closed community, but it is also a little underwhelming as we are just following an idea of something, and we are not sure what it is until we hear of a crime committed a long time ago.

> It is true that F. Tennyson Jesse's Solange Stories show a woman in the role of professional detective, but Solange Fontaine depends for her success, not on close reasoning, hard work or scientific study, but on an intuition of evil which rarely fails her. And if "intuition" isn't a typical, pet possession of the Nineteenth Century female, what is? [http://www.batteredbox.com].

Because her talents are of the mind, Solange needs to "get up close and personal" to discover who is the perpetrator and whom she can dismiss. This psychic detective trait was quite popular at this time and allows the detective to get away with so much. She can feel who is guilty and does not always have to provide evidence. Indeed, in some of her tales the villain does not get punished in the traditional way but is left to stew in their guilt. This, of course, was a tactic that Agatha Christie liked to use and often encouraged, where her guilty ones went off to commit suicide to save the disgrace of a trial, and is a common cozy crime trope. The author becomes judge and jury, but this perhaps moves away too much "from show and tell."

Clara, Baroness of Linz, is featured in *Advice Limited*, the detective agency that she runs to solve crimes in eleven stories by E Phillips Oppenheim. The book was published in 1936. Oppenheim later produced a collection featuring female sleuth Miss Mott. These two collections, along with *Miss Brown of X.Y.O.*, were the only ones of his prodigious output to have women leads. In *Advice Limited* there are eleven stories: "Thirty-Nine Wooden Boxes," "An Olympian Debacle," "Broken Engagements," "Too Many Dukes," "The Ritz Hotel Conference," "Between the Eighth Green and The Ninth Tee," "Help for Mr. Goldman," "The Lonely Man," "A Family Misunderstanding," "The Listening Lady," and "A Gift from The Gods."

We first meet Clara thus, in "The Thirty-Nine Wooden Boxes" on board a train in Dover Pier Station:

> John Woolston ... confided to his underling that he had no intention of answering another enquiry of any sort. He changed his mind, however, when the most beautiful woman from amongst his regular patrons leaned out of the coupe which according to custom he had reserved specially for her use [Phillips Oppenheim 9].

In this first story, Clara solves the mystery of "The Thirty-Nine Wooden Boxes" through intuitive means. She latches on to the protagonists of the crime by observing behavior. She is clear in thought and deed. She investigates at the dinner table and at the Club. In hotel foyers and in her office. All prerequisites of the cozy crime, the closed community. I suppose that is one of the advantages of beauty. Would he have noticed her if she was a drab third-class passenger on a train? Would he have ignored her as he implied he would to his workmates? That she gave generous tips may have helped, but it is her beauty that is emphasized. When she sits in her office meeting her clients, it is again clear that it is her looks that attract attention though not always in a positive way: "The young lady who controlled the destinies of Advice Limited was impressing enough in her personality, her pleasant but strong face, the severe elegance of her attire, the clean crispness of her sentences..." (Phillips Oppenheim 46). Prospective clients at times doubt her ability to succeed because of her looks and general demeanor.

Auden tells us, in his definitive piece on detective fiction, in cozy crime this is all too obvious, that, "The corpse must shock not only because it is a corpse, but also for a corpse it is shockingly out of place..." (2). The setting is always violated by the death. Why would we find a body in the library? Why would murder occur in the vicarage? These deaths both disrupt the community and so the cozy world is disturbed. It is this disorder that Agatha Christie sets up so well, and Oppenheim tries to do the same with Clara. Why do we find a body "Between the Eighth Green and The Ninth Tee"? The answer is a failed attempt on the life of the Greek prime minister and the assassination of a totally innocent man confuses one and all, but not Clara. She can even pinpoint the room he has been shot from. How she does this is not explained. This I feel is a failing of both Clara and Solange and does not follow through with the cozy crime format where the explanation is clear at the denouement. But her intuitive nature is constant throughout the stories, so we learn to accept it. It is her knowledge of all things Japanese that allows her to solve the tragic crime committed in "An Olympian Debacle," a true case of brains over beauty, I think. The gentle tragic nuances of the story where she defeats the blackmailer, Reisborough, are very moving. The blackmailer's remorse when confronted with the outcome of his machinations is quite the denouement.

In "An Olympian Debacle" the odious Reisborough preposterously condemns all women, detective or not, with a broad sweeping brush:

> Women are failures in every serious position in life. They have had their chances and lost them. They are objects of ridicule in Parliament or any public office. They can write inferior novels glibly but there has never been a great woman poetess, soldier, financier or diplomatist. Women are coming back to their own in this generation. They are beginning to understand again what their grandmothers knew—that they were made for love and to be loved and for nothing else [Phillips Oppenheim 56].

Clara can but laugh at him, as she does at Samuel Goldman in "Help for Mr. Goldman" when he doubts her ability because of her looks:

> You must forgive Mr. Goldman,' he [Geoffrey Montressor] begged in a pleasant tone. 'He has had rather a shock this morning and, if you will pardon my saying so, he was expecting to see an older—a different sort of lady.
> "I am afraid I cannot change my appearance," was the cold reply. "I may not be very old, but I have had some experience in helping people out of trouble. For instance, Mr. Goldman," she added, turning to him, "it is quite true that I found the thief of your nephew's bales of silk. Now, what can I do for you?" [Phillips Oppenheim 177].

When she solves the mystery of stolen dress designs, Goldman, of course, is convinced of her intelligence and "admits, despite his earlier misgivings.... 'I trust you,' he announced. 'I think you are vun smart girl'" (Phillips Oppenheim 203). As well as, "And I tell you this, young lady Baroness," he wound up emphatically, "you tell me you have got some clever helpers behind you. Maybe you have, but you know how to give advice good" (Phillips Oppenheim 203).

We never see the "helpers" at work, we never hear from them. They are her private army. All we get are solutions. The mystery is in the mystery. We accept this, partly because we want to. We don't want this cozy world disrupted any more than it must be. As Clara says in "Too many Dukes," "Scotland Yard has the facts, I have the ideas!" (Phillips Oppenheim 112).

She knows what she is doing; she just won't tell us her methods. It is interesting that Clara knows her good looks may be a problem: "Clara,

Baroness Linz, sole owner of the business of Advice Limited, was without a doubt handicapped by her looks.... Notwithstanding the fact that every article of her attire was chosen to conceal rather than exploit her personal charms and that she wore a closely fitting hat simply to hide the color of her beautiful hair..." (Phillips Oppenheim 204). Her client Goldman has his concerns, but when all is explained, Clara depends upon a lot of trust from him; she can deliver the culprits whilst keeping all happy and content.

I think that "Broken Engagements" shows Clara at her best. Once again, she can divine the causes of certain behavior and solve the mysteries of said broken engagements. In doing so, the truth almost breaks the heart of General Nightingale who almost mirrors Clara with "a curious indefinite premonition of tragedy" (Phillips Oppenheim 85). Again, it is the crime of blackmail at the core, a particularly insidious offense especially when the one involved seemed so above board.

Comparisons to Solange are unavoidable, but the characters are very different, though both share the curse of beauty. Clara is all too self-aware, and unlike Solange, we don't see an aversion to her sexuality. Perhaps this is because the writer is a male and didn't want to go that far into her psyche. It is not an area he seems to interrogate in any of his novels, which primarily investigate crime with a male antagonist.

We do not have many clues to her past and where she honed her intellect, but in the "Ritz Hotel Conference" Clara alludes to some training: "I happen to have seen a case before, though, when I was taking my course in the hospital..." (Phillips Oppenheim 148). Doctor or nurse? Medical training as what? Another mystery for us, but a confirmation of her intelligence and expertise. A knowledge we cannot argue with.

Clara even goes as far as to try to subdue her appearance, but this to no avail as she leaves smitten young men in her wake. She is not interested in a relationship as she feels her tastes are too expensive, but it is suggested that she takes up with the infatuated Roderigo at the very end of the final story. He can see through her appearance though. "I have never before met an intelligent woman who was also beautiful" (Phillips Oppenheim 132). As he takes up a more prominent role in the stories, he becomes her biggest cheerleader, and as he tells the Sovrados in "A Gift from the Gods," "...She has an acute mind, however, and she has solved many problems for people who have found themselves in difficulties. It is good advice which she gives, and it is generally worth following" (Phillips Oppenheim 290). This tale is interesting as again we have the closed community, this time where the story takes place, mainly in a restaurant, and again Clara uses intuition to solve the case of attempted fraud. Here she does avail herself of an outside agency at the Spanish Embassy, but this is one of very few occasions where outside help is alluded to. Even then, she must have a mind that can work out who Roderigo needs help from and whom to approach for that help. She is then able to uncover the fraudulent plot and save Roderigo's honor and property.

In "Too Many Dukes," the events take place on board the ultimate closed community, a ship and mostly inside a cabin, which is a constant of the cozy crime. We discover that jewels are stolen, and then said jewels are hidden. Identities confused, lies told, and Clara rises above it all to solve the case. Luckily, after a frantic search for the stolen jewels, Clara, "…was spared the catastrophe of failure" (Phillips Oppenheim 121). As if we ever thought she would fail! Ironic that the Duc de Challes, who thought he had lost his fortune and had then approached Advice Limited for help, has the temerity to ask, "…I insist upon an introduction to your principal" (Phillips Oppenheim 122). But when Clara pulls up the blind shading herself from his view, "and removed her spectacles. That intriguing smile which had captivated him…" (Phillips Oppenheim 122) is clear. He can only acknowledge her beauty and then her talent as a detective.

Clara, Baroness of Linz. What an exotic ring that has. Of its time it was a title we would associate with glamour and intrigue. What was the woman like, where did she really come from? She is indeed a woman of many characters, blessed with language skills and experiences from many European countries. She is a woman other women would love to be, a woman men would love to take into their arms. She uses her beauty to charm confessions and clues. One victim is "…encouraged by the admiration in those beautiful hazel eyes" (Phillips Oppenheim 115). And later in the same tale: "He was under the spell of the light in her beautiful eyes…" (Phillips Oppenheim 116). Intoxicated by the exotic indeed!

But above all she is a woman with the intellect to stand alone and above all others. She can see what an ill-considered relationship would be, an unnecessary liaison. She knows how men can use women and quickly disabuses any with that thought, but she also knows that by being true to herself she will succeed, and she does not have to lower her standards or capitulate to the patriarchy, just as Solange refuses to be subjugated by Men. What an exotic creature we expect to see, and we are not disappointed. Clara uses her beauty to charm all concerned, the victim as well as the villain. She is able to rise above the mere formalities of life through her very appearance and this is an asset she uses. Throughout *Advice Limited* there are constant mentions of her appearance. Her beauty is reinforced in every story unlike in Solange's world. Is this because we need the constant juxtaposition of beauty and intellect here, whereas the fact that Solange is more of a psychic detective means her charms do not have to be constantly reinforced? I am unsure, but in "Between the Eighth and Ninth Tee" we read again, "The picturesque genius of ADVICE LIMITED settled herself down to listen. She was facing her visitor ... and the half lights were upon her beautiful hair and sensitive, thoughtful face" (Phillips Oppenheim 156).

Although Oppenheim tells us in "Help for Mr Goodman" that Clara "was without doubt handicapped by her looks ... [her clients] were all struck dumb by her entrance ... despite the fact that every article of her attire was chosen to conceal rather than exploit her personal charms..." (Phillips Oppenheim 176). If Clara can see the problem, she can also see the solution, but in all the other stories there is no indication of her covering up her beauty. Indeed, it is her intelligence she tries to hide as she knows that is what will win the case. Thus, she melts, for all her beauty, into the background, uses her contacts and assistants to discover who has done what and why. She meets with success in each of the eleven tales. As one of her acquaintances wonders why she is dining with a hopeless man, her friend tells her: "Clara always has a purpose in everything she does" (Phillips Oppenheim 14). As I have already stated, we cannot always see that purpose, but it is telling that those who know her are fully aware of her methods. Later in the same point in the story, "Anyhow.... Clara seems to have succeeded in making him talk" (Phillips Oppenheim 15).

But it all begs the question as to what we want from our detective heroes. Do we want to see the female detective portrayed in films as a glamorous sex symbol as, for example, when Kathleen Turner played Sara Paretsky's V.I. Warshawski, but failed miserably in every sense from replicating the detective's written persona to failing to act in the film? Warshawski is not Kathleen Turner and vice versa. This is where the film fails whilst the novels flourish. Or should we defer to recent portrayals of female detective protagonists in Nordic Noir on TV where we don't see strikingly beautiful women, but strikingly talented actors: Angela Kovacs as Irene Huss, Sofie Gråbøl as Sarah Lund in *The Killing,* and Sofia Helin as Saga Norén in *The Bridge*? The trouble is that we then have the exception that proves the rule when Ida Engvoll, a very attractive woman, plays Rebecka Martinsson. But then am I being sexist or objectifying women to actually write that down? At the end of it all, crime fighting is not a beauty contest, and it is odious to be caught up in that!

Clara works from her office or from various night clubs and hotels. The closed cozy crime community is evident here. We don't see Clara out and about investigating. She uses her contacts and her mind. She tells Mr. Goldman in "Help for Mr. Goldman" that, of course, she does make guesses: "If I do, they are generally good ones ... but of course I have to have help. If you like to know I will tell you that I have connections with a very excellent enquiry office..." (Phillips Oppenheim 197). So part of the secret is out, but if that were the whole truth, it would lessen the excitement, and we know there is more to her crime solving than that, but ... we cannot be sure what it is and that is the joy of reading the book!

We can see in the stories of Loveday Brookes, Mrs. Gladden, and Mrs. Paschal, the plainness of the woman detectives and how they meld into the furniture and are unseen by so many allowing them to solve crime. Solange and Clara use their femininity and their looks to combat crime. They are both able to travel in a world that accepts their beauty and doesn't see it as an impediment to crime fighting. Indeed, it allows them to flourish in the circles they occupy.

As I asked before, does beauty solve a crime? I don't think so, but it is an interesting feature for any story and can lead to diversions and distractions for other members in the script. Clara has more than her beauty. As Phillips Oppenheim explains, although she was a truly beautiful woman, it was not just that that made her so special: "…perhaps few who realised that apart from her beautifully curved mouth, her steady truthful eyes, the fine shape of her head and her untouched complexion, the greatest charm which she possessed was her intense humanity" (Phillips Oppenheim 225).

Do we need masculine characteristics to be a good detective? Not particularly, but what are these characteristics? Stubbornness, fortitude, bravery? We can all share those and they are not particularly masculine. More to the point, is initiative a female only trait? Poirot would say no, and he has a nose for crime as well as the little grey cells. Does the plain Jane stand more chance of success as she blends into the background and insinuates herself into the mystery that is a mystery? In the case of Mrs. Gladden and Loveday Brookes, we would say yes, but it does not exclude beauty from the equation. Just being beautiful is not the only asset needed, but we would ask how could such an enchantress be involved in the dirty business of crime? In "A Gift from the Gods," Clara explains to a Spanish plotter: "…that intelligence in this country is not a matter of sex" (Phillips Oppenheim 290). This may be slightly over egging it as to how all women were viewed in this period, but it is a view that could be held amongst female detectives!

It doesn't follow that beauty alone solves crimes, nor that plainness does either, but both have their advantages. As I am looking at Clara and Solange, I will concentrate on this. Beauty is not a leveler. We are not put at ease by beauty, especially if in a man! But in the period in which the stories are set and with the cultural mores and norms that were employed, beauty is beneficial. Men of the social class affected by the crimes we have would expect to move in circles that involved beautiful women. Indeed, if they had been presented with a plain protagonist, what would they have thought! In the Gladden, Brookes, and Paschal series, the women detectives do not move in elite circles as equals. They appear as servants or maids or simple observers, melting into the background. Clara and Solange are at the forefront. They are the story. They are the heroes. It is because they hold a position amongst the elite that they can work their magic.

What of the opposite sex? Why are there no dalliances? Clara seems to lead the young Roderigo on to some extent, and he is constantly proposing to her. On the final page of the final story, Clara says, "I have always thought that it would be very romantic to be proposed to in a taxi." To which Roderigo responds, calling to the hotel doorman: "Taxi, please"("A Gift from the Gods," Phillips Oppenheim 312). Relationships with men are not the highlight of any of the stories. The two detectives don't overtly need men to succeed. They have their employees, whom we are never introduced to, who do the leg work, and it is an assumption that they are men. Clara, especially, has this network that she uses and that reports back to her in her offices. Solange has a smaller circle and usually depends on psychic powers as well as her nuanced intelligence. I think the main message is, however, that neither woman needs a man to succeed.

It is not that they don't have admirers, but it is a case that they are not allowed to get in the way of their work. Indeed, Clara can flirt with Felix Blondel in "The Thirty-Nine Wooden Boxes" and get him to lower his guard and tell her what she wants to know. We don't actually hear what this is, but Clara can learn enough to solve the problem of where the stolen gold might be. In "Too Many Dukes" she twists the Duc de Challes around her little finger and is able to find the stolen jewels. Her persona is such that men will tell her anything, and again she can use his advances to her advantage:

> He drew a little nearer. She avoided what was after all only a timorous attempt at an embrace.
> "Always beloved," he murmured. "But first—"
> Again she eluded him with a little laugh [Phillips Oppenheim 117]

In "Help for Mr. Goldman," the infatuation of Montressor for Clara once more helps her to solve the crime. Again, she is not inclined to fall for his wiles.

> "You won't mind, will you, if I say that I think you are wonderful?"
> The old trouble! But what an exceedingly foolish young man!
> "Don't talk to me like that, if you please," she begged...
> "Because I hate silly compliments—especially from strangers" [Phillips Oppenheim 185].

Solange does not suffer from these overt approaches from men. Indeed, she is never really put into a position where she has to deflect any man's behavior. She concentrates on her task, with no interference from the opposite sex. In this sense the stories diverge from the cozy crime definitions of relationships outlined by Erin Martin above.

Clara and Solange exist in a world of closed communities—Clara in London mainly, sometimes on a train or aboard a boat. All of these places are cut off and insular and have their own participants. Solange sees her work play out in villages which are likewise closed. They both use their intelligence to solve crimes, though we cannot always see why, but I feel we don't have to know how and why. Crimes are committed and solved. We again suspend belief and have complete faith in our detectives. Do we have to know exactly how the crime is solved? I feel we don't. We want the satisfaction of the criminal being brought to book, and because we have engaged with the story, invested in our hero, we don't have to have an ending that confuses or concerns us. We want a result and we get a result. We know Clara and Solange are experts in their field. Do we really need to know how they get to where they eventually end up? I think not. The stories stand up, and we see the result. Closure is brought in every case. Perhaps for Solange we see an explanation when Ledoux in the final story of the collection, "The Black Veil" says to her, "…your scientific sub-conscious theories may explain the facts, but not the change in that man's soul" (Tennyson Jesse 284). It is all very well having a process and a theory. However, at the end of it all, an understanding of human nature and how man leads his life provides the answer, and Solange has the knack of seeing through the shadows and can interpret what has happened, be it with a sixth sense or a more practical nature, and she will solve the crime.

Their abilities are several, but being able to deflect questions and comment through their looks does help. They do not overtly flirt or play the beauty card. They are aware of their looks, but I think no more than that. The murders are not visceral, nor are the robberies. The violence is brief and understated. They do disrupt the natural order of things à la Auden.

Clara and Solange are transgressive members of the cozy crime genre. Their beauty is their trademark, their brains a bonus. Perhaps I should leave the last word to Clara, when in "A Gift from the Gods" Rodrigo pleads, "…Forgive me, Baroness … but do you know what you're talking about?" She smiled reassuringly: "Have you ever known me when I didn't?" (Phillips Oppenheim 311).

Works Cited

Auden, W H. 1948. "The Guilty Vicarage." http://harpers.org/archive/1948/05/the-guilty-vicarage, accessed 18/07/2018. Web.
Bowen, Rhys. Message to the author. 20 July 2018. E-mail.
Bradley, Alan. Message to the author. 8 July 2018. E-mail.
Brody, Frances. Message to the author. 9 July 2018. E-mail.
Christie, Agatha. *Murder at The Vicarage*. London. HarperCollins. 1996. Print.
Christie, Agatha. *Thirteen Problems*. London. HarperCollins. 2001. Print.

Colenbrander, Joanna. *A Portrait of Fryn: A Biography of F. Tennyson Jesse*. London. André Deutsch, 1984. Print.
"The Compleat Adventures of Solange Fontaine." http://www.batteredbox.com/VicEdDetctive/SolangeFontaine.htm accessed 17/08/2018. Web.
Cozy Mystery. *GoodReads*. https://www.goodreads.com/genres/cozy-mystery. Accessed 30/07/2018. Web.
Cozy Mystery List. https://www.cozy-mystery.com/. Accessed 17/08/2018. Web.
Dunn, Carola. Message to the author. 9 July 2018. E-mail.
Edwards, Martin, ed. 1919. *Continental Crimes: The Lovers of St. Lys*. London. The British Library. 2017. Print.
Edwards, Martin, ed. 1931. *Blood on the Tracks: The Railway Carriage*. London. The British Library. 2018. Print.
Field Louise Maunsell. "What's Wrong with the Women?" *The North American Review*, 232. 3 (1931):274–280 Print.
Forrester, Andrew. 1864. *The Female Detective*. London. The British Library. 2014. Print.
Hendrey-Seabrook, Therie. "Reclassifying the Female Detective of the *fin de siècle*: Loveday Brooke, Vocation and Vocality." *Clues* 26:1 (2008):75–78 Print.
Knight, Stephen. 2010. *Crime Fiction Since 1800: Detection, Death, Diversity*. London. Palgrave. 2010. Print.
Malice Domestic. http://malicedomestic.org/about.html. Accessed 17/08/2018. Web.
Miss Brown of X.Y.O. https://www.fadedpage.com/showbook.php?pid=20140543. accessed 12/06/2018. Web.
Phillips Oppenheim, E: 1936. *Advice Limited*. London: Hodder and Stoughton. 1936. Print.
Pirkis Catherine Louisa. 1893. *The Experiences of Loveday Brooke, Lady Detective*. London. The British Library. 2014. Print.
Sayers, Dorothy. 1930. *Strong Poison*. London. Hodder & Stoughton. 2016. Print.
Sayers, Dorothy. 1935 *Gaudy Night*. London. Hodder & Stoughton. 2003. Print.
Tennyson Jesse, F. 1929. *The Solange Stories*. London: William Heinemann. 1931. Print.
Todd, Charles. Message to the author. 7 July 2018. E-mail.
Warthling Roberts, Joan. "Amelia Butterworth : The Spinster Detective." In *Feminism in Women's Detective Fiction*. Ed. Glenwood Irons. Toronto: University of Toronto Press, 1995. Print.
Wentworth, Patricia. 1961. *The Girl in the Cellar*. London. Hodder & Stoughton. 2007. Print.
Winspear, Jacqueline. Message to the author. 7 July 2018. E-mail.
Women Detectives. https://womendetectives.weebly.com/. Accessed 07/06/2018. Web.

A Likeable Man

Columbo as Cozy Detective

STEPHEN CLOUTIER

"You know Columbo, you're almost likeable in a shabby sort of way. Maybe it's the way you come slouching in here with your shopworn bag of tricks."—Leslie Williams, *Ransom for a Dead Man*

Created by Richard Levinson and William Link, the television show *Columbo* continues to enjoy a popularity amongst devotees of television crime dramas, a popularity evident from the fact that there are (or were) four different podcasts dedicated to the show (*The Columbo Podcast*, *Just One More Thing*, *The Columbo Confab*, and *The Columboys*). *Columbo*'s enduring popularity stems, in large part, from the ability of the character to transcend the show itself. As the Italian Marxist Antonio Gramsci argues, iconic popular cultural heroes are those who can transcend their source material; Gramsci suggests that "the writer's name and personality do not matter, but the personality of the protagonist does" (350). While fans of Columbo recognize the contributions of the show's writers and directors (one of whom was Steven Spielberg), it is the character of Columbo and Peter Falk's portrayal of the character, in particular, that draw in fans, allowing the character to become a cultural icon. Mark Dawidziak remarks that it is "better to have a strong character than strong writing when you want to last on commercial television. *Columbo* was blessed with both" (95). Columbo was so recognized that Falk could play the character outside the confines of the show itself, appearing in the real world as Lt. Columbo, as one of those who roasted Frank Sinatra on the July 2, 1978, episode of *The Dean Martin Celebrity Roast*. So, what is it about the character that appeals to audiences so much? I will argue that it stems from the cozy nature of the character and that, because of these cozy elements, audiences enjoyed watching this odd little ill-kempt shambling working class man humble the rich and powerful.

On the face of it, the idea that a cozy detective could reside in Los Angeles seems absurd. Surely the urban landscape of LA produces not the Jane Marples or Jessica Fletchers of *Detective* fiction but the hard-boiled Philip Marlowes or Hieronymus Bosches of *Crime* fiction. It is the world Raymond Chandler, deliberately placing himself in opposition to those who became defined as cozy, says "is not a fragrant world, but it is the world you live in, and certain writers with tough minds and a cool spirit of detachment can make very interesting and even amusing patterns out of it" (20). In Chandler's view, the detective who haunts the streets of Los Angeles should be tough and detached. These are the famous mean streets, down which "a man must go who is not himself mean, who is neither tarnished nor afraid" (Chandler, 20). This is what we have come to expect: cozy detectives do not emerge from the city but the sleepy towns and villages where crime is a rare event. As Marilyn Stasio contends, "The settings [of the cozy] are never sleazy; the atmosphere is designed to give pleasure and comfort." Los Angeles is a place of fear, filth, and degradation, not a place of pleasure and comfort.

Yet, the 1970s saw just that: a cozy detective working in a major metropolitan area. *Columbo* very much encapsulates Gramsci's idea that the personality of the protagonist is the defining characteristic of the popular drama. Everything about the show is designed to focus on the character of Columbo himself. Even its famed inverted formula, in which the identity of the killer is shown at the beginning of each episode, highlights the singular personality of the title character. By focusing not on "whodunit" but on the investigation itself, the show puts Columbo at the center of the show rather than the mystery itself. By removing the mystery, the show forces viewers to focus on Columbo's interactions with the rich and powerful and to tease out the show's social commentary. The attention of the viewers is not divided between watching the detective's investigation and trying to guess the identity of the killers themselves. The driving force of the show, therefore, becomes not the perpetrator of the crime but the way in which Columbo outwits and humbles those who see themselves as being superior to Columbo.

My argument is that the primacy of character above all else explains not only the enduring success of *Columbo*, but the enduring success of the cozy itself, and critics need to recognize this centrality of character in the cozy genre. As the academic scaffolding rises around the cozy genre and its characteristics are explicated, we need to ensure that the definitions we set are not too restrictive. If we chain the cozy genre to the more peripheral characteristics such as setting (a bold statement indeed) and fail to recognize that the cozy rests in character, we ultimately fail to give the genre credit for its vigor and versatility. An example of the robust nature of the cozy character is the two-part crossover episodes with Jessica Fletcher of *Murder, She Wrote* and Thomas Magnum of *Magnum P.I. Magnum P.I.* with its gunplay and its rugged, Vietnam vet lead character can hardly be categorized as cozy even with its luxurious Hawaiian backdrop and its self-deprecating humor; yet, the two shows successfully blended their styles. If Jessica Fletcher can successfully move out of her own cozy television series, albeit temporarily, then we must conclude that it is *character itself* that embodies the cozy spirit and *not* the surrounding elements. Thus, Columbo, despite his urban environment, can be brought under the cozy umbrella.

Columbo began as two TV movies: *Prescription: Murder* (February 20, 1968) and *Ransom for a Dead Man* (March 1, 1971). The full series premiered on September 15, 1971, with "Murder by the Book" (directed by Steven Spielberg) and ended on May 13, 1978, with "The Conspirators." There *was* a revival of the series in the 1980s and 1990s, but my focus here is on the episodes that specifically aired in the 1970s. I want to explore what initially attracted audiences to the show and to examine why the relationship between audience and detective developed. The episodes in the 1980s and 1990s with their nostalgic gloss have a significantly different tone to them.

Looking back to the 1970s episodes, then, Columbo's popularity stems, I contend, from his ability speak for the common person who felt excluded from a social and financial prosperity that was enjoyed, it seemed, only by the powerful. W.H. Auden, one of the first writers to attempt to define what has become known as the cozy, states that the

> job of the detective is to restore the state of grace in which the aesthetic and the ethical are as one. Since the murderer who caused their disjunction is the aesthetically defiant individual, his opponent, the detective, must be either the official representative of the ethical or the exceptional individual who is himself in a state of grace [154].

Columbo *is* that cozy detective who restores a sense of order and, perhaps more importantly, a sense of morality to the alienating urban environment that is Los Angeles. In his article "Tarzan and Columbo, Heroic Mediators," Gary L. Harmon suggests that Columbo acts as a mediator "in the complex issues that boggle the collective mind" (115). Harmon argues that the function of the mediating hero is "to help man get rid of the uneasiness, sometimes the fear, that chaotic, unintelligible or even hostile circumstances produce in him" (115). Thus, we can see Columbo as the cozy detective who orients the viewers in an American society that had changed so dramatically in the aftermath of the 1960s that it seemed to be almost a foreign country when compared to pre–1964 American society. I use 1964 as a convenient, if tentative, sign post because events of that year (including

Cassius Clay changing his name to Muhammad Ali, the American government sending more military advisors to Vietnam, and the Beatles performing on the *Ed Sullivan Show*) seem to signal the beginning of a cultural shift. *Columbo* uses the cozy detective as a kind of corrective to the excesses of the new society that emerged from the conflict of the 1960s. To use Auden's terminology, Columbo facilitates the restoration of a sense of grace, the restoration of the ethical, to a "disjuncted" society.

The cozy detective stands in for the audience and, thus, shares the (perceived) values of the audience. Columbo acts as proxy for the audience as viewers follow his attempts to renegotiate the massive social changes taking place. Harmon asserts that

> It is important to see that Columbo's style as a hero is inextricably linked to our particular period of history: One that is urban, complex, capitalistic, consumer-oriented, industrial, machine-supported—and one that espouses individuality, independence, logical reasoning, originality, staying within the law, status-achieving and money-making as desirable ideals [126].

Like the cozy detective, then, Columbo acts as a mediator, giving the audience clues as how to negotiate new social norms in an increasingly unfamiliar and alienating world. In the episode "Playback," for example, the writers emphasize Columbo's alienation from the new culture by placing him in an art gallery featuring contemporary art. As Francine, the gallery's curator, gives him a tour of the gallery, we see him become increasingly befuddled by the abstract post-modernist art he sees, and he marvels at the prices people are willing to pay for such art. Francine tells him that art is subjective. Art either does something for you or it does not. He replies, looking at one of the pieces hanging on the wall, "This doesn't do anything for me." The scene ends on a humorous note with Columbo mistaking the air conditioning ventilator for a work of art. Embarrassed by the mistake, he goes on to tell the curator that his wife paints paint-by-number pictures. Here we see Columbo acting as, in Harmon's terms, mediator. As seemingly strange post-modernist ideas take hold within the cultural sphere, the audience looks to Columbo for clues on how to negotiate these new cultural forms. His befuddlement gives them permission to dismiss these ideas as silly and lessen their own sense of unease when faced with artistic forms and ideas they do not understand. While the joke seems to be on Columbo in the scene, it is Columbo who emerges as the victor. The characters he interacts with in the scene may smirk and shake their heads at his performance, but, for the audience, he reveals the absurdity of contemporary avant-garde art.

The 1970s were a time of great change globally and not just in terms of aesthetics. American society was weary from the conflict and chaos of the 1960s, a decade that began with the promise of a prosperous future, symbolized in the presidency of John F. Kennedy and the imagery of Camelot.

Actor and director Peter Coyote, in the *American Experience* documentary "Summer of Love," expresses the attitude of the 1960s when he says

> It was such an exciting, heady time to find out that under the official reality there was this seething turmoil of young people learning new music, new thoughts, new ideas, new literature, new poetry, new ways of being.

By the dawn of 1970, however, that promise was gone. Kennedy, his brother Robert, and Martin Luther King, Jr., had all been victims of an assassin's gun. Rather than transforming society into an egalitarian utopia, the 1960s seemed to usher in a new violent decade as the Manson family, the Zodiac killer, and the Son of Sam terrorized their communities. American society in the 1970s seemed to have fractured along the lines of race, gender, sexuality, and generations. The dream of a coherent unified social structure seemed dead, leaving war, conflict, and an increasing sense of alienation in its place. Even Walter Cronkite announced as early as 1968 that he no longer felt that the United States could win the Vietnam War, telling viewers that "the only rational way out then will be to negotiate, not as victors, but as an honorable people who lived up to their pledge to defend democracy, and did the best they could." America seemed to be losing its way.

The attitude among young people seemed to change. Gone was the exuberance of the hippie movement espoused by the likes of Peter Coyote to be replaced by a sense of disaffection. Warren McGinnis, identified in the CNN documentary *The Seventies* as being with the Runaway Squad, delineates the differences between the children who ran away in the 1960s and those who ran away in the 1970s:

> The children that run away from home today are not the children that we had running away in the 60s. In the 60s, we had what we called then flower children, and they ran away basically for socio-political reasons. Today children are running from a situation rather than to a situation.

Culturally, the 1970s initiated a shift in ethical and moral attitudes. Gone was the idealized nuclear family portrayed by shows like *Leave It to Beaver* and *Father Knows Best* as television began to grapple with more difficult and less clear-cut social issues. The transformative power of social movements that demanded equal rights for African Americans, women, and homosexuals fundamentally changed American social relations. As Bruce J. Schulman writes, the '70s

> ushered in another sort of change in latitude. Hair was no longer an issue. Fashions became outrageous, sexual behaviour less restrained. A new ethic of personal liberation trumped older notions of decency, civility, and restraint. Americans widely embraced this looser code of conduct. Even those who had never been hippies, or never even liked hippies, displayed a willingness to let it all hang loose [xv].

These changes could be, and to some *were*, overwhelming as people tried to negotiate their way through these new social relations. Forces of the status quo were fighting to maintain their socio-political hegemony (what Gramsci would term a War of Position) as the emerging counterculture was pushing its own ideology in an attempt to wrest socio-political power from older, more conservative elements (a War of Maneuver in Gramsci's terms). Into this seemingly chaotic world shambles the figure of Columbo.

Television has always reflected the anxieties and hopes of society, and writers in the 1970s used television screens to engage in a socio-political struggle, as the forces of the status quo fought for hegemony against the emerging counterculture. Shows like *All in the Family*, *M*A*S*H*, *Good Times*, and *The Mary Tyler Moore Show* fought the social conflicts of the time. Detective shows, in particular, exposed the changing morays of American society. It did not seem to matter which side of the political spectrum a show came down on; they all tended to incorporate the hard-boiled characteristics of Chandler. This trend took shape in the late 1960s with the reboot of *Dragnet* starring Jack Webb. *Dragnet* first ran on radio from 1949 to 1957 and on television from 1951 to 1959. The series, which would run until 1970, was relaunched in 1967. Dragnet stands squarely against the rising counterculture. Christopher Sharrett states that Dragnet "wants to define 'American values' and to separate the righteous not just from the criminals but from all the misfits, oddities, and malcontents who pollute the American landscape" (165), arguing that

> Webb has a full array of "others" who serve as raw meat for his angry, voracious appetite: hippies, protestors, pot smokers, black militants, liberal intellectuals, and a gaggle of miscellaneous social misfits constitute an army of opposition that is always the fantas life of the Right [167].

In a January 12, 1967, episode (variously called "The LSD Story," "The Blue Boy episode," and "The Big LSD"), Webb tackles the increasing use of LSD. Adam Graham writes that

> The show does a great job portraying how those who are charged with enforcing the law are often frustrated by the law when it failed to deal with an issue like LSD use…. For some, this represented a hard hit back against the emerging counterculture…. Friday re-emerged as the rock solid hero we needed in a time when everything was shifting including cherished values.

Graham is undoubtedly right in this assessment. For others, however, it was an over-the-top conservative push-back against a new cultural attitude. The LSD-using character (Benjie "Blue Boy" Carver) engages in some amusingly ludicrous behavior which includes chewing the bark off the tree and burying his head in the ground. The show veers close to creating a straw man in its attack on the counterculture.

The fight against LSD also features in the 1968 episode called "The Prophet" (sometimes listed as "The Big Prophet") which, in Sharrett's words, is

> devoted entirely to Webb and Gannon verbally jousting with an LSD proponent named Brother William, clearly modelled on Timothy Leary. The show is nothing but rapid shots and countershots, as Friday and Gannon exchange verbal blows with the arrogant LSD apostle [169].

Timothy Leary, of course, is the LSD proponent who became a symbol of the counterculture. Like Webb, conservative leaders viewed Leary with hostility. In their biography of Leary, Bill Minutaglio and Steven L. Davis write that those in power saw Leary as a

> a Robespierre on acid, a kingpin hell-bent on unraveling the normal order. He is a subversive, a hippie rebel leader summoning his army, a sociocultural terrorist whose real master plan is to blow up the nation's moral compass in the name of free love and drugs [10].

This is clearly how Webb sees Brother William: as the Leary stand-in. Daniel Moyer, in the booklet accompanying the DVD, writes that "Jack believed the new version of *Dragnet* was successful because the timing was right and persons in the late 1960s were asserting that policemen should no longer be maligned" (10). Friday is the hard-nosed, uncompromising defender of the police and law and order. After Brother William tells him that "No law that restricts what I can do to myself in the privacy of my own home, on my own land is a good law," Friday responds, "If you're gonna live with the rest of us, then you'll have to learn to play the game by the rules, And, in case you've forgotten the name of the game, we call it democracy." The show's political position demands conformity rather than insisting on the freedom of the individual for which Brother William argues. Friday never seems to see the contradiction between his views and the centrality of the rugged individualism at the heart of American national identity. Perhaps Brother William's individuality represents a lawlessness that is just too extreme for Webb.

It was not just conservative shows that reflected this harder edge in its social commentary. Even a politically liberal show like *The Mod Squad* depicted a tougher social view. In his autobiography, Aaron Spelling (*The Mod Squad*'s producer) confirms that they intended for the show to be a counter to *Dragnet*: "[*The Mod Squad*] was a million light years away from *Dragnet* and other cop shows of the day. Nobody had never done a young cop show before" (62). For Spelling, politics also sets his show apart from Webb's:

> They were right wing, we were liberal. They thought everybody under 25 was a creep, we thought everybody under 25 was misunderstood. And, more importantly, *Mod Squad* had an ingredient called "soul" [67].

The Mod Squad embraced the counterculture *Dragnet* rejected, attempting to show that the fractures in society, the divisions, could be overcome. The premise is that three "kids," all in trouble with the law, join the police force to become undercover police officers in order to avoid prison. Each character represented a segment of society. Peter "Pete" Corcoran came from an affluent white family and was arrested for stealing cars; Julie Barnes was a runaway whose mother was a prostitute, and Lincoln "Linc" Hayes was the angry African America radical who had been arrested during the Watts riots. The show's liberal ideology insists that, despite the social divisions, it is possible for people from different social backgrounds to not only work together, but even care about each other. This includes bridging the generation gap. To that end, viewers see the character of Captain Adam Greer who represents the older generation, the "squares." Greer is the gruff, suit-wearing father figure who stands in for the older generation. While there are inevitably conflict between Greer and the mod squad, the show suggests that understanding is possible between the generations.

In "The Guru" episode, Greer shows annoyance at the distrust the three younger police officers have of him: "What do I have to do to win your trust? Wear beads? I read the Guru. I like the newspaper. I think it has a healthy attitude. It says something." He finishes with "Do I surprise you?" To which Linc replies, "Constantly." Greer's willingness to express admiration for an underground, counterculture newspaper (the Guru) shows that he doesn't reject youth culture out of hand (like Friday might do); it shows his willingness to listen to young people. Linc's response similarly shows his readiness to see Greer as something more than a representation of social oppression. It is significant that Linc, representing Africa Americans, is the one who makes this concession, a gesture of racial equality and harmony.

Yet, as popular as these shows were, they did not reflect the day to day experiences of their audiences. Joe Friday has no soft edges; he has no home life, no wife or kids, and, while the Mod Squad may have softer edges, they are damaged and often dark characters. Columbo, the cozy detective, offers an alternative to these portrayals. While audiences might get a vicarious thrill from *Dragnet* and *The Mod Squad*, it is Columbo, who in his rumpled raincoat seems more like a favorite uncle, viewers turn to for a sense of comfort and connection.

The *Columbophile* blog highlights the attraction of the disheveled lieutenant and stresses the cozy nature of the character:

> There's negligible on-screen violence. Barely a drop of blood. No swearing. Sex and drugs are on the periphery. And Columbo is a man with a strict moral code who is inherently respectful and knows how to treat people.

The world he must negotiate is filled with corrupt, greedy, power-hungry people, people who threaten him, belittle him, and underestimate him, and, yet, he weathers the threats to his career, and occasionally to his life, to bring the killers to justice, whether a snobbish art critic ("Suitable for Framing"), a cold haughty doctor ("A Stitch in Crime"), a politician ("Candidate for Crime"), or a Deputy Police Commissioner ("A Friend in Deed"). He remains the moral center of the show, and, by exposing the corruption and criminal behavior of the ruling class, Columbo gives viewers a sense of control in a society that seems increasingly confusing, even if that control is seen vicariously through Columbo's efforts to bring the powerful to justice. The show invites those watching to see Columbo as a surrogate for themselves. Unlike Friday or the Mod Squad, audiences see Columbo as one of them. He is the proverbial everyman, with a wife, a house, and a dog, who is trying to negotiate his way through a quickly changing world.

Despite their competing political ideologies, *Dragnet* and *The Mod Squad* consistently support the status quo. *Columbo*, however, challenges the ruling class. The moral rot at the core of American society, *Columbo* suggests, stems from the social elites. Through his investigations, Columbo lays bare social power structures and the questionable foundation on which that power lies. Antonio Gramsci posits the idea that the ruling class creates an entire apparatus of organizations to help maintain control, organizations that extend into all areas of society (government, the police, medicine, and even culture). Roger Simon writes that, for Gramsci, "social relations of civil society are also relations of power, which are embodied in the great variety of organisations making up civil society, as well as in the state apparatus" (74). *Columbo* shows how this power and corrupting influence extends into all social structures. Cozy detective stories often deal with social power (who has it, who wants it) and reveals the mechanisms of power. I would argue that there is no genre where this struggle for dominance, for hegemony, is more obvious than the detective story. It is, after all, the job of the detective, cozy or not, to engage with society, to enter the social debates and conflicts, in order to bring the criminal to justice and, thus, shine a light on how society works to reveal the power structures that exists. A detective, after all, needs to examine social relations in order to determine who had the most to gain from a crime. As a Marxist, Gramsci's views the ideology of power through the lens of class which, at first glance, may seem to disqualify his ideas as an approach to consider the cozy detective. After all, in cozy detective novels, the detectives, the criminals, and the suspects are often of the same class. J. Madison Davis writes that,

> The amateur detective who solves the perplexing case is almost invariably a person of the upper middle class, well educated and well read, with all the manners that go with that position in society. If the detective did not have such manners, he likely wouldn't

be invited to stately Postlethwaite Manor where the ten suspects and victims are isolated for the weekend [10].

While this may be superficially true, I have been trying to suggest that the cozy genre is far more complex and subtle than we give it credit for. Cozy detectives are often characters positioned on the margins of society who are seen to have little value in the society they inhabit, even when of the same class as other characters and, as such, often have no power within the society they investigate. Agatha Christie's Jane Marple is a spinster, for example; yet her position on the margin allows her to see her society more clearly and more objectively than those at the center of power.

As a spinster, Marple is seen in a negative light as she is neither a potential wife for the men nor a potential love rival to the women. In *The Murder at the Vicarage* (the first novel in which she appears), for example, her position unsettles the other characters. Griselda Clement, the vicar's wife, calls Miss Marple "terrible" (5) and "the worst cat in the village" (5) when describing her. Despite what Davis implies, an invitation to stately Postlethwaite Manor and membership in the ruling class does not guarantee one acceptance. Yet this dismissal of Marple gives her the ability to move through the novel unseen but observing everything. She has no value in her society and, thus, the other characters underestimate her. This underestimation will become a major characteristic in *Columbo*. The key to examine cozy detectives, it seems to me, is not to view them overly simplistically but to see their relation to the power structures of the society in which they live.

Focusing on power structures allows critics to find new and dynamic ways to unpack the cozy genre. Viewing the show through this lens, Columbo's class no longer becomes problematic. In fact, it helps to solidify his coziness by furthering his marginalization from the center of power. As a poor working-class police lieutenant, he has no stakes in the high-flying world he investigates, a world of such extreme wealth that it has been referred to as "Monaco rich" (Brodbeck), that is the extremely wealthy, those who are so rich that their lives seem light years from the struggles faced by Columbo and, by extension, the viewers. In the episode "Etude in Black," for example, Columbo visits the mansion of the killer Alex Benedict and the two discuss the price of the mansion. Columbo, who says he makes $11,000 a year, figures out that, to afford the price of Benedict's mansion, Columbo would have to work for ninety years. "Without eating," he adds.

This is a scene, Sheldon Catz argues, "that the program could easily do without" (137). Producers often padded episodes to meet the two-hour running time (with commercials) demanded by the television network. This scene is often used, as Catz suggests, as an example of such padding, but I would challenge that view. I would argue that, rather than being mere filler, the scene is important in establishing Columbo's cozy credentials. For the show to work, the producers need the audience to identify with Columbo. Thus, the writers need scenes that emphasize this connection. If, as I contend, *Columbo* posits the idea that moral corruption stems from the social, political, and cultural elites, then the show needs to distance Columbo from those elites to establish his surrogacy for the audience. The conversation between Columbo and Benedict does just that: it establishes Columbo as a regular working-class citizen just like the viewers. The difference is, of course, that Columbo can do the one thing that the members of the audience cannot: he can speak truth to power. Thus, we can see that Columbo's popularity comes from the fact that, while the audience may feel a lack of agency, they live vicariously through Columbo as he exerts his agency (bestowed on him by his position as a police officer) to bring the rich and powerful to justice. It should be pointed out that his position as a professional investigator (or as a man) does not necessarily push him out of the cozy umbrella. Numerous cozy detective shows feature male police officers, including *The Brokenwood Mysteries* (New Zealand), *Pie in the Sky* (Britain) *Midsomer Murders* (Britain), and *Murdoch Mysteries* (Canada).

Although the show pushes back against what it sees as the decadence of a licentiousness society, it also acts as a corrective to the reactionary conservativism fighting its war of position against the counterculture. *Columbo* tries to walk the line between conservatism and liberalism, taking the best from both ideologies. This is in sharp contrast to other police officers like Dirty Harry Callahan for example. Joe Street argues that *Dirty Harry* "offers a scathing critique of the liberal approach to crime and the law, even suggesting that liberalism facilitated Scorpio's killing spree. San Francisco thus becomes a scene of confrontation between liberals (the local power structure), conservatives (Callahan), and the counterculture (Scorpio)" (3). *Columbo*, however, takes a more nuanced view of the criminal element. In fact, the show reveals not a liberal bureaucracy that thwarts the individual citizen as Dirty Harry posits but an increasingly conservative one. The episode "A Friend in Deed" brings Columbo's conflict with his police department superiors to the foreground as he matches wits with Deputy Police Commissioner Mark Halperin. Hugh Caldwell, Halperin's friend and neighbor, has accidentally killed his wife and turns to Halperin for help. The two then hatch a plan to cover-up the murder, by staging it to look like a botched robbery and blaming it on a house burglar active in the area. Halperin then blackmails Caldwell into killing Halperin's wife so Halperin can inherit her vast wealth.

When we first see Halperin, he is seated at a backgammon table having just placed a $3200 gambling wager. He is sitting back in his chair, confident, and smoking a small cigar. A glass of brandy is before him and standing behind him is a beautiful young woman (who is not his wife) holding a glass of wine in one hand and with the other hand, which he had been fondling, gently resting on his shoulder. The image is doubled as he is seated beside a mirror. The mirror can suggest his narcissism and the double killings in the episode. Here in one image we see the quintessential representation of those rich and powerful figures Columbo targets in his investigations. We sense Halperin's feeling of entitlement even before he speaks. The decadence and dissolution of morality comes not from the street "punks" as the likes of Dirty Harry Callahan would have it but from those at the top of society. That is, to use Brodbeck's term, the Monaco rich.

The show uses Halperin to undermine the conservative ideology that the status quo and those in charge are best suited to run society. In one scene Halperin and his wife Margaret argue over Margaret's liberal philanthropic donations to, in his words, "a motley assortment of junkies, pushers and losers" and her handing her money out like candy to "grifters who've never done a day's work in their life." She argues the liberal idea that money is a tool to help ex-convicts get jobs to help them reintegrate back into society. He suggests that she should give him her millions; he would happily spend it on his own desire with no guilt at all. Halperin defends the wealthy from the poor at a press conference, saying "We will provide protection for all of our citizens, not just for those in the inner city or in the so-called problem areas." While a statement like this seems eminently reasonable, as all citizens of a society deserve to be protected by the law, the viewer already knows Halperin says this not as a statement of equality and fairness but to protect his own interests.

To underscore this point, we cut immediately to a bar where we are introduced to Artie Jessup, the house burglar being set up for the murders. He finds it difficult to reintegrate back into society after prison. When we first see him, he is being harangued by his lady-friend who wants him to buy tickets for the roller derby. Trying to sell what he stole in his latest robbery, Jessup meets with Sharkey, a fence, who tells him that the increased police activity means that he cannot sell Jessup's items. Sharkey tells him, "Times change. It's tougher on the outside now. You know you spent so much time up in that prison you don't know how it is anymore." Jessup is not one of Halperin's "losers." He is a man trying to negotiate his way through a drastically changed society. By this point in the series ("A Friend in Deed" was the final episode of the third season and the twenty-fifth episode overall), the tropes that have come to define Columbo have been set, and audiences know where the sympathies of the show lie: those who are powerless in the face of the powerful and selfish forces that work to maintain their own hegemony at the expense of those further down the social ladder trying to make ends meet.

Another characteristic of the cozy *Columbo* follows is the rejection of violence and gore. Marilyn Stasio points out that violence, in the cozy story, "is kept to a minimum and described discreetly," and they do not go into detail about the gore. Remember one of the qualities of *Columbo* The Columbophile blog, quoted earlier, highlighted as part of the show's appeal: "There's negligible on-screen violence. Barely a drop of blood." Columbo responds to the violence of the world with a non-violence that borders on pacifism. This would be a welcome sight for the viewer as violence seemed to be on the rise. Riots exploded in Harlem (1964), Philadelphia (1964), Watts (1965), Newark (1967), Chicago (1968), and Washington, D.C. (1968). The violence was not limited to those perceived to be "thugs" or "hippies." The police response seemed to be equally violent. Never was this as clear as during the 1968 Democratic National Convention (DNC). Bruce J. Schulman writes that the events of the DNC "vividly showcased the smashed remains of the old consensus—the sense that Americans, however much they might disagree on specifics, shared fundamental values and could solve disputes peaceably" (12). Television viewers were horrified as the police, in Schulman's words, "suddenly snapped. They charged into the crowd, swinging billy clubs indiscriminately, seizing demonstrators, clubbing them, and tossing them into paddy wagons" (13). America seemed to be degenerating into an orgy of violence from both sides of the law.

This violence was spreading to the television and movie screens as well. Police shows become increasingly violent with gunplay becoming a staple. The attitude of the viewers might best be summed up by Donald Horton, the narrator of Harlan Ellison's 1977 short story "Jeffty Is Five," when he says

> When I was fourteen years old, I used to go to the movies on Saturday afternoons [...] and I could always be sure of seeing a western like Lash LaRue, or Wild Bill Elliott as Red Ryder with Bobby Blake as Little Beaver, or Roy Roy Rogers, or Johnny Mack Brown[....] Today, I go to movies and see Clint Eastwood blowing people's heads apart like ripe cantaloupes [10].

On television, the "Death on Credit" episode of the anthology series *Police Story*, created by former police officer and novelist Joseph Wambaugh, featured, for its time, a graphic rape scene, and the controversial "Flowers of Evil" episode of *Police Woman* stirred protests due to its homophobic portrayal of lesbianism. Not only were the lesbians portrayed as crazed murderers, but Pepper Anderson (the policewoman of the title) comments that she understands "what a love like yours can do to a person." This growing focus on a hyperrealism and graphic nature of detectives shows culminates in a show like *Starsky and Hutch* which shows one of the detectives, Ken "Hutch" Hutchinson, becoming addicted to heroin.

Columbo seemed to hearken back to a time when the police served as the moral center of a police drama rather than a near-executioner distributing what borders on vigilante justice. When so many police resort to violence, Columbo uses his wit, charm, and unassuming character to disarm those who threaten him with violence. This is sometimes a literal disarming as is the case when the killer in "Lady in Waiting," Beth Chadwick, pulls a gun on Columbo as he tries to arrest her. He calmly says "No, you really don't want to do that. With policemen outside, what would be the point? Besides you're too classy a woman." His recognition of her as a "classy" woman pleases Chadwick, and she hands over the gun. Columbo seems to be trying to bring back the idea Schulman highlighted that disputes, even murder, could be solved peaceably by showing Columbo appealing to the basic decency of the killer.

The show constantly reinforces Columbo's rejection of gun culture that seemed to be embraced by most other television shows (except for *The Mod Squad* who never carried guns either). In "Forgotten Lady," Columbo spends most of the episode trying to avoid going to the gun range to prove his shooting proficiency, as required by regulations. At one point, Columbo is warned that he could be suspended for not complying with the gun-range regulations. The subplot ends with Columbo giving his badge to another detective and asking him to take Columbo's place at the gun range. Sheldon Catz points out that "Playback" is the only episode in which Columbo fires a gun during the complete run of the show (283). Even then, it is not fired in anger but as an experiment to determine the time the murder took place. He is so skittish around the gun he uses that he asks a uniformed police officer to take the safety catch off, saying to Harold Van Wick, the killer, "Hate guns." Just as Columbo is about to shoot the gun into a box filled with sand, he tells Van Wick that Van Wick can put his fingers in his ears as the sound will be loud. When Van Wick replies that he can handle the sound, Columbo replies, "I wish I could say the same." He then turns his head away, puts a finger in his ear closest to the gun, and fires the gun. In the earlier episode "Troubled Waters," Columbo wants to fire a gun into a mattress in order to test the ballistics but, in this case, asks the murderer (Haydn Danziger) to fire the gun for him, saying "I hate guns. Besides, I'm a bad shot. I'm liable to miss."

Columbo, then, *is* the quintessential cozy detective, a cozy detective transplanted into an urban landscape to be sure, but this allows the character to act as a mediator between the audience and an American society that is being radically transformed. As new ideas, modes of behavior, and social relations come into existence, Columbo helps the audience to negotiate a new and often bewildering world. He acts as a corrective not only to the disorienting liberal excesses of the 1970s, but also to the extreme brutal violence of the conservative backlash. Thus, Columbo offers an ideologically centrist social space (a kind of "normal" position) which the audience can inhabit. In broader terms, the television show *Columbo* allows us to see the adaptability of the cozy detective. Recognizing the dynamic characteristics of a subgenre not normally seen in this way and focusing on the primacy of *character* offers critics and readers a way to gain an even greater appreciation for the cozy detective and those who write them.

WORKS CITED

Auden, W.H. "The Guilty Vicarage." *The Dyer's Hand and Other Essays*. (London: Faber & Faber, 1963): 146–158. Print.
"The Big LSD." *Dragnet*, season 1, episode 1, 1967.
Brodbeck, David, Anthony Marco, Bob Goyetche. "Monaco Rich." *Best Episode Ever Podcast*. S5E14. 24 Feb 2014. http://bestepisodeever.com/?page=10.
Catz, Sheldon. *Columbo Under Glass: A critical analysis of the cases, clues and character of the Good Lieutenant*. BearManor Media, 2006. Print.
Chandler, Raymond. "The Simple Art of Murder: An Essay." *The Simple Art of Murder*. Ballantyne Books, 1977. Print.
Christie, Agatha. *The Murder at the Vicarage*. William Morrow, 2011. Print.
"Crimes and Cults." *The Seventies*, episode 4. CNN. July 9, 2015.
Cronkite, Walter. "How Walter Cronkite's broadcast changed the way we perceived the Vietnam War." *The Washington Post*. May 25, 2018. https://www.washingtonpost.com/national/did-thenews-media-led-by-walter-cronkite-lose-the-war-in-vietnam/2018/05/25/a5b3e098-495e-11e8827e-190efaf1flee_story.html.
Davis, J. Madison. "So Who Has Time to Read? Social Class and Crime Writing, Part 1." *World Literature Today*. 87.5 (September/October 2013): 9–11. https://www.jstor.org/stable/10.7588/worllitetoda.87.5.0009.
Dawidziak, Mark. *The Columbo Phile: A Casebook*. Mysterious Press, 1989. Print.
"Death on Credit." *Police Story*, season 1, episode 8, 1973.
Ellison, Harlan. "Jeffty Is Five." *The Magazine of Fantasy and Science Fiction*. 53.1 (July 1977): 8–27. Print.
"Etude in Black." *Columbo*, season 2, episode 1, 1972.
"Flowers of Evil." *Police Woman*, season 1, episode 8, 1974.
"Forgotten Lady." *Columbo*, season 5, episode 1, 1975.
"Frank Sinatra." *The Dean Martin Celebrity Roasts*. July 2, 1978. *YouTube* uploaded by Ccvanl4, 16 June, 2018, https://www.youtube.com/watch?v=3_UN2S8SasY.
"A Friend in Deed." *Columbo*, season 3, episode 8, 1974.
Graham, Adam. The Top Twenty-Five Dragnet Programs, Part Five." March 2. Retrieved February 22, 2019. http://www.greatdetectives.net/detectives/?s=dragnet+the+lsd+story.
Gramsci, Antonio. *Selections form the Prison Notebooks*. Edited by Quintin Hoare and Geoffrey Nowell Smith. International Publishers, 2003. Print.
"The Guru." *The Mod Squad*, season 1, episode 12, Thomas/Spelling Productions, 1968.
Harmon, Gary L. "Tarzan and Columbo, Heroic Mediators." *The Hero in Transition*. Edited by Ray B. Browne and Marshall W. Fishwick, Popular, 1983, pp. 115–130. Print.
"Lady in Waiting." *Columbo*, season 1, episode 5, 1971.
"Magnum on Ice: Part 2." *Murder She Wrote*, season 3, episode 8 1986.
Minutaglio, Bill and Steven L. Davis. *The Most Dangerous Man in America: Timothy Leary, Richard Nixon and the Hunt for the Fugitive King of LSD*. New York and Boston: Twelve, 2018. Print.
Moyer, Daniel. "Notes," Commemorative Booklet. *Dragnet: 1968*, Shout Factory, 2010. Print.
"Novel Connection." *Magnum P.I.*, season 7, episode 9, 1986.

"Playback." *Columbo*, season 4, episode 5, 1975.
"The Prophet." *Dragnet*, season 2, episode 18, 1968.
Schulman, Bruce J. *The Seventies: The Great Shift in American Culture, Society, and Politics.* The Free Press, 2001. Print.
Sharrett, Christopher. "Jack Webb and the Vagaries of Right-Wing TV Entertainment." *Cinema Journal*. 51.4 (Summer 2012): 165–171. Print.
Simon, Roger. *Gramsci's Political Thought: An Introduction*. Lawrence and Wishart, 1991. Print.
Spelling, Aaron, with Jefferson Graham. *A Prime-Time Life: An Autobiography*. St. Martin's Press, 1996. Print.
Stasio, Marilyn. "Murder Least Foul: The Cozy, Soft-Boiled Mystery." *The New York Times*, section 7 (October 18, 1992): 42. https://www.nytimes.com/1992/10/18/books/crime-mystery murder-least-foul-the-cozy-soft-boiled-mystery.html.
Street, Joe "Dirty Harry's San Francisco," *The Sixties*, 5:1, 2012. 1–21, DOI: 10.1080/17541328. 2012.674850.
"Summer of Love." *American Experience*. PBS. April 23, 2007.
"Television Gets Real." *The Seventies*, episode 1. CNN. June 11, 2015.
"Why Columbo Matters as Much as Ever." *The Columbophile*. June 23, 2018. https://columbophile.wordpress.com/2018/06/23/why-columbo-matters-as-much-as-ever/ Accessed July 14, 2018.

The Best of Both Worlds
Being Cozy and Hard-boiled in Rex Stout's Nero Wolfe

SALLY BERESFORD-SHERIDAN

Nero Wolfe will tell anyone who is around—whether they care to hear or not—that the ingredients down to the last pinch of tarragon make or break the final meal. Throughout his career in the 75 stories written by Rex Stout, we see Wolfe storm out of the kitchen, or worse, refuse to eat a meal, when his personal chef Fritz Brenner has dared to deviate from the prescribed menu. When the success of the final meal is determined by the exact quality of the ingredients, it is the ingredients which are important to define, determine, and examine to understand the final result.

How do you define the elements that belong to the successful murder mysteries of Rex Stout? How do you narrow down the definitions enough to determine what elements make up this mystery and the subsequent sub-genre it should be labeled? Robert S. Paul, in *Whatever Happened to Sherlock Holmes*, writes that detective fiction manifests itself in two basic forms: the "classic ratiocinative puzzle" (or, as Stephen Knight calls it, the clue-puzzle) in the tradition of Edgar Allan Poe and Sir Author Conan Doyle, and the hard-boiled, non-conforming mystery more seriously developed by American authors (244). From here, critics and readers further narrow down the genre, creating sub-genre categories and labels to alert readers of what they can expect from the story itself. Indeed, there are several words and phrases used to describe the myriad of stories that comprise the world of detective fiction such as hard-boiled, Golden Age, cozy, soft-boiled, a locked room mystery, and even old-fashioned clue puzzles.

The Nero Wolfe series has had many labels attached to it by various critics: Charles J. Rzepka includes Rex Stout as a Golden Age interwar writer (*Detective Fiction* 155); Stephen Knight calls the Wolfe series "American clue-puzzles" and characteristic of the Golden Age (*Crime Fiction: 1800–2000* 87); while John McAleer, Stout's biographer, claims that Rex Stout saved the detective genre by writing stories which fuse the best elements of both the hard-boiled and the formal detective story (*Rex Stout: A Biography* 6). In the "Introduction" to the 1990s reprint of Rex Stout's *And Be a Villain* (1948), husband and wife team Martin Meyers and Annette Meyers (known jointly as Maan Meyers) write, "[s]omewhere between the hard-boiled detective story and the cozy mystery, Nero Wolfe sits alone, the master, in his huge specially constructed brown leather Brazilian Mauro chair" (ix).

In this essay I argue that the Nero Wolfe mystery stories by Rex Stout straddle the border between two subgenres of detective fiction, the hard-boiled and the cozy. While the hard-boiled mystery is well defined and assumes set expectations, the cozy mystery lacks such parameters and thus must be examined within the context of actual stories to determine its ideal ingredients. This being the case, I suggest that the Nero Wolfe stories, in their liminal position of neither hard-boiled or cozy, can help to determine the parameters of the cozy label more clearly and help to set readerly expectations of the fiction. As Nero Wolfe states in *Too Many Cooks* (1938), "I've often told you, a search for negative evidence is a desperate last resort when no positive evidence can be found. Collecting and checking alibis is dreary and usually futile drudgery. No. Get your positive evidence, and if you find it confronted by the alibi, and if your evidence is any good, break the alibi" (153). Thoroughly examining the hard-boiled aspects will leave the cozy aspects of the mysteries accessible for scrutiny.

It must be noted that when defining the sub-genres of what Robert S. Paul states were the two types of detective fiction—the clue puzzle and the hard-boiled (244)—labels will overlap, time periods and societal concerns will change, and thus definitions will be fluid. As Stephen Knight writes, "to think in terms of specific periods as if they belong exclusively to a sub-genre is to falsify the complex, overlapping and multiple ways in which sub-genres and their audiences operate" (86).

My essay is broken into sections which examine different aspects of the Wolfe corpus. Before I start to investigate the aspects of the stories, however, I discuss the assumptions of a "cozy" mystery articulated by various cozy authors and readers. I examine the hard-boiled aspects of the stories themselves, question how women and relationships play into the hard-boiled or cozy aspects of the series, and finally, speculate on how the Wolfe series participates in cozy conventions to further clarify the cozy mystery definition.

Doing the "Legwork": Current and Prevailing Cozy Definitions

It is important to begin by questioning the term "cozy." Then, in turn, how do we read this term in relation to the mystery stories themselves? Do we impose the label retrospectively on the stories or is it simply applicable for a new genre of writing? Knight defines "cozy mysteries" as continuations of the Golden-Age British clue-puzzle which had declined in the aftermath of the Second World War and taken on a new attempt at realism (136–139). This realism was based, he claims, in characters and/or context and relied more heavily on the police detective in a longer series called "cosies" or, in the U.S., "cozies." He writes, "These are usually set, with some credible detail and cross-class sociology, in a provincial region of England, where a senior detective investigated an exotic crime with its roots in local and usually familial hostilities and obsessions" (136). Knight seems to have a different interpretation of the term "cozy" than is often discussed by the new so-called/self-entitled "cozy" authors themselves as I outline below.

This anthology works towards defining the "cozy," a term already frequently used by authors and readers alike. As these authors and readers have preconceived assumptions of what the cozy mystery is, I refer to their expectations using sources perhaps not considered "academic," in addition to critical works. George N. Dove writes in *The Reader and the Detective Story* that detective fiction is unique in that the reader is directly involved in its structure, and therefore the fiction must take the reader into consideration (1). To further justify my use of blog postings and reviews, I turn to Dorothy L. Sayers, a founding member and third president of the Detection Club.[1] Sayers published reviews of mystery stories for several years and her standards for the strength of the stories have come to be recognized as criteria for defining Golden-Age detective fiction (Edwards, "Introduction" 3). Her reviews have recently been brought together into an edited collection *Taking Detective Stories Seriously: The Collected Crime Reviews of Dorothy L. Sayers* and provide Sayers' witty and insightful comments on many detective stories to fans of the genre. Therefore, blog postings and online reviews by self-entitled cozy authors and readers are essential when looking at the expectations and definitions of a cozy mystery.

In a *New York Times* article from 1992 entitled, "Murder Least Foul: The Cozy, Soft-Boiled Mystery," journalist Marilyn Stasio comments on the "new publishing rage" of the cozy mysteries. She argues that audiences were ready for gentler reading material after the blood, gore, and psychological stress from thrillers such as *Silence of the Lambs*. She explains that these "polite, 'cozy' mysteries, [are] remarkable for their nonthreatening content and nonviolent characters. ... [M]ystery readers were probably ready for more civilized killers with more agreeable manners." Stasio takes her loose definition of the cozy from the Malice Domestic Advocacy Group started in the 1980s by authors and fans of the genre. She writes that while there is no formal definition of the contemporary cozy, seven key attributes are identifiable:

    1. no gore
    2. the detective is an amateur who also works at another interesting profession such as bookkeeping
    3. the crime is in an enclosed community (in a series, the author must send their sleuth out of town before the population is wiped out by the several murders which must necessarily continue to be committed)
    4. "the settings are never sleazy; the atmosphere is designed to give pleasure and comfort"
    5. the characters have no affiliation with professional institutions such as the CIA or mafia and the mysteries are solved through personal motivation
    6. In terms of the physical bodies of the sleuths themselves, sex and violence are described discreetly—often the sleuth will be in romantic relationships though sex is unmentioned and she/he is most likely never beaten up.

The seventh and most important definition of the cozy mystery as mentioned by its advocates, Stasio writes, "is the belief that it is an updated version of the traditional British detective story."

This definition is at odds with that of Knight's above, where he reiterates the pastoral countryside of England as being the ideal setting for the post-war "cozy" and cites P.D. James as an innovator of the genre (136–137). Stasio discusses a North American setting, or an "Americanization and modernization of the classic English mystery." This being the case, perhaps a distinction between the English "cozy" and American "cozy" can be proposed. As the Nero Wolfe stories take place in the United States, I focus on shaping an American definition of the "cozy" for the purposes of this essay rather than Knight's use of the English "cozy" as the need for post-war realism in small pastoral English settings.[2]

Self-described cozy mystery author Barbara Ross, author of the Maine Clambake Mystery series, wrote a three-part blog post defining the cozy mystery[3] and she acknowledges that the definition mostly sounds like the traditional mystery story, or what Stephen Knight would call the "clue-puzzle"[4] mystery. She further adds to the cozy definition that, "many people append, 'In a cozy mystery, cursing is kept to a minimum and most sex and gore are kept off the page'" ("How I Learned to Relax About Being a 'Cozy' Author and Just Write the Damn Books—Part III"). A common factor in trying to define the cozy mystery seems to be that, much like the Greek tragedies, the action happens off-stage.

Other opinions of the cozy mystery include character development; one commenter on Ross's post writes: "I believe character development is what defines a cozy.... I'm especially fond of books in a series simply because the characters become like old friends (or sometimes old enemies). Even the place becomes a character" (comment by "nohausfrau," July 23, 2015, at 7:52 a.m.).

As is clear, there are many discussions surrounding the definition of the "cozy" mystery which call for scrutiny. It might even be noted that perhaps sub-sub-genres of the cozy mystery need to be identified such as the modern cozy, the American cozy, and the English cozy. Both Stasio and cozy authors additionally now seem to see the modern cozy as having more accidental/superfluous definitions included in the cozy criteria such as having cats on the cover page, puns as titles, and generally more female than male authors of the genre.[5]

While Stasio's article seems to be a comprehensive list of what the cozy is, she also calls for a standard of quality for the cozy genre. She warns against authors who simply include what they think are so-called classic tropes of the cozy genre, (as mentioned above: cats on the cover page; puns for titles etc.) and writes that, "[u]nless its leading practitioners keep their literary priorities straight, however, the only place the cozy might be going is to the dogs—er, cats." Though Stasio was primarily reviewing the so-called cozy genre as a whole, she seems to agree with Sayers on the importance of literary style and cautions against allowing clichés of the genre to take over the literary merit of the stories themselves. As Sayers wrote about her reviews: "People sometimes complain that I am harsh.... I give you my word that when I meet the least touch of real originality ... or glamour, or humour.... I hail it with cries of joy. But 99 times out of 100 I find only bad English, cliché, balderdash, and boredom" (*Taking Detective Stories Seriously* 8). No matter the sub-genre, in order for the stories to be taken seriously, originality and effective writing must be displayed; all of which are key ingredients in Rex Stout's series.

From these definitions of the American cozy, it seems at first that the Nero Wolfe stories do not quite fit into the "ideal" cozy mystery. And as I stated in my introduction, there are certainly elements of the hard-boiled story in the Nero Wolfe corpus. In taking these hard-boiled aspects apart however, I argue that there are indeed cozy elements present in Nero Wolfe stories and these can help highlight a more precise definition of the "cozy" mystery itself.

The Case for Being Hard-boiled

Archie Goodwin opens the first Nero Wolfe novel, *Fer-de-lance* (1934), seven years into his working relationship with Nero Wolfe. Consequently, our first introduction of the two—Wolfe and Archie—shows them in an established relationship and as a working team. The tone of *Fer-de-lance* differs slightly from the other Wolfe stories: Archie's snappy character and narration is more stilted: he is less accustomed to his role as narrator than in subsequent stories. In taking his role as narrator to Nero Wolfe as the "Great Detective," Archie participates in two detective fiction traditions simultaneously: Christopher Breu in *Hard-boiled Masculinities* states that a first person narrator in stories characterizes the hard-boiled genre (13), yet Archie additionally plays a "Watson" role to Nero Wolfe, laying out the story for the reader so as not to let us into the mind of the "Great Detective" himself who ultimately solves the case. John McAleer in his biography of Rex Stout writes that while Nero Wolfe is a "'Great Detective' in the classic mold. Archie Goodwin is hard-boiled" (6). And it is the mingling of the two that presents aspects of both a hard-boiled and cozy mystery in the Rex Stout series.

P.G. Wodehouse, in his Forward to McAleer's biography, claims that "Stout's supreme triumph was the creation of Archie Goodwin" (xv). He goes on to state that "Telling a mystery story in the third person is seldom satisfactory. ... A Watson of some sort to tell the story is unavoidable. Archie is a Watson in the sense that he tells the story, but in no other way is there anything Watsonian about him" (xv-xvi). Archie fulfills his role as Watson insofar as he narrates the story, but really, he does much more. As Wolfe refuses to leave the house, Archie becomes the active partner of their alliance, giving him the agency to go where Wolfe should go, when Wolfe refuses. In being the active partner, Archie participates more in the hard-boiled detective tradition than the sedentary Wolfe. As Breu writes, "The story also requires that the hard-boiled male be in motion ... gaining agency as he moves knowingly through seemingly opaque urban spaces" (13). Archie is the narrator, but is also given the role of active detective, since Wolfe, his reputation for genius well established, eccentrically declines to leave the house. Archie becomes Wolfe's eyes and ears when Wolfe refuses to leave the house, to become mobile, or to enter into potentially dangerous situations: "I repeat, Mr. Frost, it is useless," he declared. "I never leave my home on business. ... You observe my bulk. I am not immoveable, but my flesh has a constitutional reluctance to sudden, violent or sustained displacement" (*The Red Box* 7, 8). And Wolfe explains to Archie in a later short story, after Archie has used subterfuge to bring Wolfe to investigate a murder:

> You regard my rule not to leave my house on a business errand as one of the stubborn poses of a calculated eccentricity. It is no such luxury; it is merely a necessity for a tolerable existence. Without such a rule a private detective is the slave of all the exigencies of his neighbors, and in New York there are ten million of them [*Invitation to Murder* 41].

While Archie enjoys his freedom to go out and detect, he, for the most part, follows Wolfe's instructions when moving around the city. New York City is so well known to Archie that he knows all its nooks and crannies, while Wolfe, despite having the gargantuan globe in his office, displays an embarrassing lack of knowledge about New York and its outer limits. Archie possesses agency in motion through the city; he knows, loves, and understands it. Wolfe is motionless and unaware of the physical layout of the land, yet it is he who demystifies the mystery. In terms of moving through the dangers of the city, Archie is the hard-boiled male detective who fights his way through the mean streets of the metropolis.

Additionally, it appears that Rex Stout was concerned with how his fiction would be labeled and introduces the adjective hard-boiled almost at the beginning of *Fer-de-lance*. Wanting to discuss a new development in the case with Wolfe, Archie states, "I just waited, thinking I would show him that other people could be as hard-boiled as he was" (58). In his statement, Archie seems to convey that both he and Wolfe are hard-boiled: right from the beginning of the series we see the assumption that a hard-boiled element will be present in the stories themselves. After Archie refers to himself as hard-boiled in the first book of the series, several clients continue to utilize the term in relation to themselves and the cases that they are bringing to Wolfe to solve: "I persuaded my uncle to come see you. ... I told my uncle he was a sentimental romantic. ... I'm not. I'm hard-boiled" (*The League of Frightened Gentlemen* 19). We can theorize that Stout was still debating on the impact of the hard-boiled story on his fiction and wanted to make his readers aware of the potentiality of hard-boiled aspects in the stories. His use of the term diminishes as he continues to write his stories.

The action that characterizes hard-boiled stories, according to Breu, "is reserved for the kinds of violent action that were the stock-in-trade of most pulp magazines.... Action usually comes in quick bursts in the hard-boiled narrative and is represented as chaotic and potentially disorientating" (14). Conversely, cozy author Patricia Sprinkle, in her Introduction to Stout's *In the Best Families* (1950), writes that Nero Wolfe taught her to love the intelligent detective rather than the ones who "lead with their fists or their gonads"[6] (vii) such as is characterized by the hard-boiled genre. While there might be violence or the occasional swear word in the Nero Wolfe corpus, for the most part these happen off the page or are censored by Archie's narration. Wolfe absolutely refuses to use physical violence when solving a case and declares in *Too Many Cooks* that "I wouldn't use physical violence even if I could, because one of my romantic ideas is that physical violence is beneath the dignity of a man, and that whatever you get by physical aggression costs more than it is worth" (112). In *The Red Box* (1937), Archie goes to the police station to witness a suspect being questioned by the police and portrays disgust at the physical interrogation techniques utilized on the suspect (146–149). While Archie is not above using some violence himself—as he says "though the ethics of it was none of my business, I admit I had my prejudices. I can bulldog a man myself, if he has it coming to him, but I prefer to do it on his home grounds, and I certainly don't want any help" (*The Red Box* 147)—he is shown to be adept in hand-to-hand combat, always carries a gun when investigating murder, and for the most part he uses violence as a last resort to protect Wolfe or a client. In a humorous twist, Rex Stout has Archie as the narrator comment on this censorship. In *Death of Dude* (1969), Archie tells the reader:

> Actually that isn't what he said. But about a year ago I got a four-page letter from a woman in Wichita, Kansas, saying that she had read all of my reports and that as each of her fourteen grandchildren reached his or her twelfth birthday she gave him or her copies of three of them just to get them started. If I go ahead and report what Emmett Lake actually said I would almost certainly lose that nice old lady, and what about the grandchildren who aren't twelve yet? I don't like censorship any better than you do, and if the payoff was going to be that it was Emmett who shot Brodell, I would have to report him straight and kiss Wichita good-by. But he just happened to be around because it was a ranch and he was a cowhand, so I'll edit him. Those of you who like the kind of words he liked can stick them in yourselves, and don't skimp [102].

Tragedy, violence, and foul language, according to Wolfe, Archie, and Stout, are best left off-stage.

At the start of the series Archie wants the reader to believe that both he and Wolfe are hard-boiled. Wolfe, however, refuses to conform to the ideal of the hard-boiled detective, who, according to Knight, "rarely detects very much, using his movements, observations, consciousness (and his frequent unconsciousness) as his primary method of unraveling a mystery" (112). Rather, from the beginning of the series in *Fer-de-lance*, Wolfe tells Archie that he is an artist:

> Must I again demonstrate that while it is permissible to request the scientist to lead you back over his footprints, a similar request of the artist is nonsense, since he, like the lark or the eagle, has made none? Do you need to be told again that I am an artist? [40]

And, as he explains in *The Golden Spiders* (1953):

> [Y]ou must thoroughly understand that primarily you are practicing an art, not a science. ... Science in detection can be distinguished, even brilliant, but it can never replace either the inexorable march of a fine intellect through a jungle of lies and fears

to the clearing of truth, or the flash of perception along a sensitive nerve touched off by a tone of a voice or a flicker of an eye [9].

Wolfe is a self-declared artist and throughout the series, Archie, amongst others, acknowledges him as a genius. As an artist and genius, Wolfe does not always feel the need to let Archie, and therefore the reader, in on his thought process nor to explain how he is going to solve the mystery. In the same style of Holmes and Poirot, Wolfe does not always let his "Watson" share his secrets. This allows for staging and a big reveal at the end of the story, a moment which Wolfe, much like Poirot or Holmes, revels in. This aspect of the Wolfe series brings it fully in line with both the Golden Age traditional mysteries, which are sometimes also characterized as clue-puzzles. These Golden Age stories place high value on rationality and plot intricacies, both of which are abundant in the Wolfe corpus. Set in the United States and spanning the Golden Age and into the 1970s, the Wolfe stories overlap or break out of many categories. As mentioned above, Marilyn Stasio quotes aficionados of the cozy genre who believe that "the strongest article of faith held by champions of the cozy mystery is the belief that it is an updated version of the traditional British detective story ... the Americanization and modernization of the classic English mystery." With his self-acknowledged artistic ability for solving cases, Wolfe removes himself from the hard-boiled tradition and places himself firmly in the tradition of Holmes and Poirot, both of whom are quintessential classic English detectives.

It is important to note that Stout plays fair with his readers and does not hide clues from them; rather, it is Wolfe who keeps information from Archie, who, as the narrator, shares in the readers' myopia. Archie aligns himself with the reader by stating that

> There was nothing new about it, but that didn't make me like it any better. ... [H]is theory [is] that the less I know the more I can help, or to put it another way, that everything inside my head shows on my face. It only makes it worse that he doesn't really believe it. He merely can't stand it to have anybody keep up with him at any time on any track [*Instead of Evidence* 207–208].

Archie also assumes that the reader keeps up with or surpasses him in solving the mystery. Several times throughout the series, Archie breaks the fourth wall and addresses the reader, acknowledging that they may have solved the case before he did. In the final Wolfe book, *A Family Affair* (1975), Archie declares:

> When I heard him say that, I knew. It came in a flash, like lightening. It wasn't a guess or a hunch, I *knew*. I'm aware that you probably knew a while back and you're surprised that I didn't but that doesn't prove that you're smarter than I am. You are just reading about it, and I was in it, right in the middle of it [original emphasis, 114].

In addressing the reader in this manner, Archie assumes their cleverness, as well as establishing a relationship with them. And relationships are key in the solving of these mysteries, and the mystery of defining the cozy.

On Women and the Femme Fatale

The most complex aspects surrounding the discussion of the Wolfe series as hard-boiled or not arise in the manner by which Stout deals with women and various personal relationships. Some critics accuse Stout of misogyny while others defend his portrayal of women (as detective fiction author Sandra West Prowell comments on in her Introduction [1995] to *Death of a Doxy* [1966]), and though the relationships involving women at first appear to highlight the hard-boiled features of the stories, ultimately the "women question" points to the most "cozy" element of the series: the personal relationship between Wolfe and Archie.

Nero Wolfe's relationship with women is difficult; even Archie finds it so. On many occasions, Wolfe declares his attitude towards women: "Not like women? They are astounding and successful animals. For reasons of convenience, I merely preserve an appearance of immunity which I developed some years ago under the pressure of necessity" (*Too Many Cooks* 107). What this pressure of necessity was, the readers are never told. When examining the Nero Wolfe stories for hard-boiled aspects, however, the case could be made that Wolfe may be justified in remaining aloof from women. Stephen Knight writes that in the hard-boiled genre, it is often the woman who poses the biggest threat to the detective: "in the private-eye novels the real crimes solved, the deepest threats faced by the private eyes, come from personal betrayals, mostly by women" (112). He writes in addition, that "if the threat of gangsters and corruptions is in Chandler's novels a charade, real villainy is simple and consistent; it was a woman who did it" (119). Perhaps Wolfe's fear of women stems from a fear of becoming a hard-boiled detective. Additionally, if it is the woman who "did it" in the hard-boiled stories, Breu writes that the action of the hard-boiled mystery "often exceeds *any relationship to the solution of the mystery* or resolution of the narrative" (emphasis added, 14). He then continues that "The hard-boiled male's relationship to other men is generally antagonistic, forming the locus of much of the narrative's violent action" (15). Thus, in the hard-boiled genre, the antagonistic relationships between the men in the story drive the action and narration, while women become the catalyst for the downfall of the detective. The Wolfe stories do not participate in this hard-boiled trope. It is the relationships and the mutual understanding, specifically between Wolfe and Archie, which brings conclusion to the stories themselves. These relationships also encompass Wolfe's broader household established in the brownstone where Wolfe, Archie, Fritz (the chef) and Theodore (the orchid man) all live, and the additional operatives Saul, Fred, Orrie, and Jonny,[7] whom Wolfe utilizes when necessary. While at first it appears that Wolfe's mistrust and relationship with women solidly categorizes the series as hard-boiled fiction, in actual fact, it is this quirk that amplifies his existent relationships within the household which the series is built upon. Consequently, we can state that this creates the coziest aspects of the books.

In order for the cozy relationship between Wolfe and Archie to be understood, the potential hard-boiled nature of Wolfe's relationship with women must first be discussed. Wolfe is certainly more hard-boiled than Archie regarding women. He often mistrusts Archie's relationship with women and sometimes feels compelled to act outside of his comfort zone to protect his and Archie's relationship from a possible threat. In *Christmas Party* from the omnibus *And Four to Go* (1958), Wolfe leaves his home, dressed up to play Santa Claus, to verify for himself Archie's announcement of marriage: "The point was this, that he had shown what he really thought of me. He had shown that rather than lose me he would do something that he wouldn't have done for any fee anybody could name" (30). In this case, Wolfe is justified in his fear for Archie, since Margo's relationship with Archie is entirely self-serving; she kills the man that she truly loves, counting on Archie's good feelings to hide her part in the murder. Archie's potential marriage demonstrates for the reader, and for Archie, both Wolfe's dependence on Archie as well as his regard for him. Wolfe insists on keeping his relationship with Archie while at the same time rushing to save Archie from a potential *femme fatale*.

The character of Lily Rowan is introduced six books into the series and her function could be seen as a prospective *femme fatale*. Throughout the rest of the series she plays the role of potential romantic interest for Archie. In *Some Buried Caesar* (1938), Archie is introduced to Lily when, after he has hurdled over a fence escaping a charging bull, Lily, who was watching, calls him Escamillo (15). This establishes the tone of their relationship from the beginning, and it is clear that Lily is able to repartee with Archie no matter the situation. Lily catches Archie's eye when he looked up to see her gazing at him. As Breu notes, the hard-boiled male controls the gaze throughout the story (13), and Archie characterizes the gaze for the audience in his descriptions of the women within the series. He describes Lily:

> The girl in yellow slacks was there close. I realized with surprise that her head came clear to my chin or above, and she was blonde but not at all faded, and her dark blue eyes were not quite open, and one corner of her lips was up with her smile.... She brushed against me as we walked and said, "I'm Lily Rowan." ... Then we sat again, with

Lily the blonde doing a languid drape on a canvas swing and a beautiful calf protruding from one leg of her yellow slacks [15, 16, 22].

The readers have by now been used to participating in Archie's voyeurism and his treatment of Lily is routine. What signals her as a *femme fatale* comes to Archie in the form of a warning from another woman. Caroline tells Archie that Lily is dangerous and hires Archie to protect her brother from being enthralled in Lily's clutches. Caroline tells Archie:

> She's a vampire. She's dangerous.... I used to think the talk about some women being dangerous, you know, really dangerous, was romantic hooey, but it isn't. Lily Rowan is one. If she wasn't too lazy to make much of an effort there's no telling how many men she might ruin [*Some Buried Caesar* 45].

Naturally, these warnings only serve to pique Archie's interest, and Lily weaves in and out of the plots throughout the series. Though her potential as a *femme fatale* is there, and Lily upsets Wolfe's relationship with Archie quite a few times, she ultimately does not bring about either of their downfalls. Lily serves, rather, as a fun romantic partner for Archie, highlighting his dancing skills at their favorite club, the Flamingo.

The Wolfe series seems to play humorously with the notion that women upset the balance of order or cause the downfall of the detective from the hard-boiled tradition while at the same time refusing to fully engage with *femme fatales*. In *The Rubber Band* (1936) Clara Fox, Wolfe's client who is forced into hiding at the brownstone, tells Archie:

> You know, Mr. Goodwin, this house represents the most insolent denial of female rights the mind of man has ever conceived. No woman in it from top to bottom, but the routine is faultless, the food is perfect, and the sweeping and dusting are impeccable. I have never been a housewife, but I can't overlook this challenge. I'm going to marry Mr. Wolfe, and I know a girl that will be just the thing for you, and of course our friends will be in and out a good deal. *This place needs some upsetting* [emphasis added, 115].

Ideas about women's place in domestic duties aside, Clara claims that bringing women into the house would "upset" or turn upside down the apparently smooth arrangements in the male household. Archie also tells us that Fritz Brenner, the cook, is wary of any female presence, worried that she will marry Wolfe and thus usurp his right in the kitchen:

> I was glad Fritz wasn't there. He suspects every woman who ever crosses the threshold of wanting to take over his kitchen, not to mention the rest of the house. He would have been squirming. Dol Bonner's caramel-colored eyes and long dark lashes were by no means her only physical attractions, and she was the right age, she had shown some sense and had done a pretty good job of reporting, and she was a companion of misery, having also been made a monkey of by Donahue [*Too Many Detectives* 160].

While drolly crediting the hard-boiled tradition that women upset relationships between men and destroy the male detective, Stout additionally uses this ploy to illuminate the main relationship in Wolfe's Brownstone which provides the cozy aspects to the series.

Being Cozy in Relationships

Stout makes it clear that Archie and Wolfe know each other well. Archie tells the readers again and again that he knows Wolfe in all moods and knows how to manage him. The following quotation from *If Death Ever Slept* (1957) has an intimate quality about it that signals the importance of the relationship between Wolfe and Archie:

> It was at the table that I caught on that something was up. Wolfe wasn't being crusty because the outlook was dark; he was being smug because he had tasted blood, or was expecting to. He always enjoyed his food, whether in spite of circumstances or in harmony with them, and after ten thousand meals with him I knew all the shades. The way he spread his pâté on a cracker, the way he picked up the knife to slice the filet of beef in aspic, the way he used his fork on the salad, the way he made his choice from the cheese platter—no question about it, he had something or somebody by the tail, or at least the tail was in sight [138].

Ultimately it is the relationship between Archie and Wolfe which constructs these stories and continues to make us read them. As mentioned above, a common concession regarding the cozy mystery is character development, sometimes, even to the detriment of plot. While Stout's stories have carefully constructed plots (McAleer mentions some heretical claims that the plots are overwhelmed by Stout's characterization of Wolfe and Archie [7]), they also have characters who grow and continue to delight in the decades in which they were portrayed. In his biography of Rex Stout, John McAleer writes that Stout never dreamed of reporting Wolfe's death as Agatha Christie and Conan Doyle did with their heroes. Rather, he hoped that Wolfe "lives forever" (McAleer 13).

The Wolfe stories are new and continually fresh: they combine character development with complicated puzzles to solve. And while there is character growth and development within the Brownstone over the many decades that Wolfe and Archie solve crime, they are ageless and thus continually able to perform their duties as when we first met them. Archie can never be over thirty-four (he is twenty-four years Wolfe's junior [McAleer 10, 27]) because he will continually be going out with Lily Rowan and breaking hearts in every case that he gets. Wolfe is forever fifty-eight (McAleer 12); he cannot grow old and die for then the city of New York would be bereft of him solving its cases. And most importantly, Wolfe and Archie continue their unique relationship, creating cozy comforts for the reader of the Nero Wolfe series.

Participating in Cozy Traditions

While I have argued that the relationship between Nero Wolfe and Archie is the most important aspect to define the cozy mystery, there are other "cozy" conventions which the series also participates in. The cozy mystery usually takes place in a confined setting whereas the hard-boiled narratives "dispense with the device of a bounded space" (Horsley 27). While at first the Nero Wolfe stories seem to belie this description, offering the entirety of New York and millions of inhabitants as potential suspects, Wolfe relates the cases to himself and therefore confines the scope of the investigation. While he sometimes makes reference to searching the entire metropolis of New York for his suspect, his clients—those that solicit favors from him or can afford to pay his fees—bring with them problems that immediately narrow down the list of suspects to a certain group of people: Nero Wolfe's cases for the most part do not engage with a seedy underworld. Wolfe's draw and ability as a detective, as well as the large fees he charges, offer an enclosed setting for the cases to inhabit. David Anderson writes in *Rex Stout* that the opening and closing scenes of the Wolfe corpus, from *Fer-de-Lance* (1934) to *A Family Affair* (1975) take place on the steps of the brownstone and "all of the intervening scenes owe something to the stability, solidity, and impregnability of the world represented by that structure" (15). The world within the Wolfe series revolves around the household Nero Wolfe has created.

The Wolfe series renews the idea of the Golden Age gentleman detective, or the novel of manners, yet does not become those as it takes place in different world—America—and thus enters into the cozy tradition of becoming the "Americanization of the British tradition." The Nero Wolfe corpus revisits the elements that made the Golden Age of detective fiction timeless, solving mysteries in a small space or place, presenting limited characters with whom to interact, and by presenting criminals and detectives that exist in a certain echelon of an ordered society—not the "seedy underbelly" so often presented in the hard-boiled genre. Additionally, though Wolfe is not a "gentleman," and he does not solve crimes for the sake of humanity as he so often tells the reader, we know that Wolfe feels the bonds of relationship and the human element in his cases. In as many stories as he charges exorbitant fees, he also assumes cases where he acts out of his sense of duty and justice for the victim; Archie always makes this clear to the readers. One example is found in the short story "Kill Now-Pay Later" (1961) wherein the shoeshine man Nero Wolfe employs is murdered and Archie tells the bereaved daughter that Wolfe will accept the case *pro bono*: "Skip it. That's no inducement for him. And don't thank him. He would rather miss a meal than have anyone think he's a softy, that he would wiggle a finger to help anyone" (32).

Nero Wolfe is further proved to be an honorable man. In *If Death Ever Slept* (1957), Inspector Cramer, certainly no friend to Wolfe and Archie, holds a grudging respect for them because he knows that Wolfe is an honorable man. Wolfe asks Cramer:

> "Do you believe in words of honor?"
> "I do when the honor is there."
> "Am I a man of honor?"
> Cramer's eyes widened. He was flabbergasted. He started to answer and stopped. He had to consider. "You may be, at that," he allowed. "You're tricky, you're foxy, you're the best liar I know, but if anybody asked me to name something you had done that was dishonorable I'd have to think."
> "Very well, think."
> "Skip it. Say you're a man of honor" [120].

Wolfe always holds himself to his code of honor when solving his cases, and outlines in *The Golden Spiders* (1953) the importance of integrity, honor, and putting detecting ability to good use. Wolfe and Archie hold definite notions of right and wrong throughout the stories and only accept a certain kind of case. Stout inserts Wolfe's philosophy thus:

> I shall confine myself to the problems and methods of the private detective who works at his profession for a living. ... It is desirable that you should earn your fees, but it is essential that you feel you have earned them, and that depends partly on your ego. ... with a robust ego, your feeling about earning your fees can safely be left to your intelligence and common sense.... As for your methods, they must of course be suited to your field. I pass over such fields as industrial espionage and divorce evidence and similar repugnant snooperies, since the ego of any man who engages in them is already infested with worms, and so you are not concerned [*The Golden Spiders* 7, 8, 9].

Any client of Wolfe's, while more than likely charged an exorbitant fee, also deals with a man who honorably protects their interests.

The "Big Reveal" or the Cozy Conclusions

In her *New York Times* article, Marilyn Stasio notes the biggest difference between the cozy mystery and the more classic forms of detective mysteries such as that by Christie and Sayers is the de-emphasis of what she calls the "puzzle plot." While the Nero Wolfe stories rely on plot and do not devalue the effect of the mystery and its resolution, they simultaneously use Archie as the narrator to bring the reader into the story and assume that the reader makes their own deductions about the case. As was established earlier, the relationship between Wolfe and Archie brings this series together, and Archie further ensures that the reader is brought into this relationship. This is compelling evidence for the labeling of the Nero Wolfe stories as cozy, and additionally what, I argue, helps to point to a definition of the cozy mystery—its use of relationships within the stories themselves, how these relationships interact with the mystery, and how both are presented to the reader taking into consideration readerly expectations and investment into the relationship of the characters. While the plots are obviously important, for they determine the story in the genre of detective fiction, perhaps cozy can be more narrowed down to how the characters' relationships play out in the books, and how the main characters act towards one another.

I have offered a definition of the cozy mystery—placing the axis on the relationships surrounding the stories. This is most important, but there are obviously other defining aspects of the cozy which have been contested by authors, critics, and readers as I considered near the beginning of the essay. This discourse will no doubt continue, but it is important to keep in mind several aspects for this discussion as I outline below. In the *Cozy Mystery Blog*, the author "Danna" compiles titles of cozy mysteries alphabetically by author and includes outlines of what she determines the cozy to be. Danna writes that "Also included in the 'S' list of mysteries are Rex Stout and Dorothy L. Sayers. Both Stout and Sayers are mystery authors who are considered staples of the genre. The 'S' list of cozy mystery book authors isn't complete without them!" ("Cozy Mystery List, Authors—S"). She goes on to note that one defining aspect of the cozy is that these "rules" or outlines are evident in most cozy stories, but *not all* ("What makes a cozy just that?"). This seems to be the general assumption when defining any particular story, cozy or otherwise. Most often there are stereotypes or boundaries which confine the stories, yet it is in breaking them that literature achieves greatness and genres are defined. Labeling a typical cozy, or other types of sub-genres, is only possible by looking back at stories or series, and then defining what works and what does not work to fit in with the genre itself.

I would also argue that the cozy, like all detective fiction as Dove states in *The Reader and the Detective Story*, has readerly expectations, which include bringing comfort and not introducing too much gore, violence, sex, etc. What the reader's expectations are and what brings comfort will necessarily change with time and the fluctuating social conditions. Detective stories are often thought to be an anodyne for social ills, and the cozy mystery will incorporate this into its plots. As social ills and domestic settings change, perhaps even what is permitted to be "cozy," including the definition I offer regarding relationships, will be expanded. Indeed, "Danna" in her blog writes that "I have to admit that lately, authors of what are considered to be Cozy Mysteries are adding more graphic language and 'adult situations.' I am not sure if this is because their publishers/editors want this or if it is because the public wants (buys) more 'adult situations' Cozy Mysteries" ("What makes a cozy just that?"). Audience willingness and acceptance for certain dialogue and relationships have altered since both the era of Wilkie Collins' *The Moonstone* (1868) (often credited as the first mystery story) and of the Golden Age of Detective Fiction (c. 1913–1945). Attributes of the cozy are already shifting given audience and reader willingness towards certain tropes in the literature. The Nero Wolfe series is an excellent example of this, as the un-aging Nero Wolfe and Archie Goodwin nevertheless modify their language and their interest in political affairs to keep pace with the times. Archie starts out smoking cigarettes but stops; Cramer starts smoking cigars, then simply chews them. In *Fer-de-lance*, we first meet Wolfe as he is trying out prohibition beer; Wolfe and Archie are involved in the Second World War; Wolfe deals with communism and the McCarthy era; and in the last novel, *A Family Affair* (1975), Wolfe initially thinks his case has connections with President Nixon and the Watergate scandal. What remains unaffected, what remains the main cozy attribute of the series, is the emphasis on the relationships, especially that of Nero Wolfe and Archie Goodwin.

This anthology defines the parameters of the cozy mystery. The important notion to be conscious of when defining strictures for detective fiction is that parameters most likely will, and should, be broken in order to continually make the genre new and exciting for its readers. Detective fiction authors continually break the bounds of fiction; the famous Decalogue or Ten Commandments of detective fiction written by the founders of the Detective Fiction Club were seemingly broken before the ink was dry, most famously by Agatha Christie, the "grandmother of the cozy," in her *Murder of Roger Ackroyd* (1926). Additionally, as Charles Rzepka and many other critics argue, the detective fiction genre is best suited for breaking out of its own bounds which then makes social statements, political statements and most especially, really great fiction.

Notes

1. Sayers is also put on the list of "cozy" authors. To define how Sayers is cozy would be another essay in itself. However, it seems as if the label of cozy can also be attached to the clue-puzzles of the Golden Age, known for their gore and violence being kept off the page, an insistence on character development, and rational plotting of the mystery itself. Marilyn Stasio, in her *New York Times* article writes: "Cozy authors do, indeed, draw from classic models; their declarations of admiration for the novels of Agatha Christie and Dorothy L. Sayers, in particular, have a heartfelt ring. But to view the cozy mystery as the continuation of an earlier tradition is to ignore its many modifications on the original golden-age mystery of the 1920's and 30's and to overlook some of its brand-new tricks. Whatever its superficial resemblances to the classic detective story, the modern cozy is a hybrid mystery with a life of its own."

2. The difference between the (English) "cosy" and the (American) "cozy" perhaps calls for greater nuance and a creation of yet another sub-genre. As I argue in the conclusion of this chapter, definitions in the detective fiction genre are meant to be broken; this is how detective fiction is continually made new. Perhaps definitions are created by looking back at what was done and applying post-critical definitions to past fiction to make accessible new fiction in the genre.

3. Barbara Ross writes a three-part blog post focusing on the lack of respect that cozy authors receive from other fiction authors. She creates a list of what she calls the hierarchy of fiction writers which I include here:

- The literary fiction writers look down on the mystery writers
- The mystery writers look down on the romance writers
- The romance writers look down on the poets
- The poets look down on the literary fiction writers
- (cycle starts again)

4. See Stephen Knight's chapter, "The Clue-puzzle Forms" in *Crime Fiction 1800-2000* for his extensive commentary on the authors who contributed and participated in the clue-puzzle format.

5. Alex Erickson, a male cozy author, writes a guest blog post on *The Wickeds Blog*, on how people react when he tells them he writes cozy mysteries. He additionally comments on how he does not reflect the cozy stereotypes presumed upon the cozy mystery authors. See "Alex Erickson" When the Not So Cozy Gets Cozy."

6. In *Murder by the Book* (1951), Archie flies to L.A. to pursue a lead. Rex Stout pokes fun at the hard-hitting/hard-boiled detective (who was most likely to be based in L.A.) and Archie describes an operative he potentially wants to hire to help in his case: "I gave him one look and one was enough. He had a cauliflower ear, and his eyes were trying to penetrate a haze that was too thick for them. ... 'No,' I said emphatically, 'not the type. Not a chance'" (130).

7. Though Jonny and Orrie are eventually killed off in the series, I include them here as they do enter into most of the stories and create opportunities to discover loyalties which exist between the men themselves. Jonny is murdered while working on a case for Wolfe in *Might as Well be Dead* (1956), and though there is no love lost for Jonny between Wolfe, Archie, and co., they wish to solve the case and avenge his death. Orrie is on trial for murder in *Death of a Doxy* (1966) and Archie, Saul, Fred, and Wolfe conclude he is innocent and help him out. Though these same sentiments contribute to their misunderstanding of the case in *A Family Affair* (1975), when they discover that Orrie is the murderer, Stout gives insight into how Wolfe, Archie, Saul, and Fred feel betrayed by him which gives us a glimpse of the trust that their working relationship had been built upon. Ultimately, Orrie commits suicide on the steps of Wolfe's house, locked outside of the "family," he destroys himself on the foyer of the relationships he betrayed.

Works Cited

Anderson, David R. *Rex Stout*. Frederick Ungar Publishing Co., 1984.
Breu, Christopher. *Hard-boiled Masculinities*. University of Minnesota Press, 2005.
Danna. *Cozy Mystery Blog*. 2019. https://www.cozy-mystery.com/.
_____. "Cozy Mystery List, Authors—S." https://www.cozy-mystery.com/authors-s.html.
_____. "What makes a cozy just that?." https://www.cozy-mystery.com/Definition-of-a-Cozy-Mystery.html.
Dove, George N. *The Reader and the Detective Story*. Bowling Green State University Popular Press, 1997.
Edwards, Martin. "Introduction" in *Taking Detective Stories Seriously. The Collected Crime Reviews of Dorothy L. Sayers*. Edited with an Introduction and Commentary by Martin. Tippermuir Books Ltd., 2017, pp. 3–6.
Erickson, Alex. "When the Not so Cozy Gets Cozy." *The Wickeds: wicked good*

mysteries, July 10, 2018. https://wickedauthors.com/2018/07/10/alex-erickson-when-the-not-so-cozy-gets-cozy/.

Horsley, Lee. *Twentieth-Century Crime Fiction*. Oxford University Press, 2005.

Knight, Stephen. *Crime Fiction 1800–2000: Detection, Death, Diversity*. Palgrave MacMillan, 2004.

McAleer, John. *Rex Stout: A Biography*. Little, Brown and Company, 1977.

Meyers, Maan. "Introduction." In *And Be A Villain*, Rex Stout. Bantam Books, 1994, pp v–ix.

nohausfrau. Comment on "How I Learned to Relax About Being a 'Cozy' Author and Just Write the Damn Books—Part III." *The Wickeds: Wicked Good Mysteries*, 23 July, 2015, 7:52 a.m., https://wickedauthors.com/2015/07/23/how-i-learned-to-relax-about-being-a-cozy-author-and-just-write-the-damn-books-part-iii/.

Paul, Robert S. *Whatever Happened to Sherlock Holmes? Detective Fiction, Popular Theology, and Society*. Southern Illinois University Press, 1991.

Prowell, Sandra West. "Introduction" (1995). In *Death of a Doxy*. Rex Stout. Bantam Books, 1995, pp. v–viii.

Ross, Barbara. "How I Learned to Relax About Being a 'Cozy' Author and Just Write the Damn Books—Part I." *The Wickeds: wicked good mysteries*, 26 Feb., 2015, https://wickedauthors.com/2015/02/26/how-i-learned-to-relax-about-being-a-cozy-author-and-just-write-the-damn-books-part-i/. Accessed 31 Oct., 2019.

_____. "How I Learned to Relax About Being a 'Cozy' Author and Just Write the Damn Books—Part II." *The Wickeds: wicked good mysteries*, 26 March, 2015, https://wickedauthors.com/2015/03/26/how-i-learned-to-relax-about-being-a-cozy-author-and-just-write-the-damn-books-part-ii/. Accessed 31 Oct., 2019.

_____. "How I Learned to Relax About Being a 'Cozy' Author and Just Write the Damn Books—Part III." *The Wickeds: wicked good mysteries*, 23 July, 2015. https://wickedauthors.com/2015/07/23/how-i-learned-to-relax-about-being-a-cozy-author-and-just-write-the-damn-books-part-iii/. Accessed 31 Oct., 2019.

Rzepka, Charles J. *Detective Fiction*. Polity Press, 2005.

Sprinkle, Patricia. "Introduction" (1995). In *In the Best Families*, Rex Stout, 1950. Bantam Books, 1995, pp. v–viii.

Stasio, Marilyn. "Murder Least Foul: The Cozy, Soft-Boiled Mystery." *The New York Times*, Oct 18, 1992, Section 7, Page 42. Accessed June 20, 2019. https://www.nytimes.com/1992/10/18/books/crime-mystery-murder-least-foul-the-cozy-soft-boiled-mystery.html.

Stout, Rex. *Fer-de-lance*. 1934. Pyramid Books, 1967.

_____. *The League of Frightened Gentlemen*. 1935. In *Full House: A Nero Wolfe Omnibus*. The Viking Press, 1955, pp. 3–212.

_____. *The Rubber Band*. 1936. Bantam Books, 1982.

_____. *The Red Box*. 1936. Pyramid Books, 1976.

_____. *Too Many Cooks*. 1938. Pyramid Books, 1966.

_____. *Some Buried Caesar*. 1938. Bantam Books, 1994.

_____. *Instead of Evidence*. In *Trouble in Triplicate*. 1945. Comprised of "Before I Die" pp. 1–76; "Help Wanted, Male" pp. 77–151; "Instead of Evidence" pp. 153–223. Bantam Books, 1993.

_____. *And Be A Villain*. 1948. Bantam Books, 1994.

_____. *In the Best Families*. 1950. Bantam Books, 1995.

_____. *Murder by the Book*. 1951. The Viking Press, 1951.

_____. *Invitation to Murder*. In *Three Men Out*. 1952. Comprised of "Invitation to Murder" pp. 3–61; "The Zero Clue" pp. 65–123; "This Won't Kill You" pp 127–181. Vail-Ballou Press, Inc., 1954.

_____. *The Golden Spiders*. 1953. Bantam Books, 1969.

_____. *Christmas Party*. 1956. In *And Four to Go: A Nero Wolfe Foursome*. Comprised of "Christmas Party" pp. 7–64; "Easter Parade" pp. 65–106; "Fourth of July Picnic" pp. 107–146; "Murder is No Joke" pp. 147–190. The Viking Press, 1958.

_____. *Too Many Detectives*. 1955. In *Three For the Chair*. Comprised of "A Window for Death" pp. 3–64; "Immune to Murder" pp. 65–120; "Too Many Detectives" pp. 121–183. The Viking Press, 1957.

_____. *If Death Ever Slept*. 1957. Bantam Books, 1983.

_____. *Might As Well Be Dead.* 1956. Bantam Books, 1980.
_____. *Kill Now-Pay Later.* 1961. In *Trio for Blunt Instruments.* 1964. Comprised of "Kill Now-Pay Later" pp 1–87; "Murder is Corny" pp. 89–167; "Blood Will Tell" pp. 169–247. The Viking Press, 1964.
_____. *Death of a Doxy.* 1966. Bantam Books, 1995.
_____. *Death of a Dude.* 1969. Bantam Books, 1981.
_____. *A Family Affair.* 1975. The Viking Press, 1975.
Taking Detective Stories Seriously. The Collected Crime Reviews of Dorothy L. Sayers. Edited with an Introduction and Commentary by Martin Edwards. Tippermuir Books Ltd., 2017.
Wodehouse, P.G. "Forward." In John McAleer *Rex Stout: A Biography.* Little, Brown and Company, 1977, xv–xvi.

About the Contributors

Sally **Beresford-Sheridan** is a doctoral candidate at the University of Waterloo. Her research interests include British women's detective fiction, how language constructs communities of readers, female sleuths, discovering interwar narratives of social history within detective fiction, and the cozy mystery.

Phyllis M. **Betz** is an associate professor of English of La Salle University in Philadelphia, PA. She has published four books with McFarland on lesbian genre fiction. She teaches courses on American Literature as well as popular fiction.

Stephen **Cloutier** teaches part-time in the English and Cultural Studies departments at Mount St. Vincent University and in the English department at St. Mary's University in Halifax, Canada. He received his PhD from the University of Leicester (United Kingdom). Areas of research include literature of the two world wars, Marxist theory, literature of the Vietnam War, and detective fiction.

Paula T. **Connolly** is a professor in the Department of English at the University of North Carolina at Charlotte where she teaches courses in mystery novels, genre fiction, film, and children's literature. She has published on topics of culture and children's literature, including her book, *Slavery in American Children's Literature: 1790–2010*.

Mary P. **Freier** is a professor at Northern Michigan University who studies the portrayal of information literacy, librarians, and libraries in mystery fiction. She has published on the librarian in the Harry Potter series and edited an issue of *Clues: A Journal of Detection* on information literacy and the detective novel.

Jessica **Gildersleeve** is an associate professor of English literature at the University of Southern Queensland. She has published works on the Gothic and detective fiction, including articles on Agatha Christie, Sarah Waters, and the recent *Don't Look Now*. She is currently at work on a study of the contemporary Australian Gothic.

Marty S. **Knepper** is a professor of English, Emerita, at Morningside College, having served as English chair for 31 years and taught many courses including detective fiction and popular culture. Past President of the Popular Culture Association, she has published articles on film, gender issues, mysteries, and especially Agatha Christie.

Susan K. **Martin** is a professor of English at La Trobe University and researches in literary studies, environment, book culture, and Australian literature, with international journal publication, books including *Women and Empire: Australia*, *Reading the Garden* with Katie Holmes and Kylie Mirmohamadi, as well as, with Kylie Mirmohamadi, *Sensational Melbourne* and *Colonial Dickens*.

Kylie **Mirmohamadi** is a research associate at La Trobe University. Her most recent book is *The Digital Afterlives of Jane Austen: Janeites at the Keyboard*. She has co-authored and co-edited a number of scholarly books including, with Susan K. Martin, *Sensational Melbourne* and *Colonial Dickens*.

Jennifer S. **Palmer** is a retired historian in England who lectures on historical controversies, real crimes, and crime fiction topics, particularly the Golden Age. She has previously contributed chapters on the New Woman detective and Conan Doyle as a detective in historical crime fiction anthologies.

Susan **Rowland** is the author of two book on detective fiction by women: *From Agatha Christie to Ruth Rendell* and *The Sleuth and the Goddess*. She teaches at the Pacifica Graduate Institute, and published *Jungian Literary Criticism: The Essential Guide* in 2019.

Kathryn Heltne **Swanson** is a professor of English, Emerita, at Augsburg University in Minneapolis where she taught courses in writing as well as literature, language and power, composition theory, women and fiction, and mystery and detective fiction. She also oversaw the licensure program for language arts teachers and the Augsburg Writing lab

Jon **Wilkins** is an independent scholar and writer. He has written one crime novel set in Utrecht and is planning a series set in the city. He is also the editor of the website *www.UtrechtCentral.com*. He has presented papers on the mystery at several conferences and contributes to various blogs.

Index

abuse domestic 60; physical 60
academic mystery 131–138
Adams, Ellery 113–116
agency 209–210
Albert, Susan Wittig 82, 85–87
Angelotta, Eve 98–112; *see also* Costa, Shelly
archetype 50, 59, 62, 120
art 74, 77

Beaton, M.C. 114–125
bias 96
books 114–115
Bowen, Rhys 82–92
Brexit 114, 120, 124, 125
Brooke, Loveday 169–179, 184

Casarett, David 138–142; *The Missing Guests of the Magic Grove Hotel*; *Murder at the House of Rooster Happiness*
Cawelti, John 22, 34
Chandler, Raymond 189
characters 2, 4, 10, 14, 18, 82, 94
Christie, Agatha 12, 18–40, 52, 114–114, 149, 171, 178; *The Body in the Library* 144; *Murder on the Orient Express* 23, 32; *Three Blind Mice* 12, 30–32
Clara, Baroness of Linz 15, 169, 179–187; *see also* Oppenheim, E. Phillips
class 10, 22, 83, 95, 107–111, 114, 124, 196
classic detective story *see* traditional mystery
Colombo 15, 188–202
community 18, 31, 39, 55, 58, 60, 65, 72, 86, 96, 101, 116, 130, 134, 144, 151, 157, 163, 178, 182
convention 3, 4–8, 11
Costa, Shelly, 98–112; *Basil Instinct* 98–112; *You Cannoli Die Once* 98–112
Cotswolds 13, 116–117
countryside *see* landscape
cozy definition 12–13, 18–40; composite 39–40, 50, 62, 65–67, 81–82, 130; cultural 34–39; formulaic 21–29; literary 30–34; market 18–22

Dalrymple, Daisy *see* Dunn, Carola
Darlings Dahlias 85–87; *see also* Albert, Susan Wittig
Davidson, Diane Mott 60–62; *Dying for Chocolate* 60–62
democracy 144, 146, 152
Depression, 79, 82, 85, 88
Dobson, Joanne 136–137; *Death Without Tenure* 136–137
Dove, George 6–8, 10, 206, 209
Dragnet 193–195
Dunn, Carola 82–92

England 13, 113–125
ethnicity 98, 102–107, 111, 124

Falk, Peter 188
family 50, 55, 57, 60, 61, 62
fantasy 18, 39, 114, 120, 121
femme fatale 213–216
Fisher, Phyrne 82, 92
Fitgar, Jason *see* Schumacher, Julie
Flowers, Amanda 12, 19- 40; *Assaulted Caramel* 12, 18, 19, 30–34
Fontaine, Solange 15, 169–179, 181–187; *see also* Oppenheim, E. Phillips
food 66, 69–70
formula 2, 6, 22
Friday, Sgt. Joe 193–195

Gamache, Inspector Armand 67, 69, 70, 76; *see also* Penny, Louise
garden 121–122
gender 10, 22, 38, 59, 95, 114, 159, 166, 192
genre 2, 4, 6, 8, 16, 29, 50, 53, 60, 62, 66, 116, 117, 122, 156, 166, 170, 171, 206, 208, 219
geography 94, 98, 106, 111, 121, 159
Gladden, Mrs. 187, 188
goddesses 53–55; Aphrodite 58; Artemis 57, 58, 59, 63; Athena 58, 59; Hestia 57, 59, 60, 62, 63
Golden Age 20, 28, 39, 49, 55, 80, 84, 113, 125, 144, 151, 157, 162, 169, 204, 212, 217
Goodwill, Susan 98–112; *Brigadoom* 101; *Little Shop of Murders* 101

Index

Goodwin, Archie 204, 209–220
gothic 156–159, 164, 165, 166
Gramsci, Antonio 188, 191, 193, 196
Green, Anna Katherine 55–56; *The Leavenworth Case* 55–56, 63, 144
Greenwood, Kerry 82–92

Hallmark 159, 163, 165
Hambly, Barbara 58–50, 63; *Graveyard Dust* 58–60
hard-boiled detective 50–52, 62–63, 204, 209–220
Harris, Charlaine 156–166
Harris, Sherry 5, 98–112; *The Longest Yard Sale* 100; *Tagged for Death* 110
historical cozy 79–92
hospital 14, 138–142

Innes, Rachel *see* Rinehart, Mary Roberts

January, Benjamin *see* Hambly, Barbara
Jung, Carl 50, 52, 76

King, Baily *see* Flowers, Amanda

landscape, 116, 117, 120, 121
library 14, 144–155, 160, 162
London, Kate *see* Goodwill, Susan
Los Angeles 189, 190

Malice Domestic 17–18, 29, 207
maps 116, 118, 123
Marple, Jane 50, 52, 197
The Mod Squad 194

narrative 2, 4, 9, 10, 31, 66, 68, 94, 101, 105, 106, 157, 164, 210
neoliberalism 36–38

Oppenheim, E. Phillips 169–187

Patalung, Ladarat *see* Casarett, David
Pelletier, Kare *see* Dobson, Joanne
Penny, Louise 12, 65–77; *The Beautiful Mystery* 69, 71; *The Brutal Telling* 68, 75; *The Nature of the Beast* 68, 75; *Still Life* 67, 68, 71, 75
pets 53, 58, 66, 71
power 196–197, 199

race 10, 22, 95, 103, 102–107, 111, 114, 124, 143, 163, 165
Raisin, Agatha *see* Beaton, M. C.
Rannock, Georgiana (Georgie) 82–92
reader 3–8, 20, 54, 66, 130, 205, 211, 212
Real Murders Club 156, 160, 162
relationships 31, 34, 39, 61, 87, 109, 139, 140, 185, 209, 213, 214, 216, 219
Rinehart, Mary Roberts: *The Circular Staircase* 56–58, 63
Rowan, Lily 214–216

Schulz, Goldy *see* Davidson, Diane Mott
Schumacher, Julie 133–136; *Dear Committee Members* 133–136
secrets 65, 70, 75
setting 12–14, 31, 65, 77, 85, 99–112, 137, 172
sex 18, 65, 160
sexuality 11, 159, 166, 174, 175, 176, 181, 192
small town 97–98, 101, 107, 111, 116, 157, 159
Southern gothic *see* gothic
space 66–67, 68, 72, 75, 76
stereotypes 10, 99, 102, 104, 106, 129, 162, 219
Stout, Rex 204–220

Teagarden, Aurora 2, 14, 145, 156–166
Three Pines *see* Penny, Louise
traditional mystery 18, 28, 49, 52, 55, 144
transgression 173, 197
trauma 72–72, 74, 77

values 22, 39, 65, 191
village 113–125, 177
violence 18, 69, 62, 73, 88, 96, 159, 160, 200–201

Willet, Amy 132–133; *The Writing Class* 132–133
Winston, Sarah *see* Harris, Sherry
Wolfe, Nero, 15, 204–220

www.ingramcontent.com/pod-product-compliance
Lightning Source LLC
Chambersburg PA
CBHW032040300426
44117CB00009B/1127